CW00370352

INTO THE DARKNESS

Also by Lothrop Stoddard

Clashing Tides of Color
The French Revolution in San Domingo
Racial Realities in Europe
Reforging America
The Revolt against Civilization
The Rising Tide of Color

INTO THE DARKNESS

*A Sympathetic Report
from Hitler's Wartime Reich*

LOTHROP STODDARD

The Noontide Press

Introduction copyright 2000 by Noontide Press

Published in the United States by
The Noontide Press
P.O. Box 2719
Newport Beach, CA 92659

Library of Congress Cataloging-in-Publication Data

Stoddard, Lothrop
Into the Darkness: A Sympathetic Report from Hitler's
Wartime Reich
ISBN 0-939482-59-2
1. Nationalsozialistische Deutsche Arbeiter-Partei.
2. Germany—Description and Travel—1919-.
3. Germany—Politics and government.
4. Germany—Economic conditions—1919-.
5. Germany—Social conditions.
DD253.S724
943.985   99-076756
                                                           CIP

This Noontide Press paperback edition of *Into the Darkness*
is an unabridged republication of the edition published in
New York by Duell, Sloan, and Pearce in 1940, with the addition of a new introduction by Rachel F. Dixon.

CONTENTS

'THIS MAN STODDARD':
A CRITICAL APPRECIATION

> "Civilization's going to pieces," broke out Tom violently. "I've gotten to be a terrible pessimist about things. Have you read 'The Rise of the Colored Empires' by this man Goddard?"
>
> "Why, no," I answered, rather surprised by his tone.
>
> "Well, it's a fine book, and everybody ought to read it. The idea is if we don't look out the white race will be utterly submerged. It's all scientific stuff; it's been proved."
>
> (F. Scott Fitzgerald, *The Great Gatsby*)

FEW THINGS GO STALE FASTER THAN TOPICAL HUMOR. When Charles Scribner's Sons published *The Great Gatsby* in 1925, most readers would have spotted the foregoing as a witty reference to one of the major nonfiction books of recent years, *The Rising Tide of Color against White World Supremacy*. Scribner's published that blockbuster in the spring of 1920 (the same season, incidentally, that it brought out Scott Fitzgerald's first novel). By year's end *The Rising Tide of Color* had gone through five printings and its author was one of America's most sought-after journalists and lecturers.

Three-quarters of a century later, *The Great Gatsby* is a classic, still doing very well for Scribner's. But whatever happened to that other best-seller, *The Rising Tide of Color?* Oh, you can still find it up in the dusty high shelves of university libraries, but it hasn't seen a major reprint since the 1920s. Worse, its author is all but forgotten.

So who was "this man Goddard"? Literate Americans of the 1920s knew very well who he was: Mr. T. Lothrop Stoddard — history writer, journalist, amateur ethnologist, and one of America's bright young intellectuals of the early twenties. His byline turned up regularly in a half-dozen magazines, from the popular *Saturday Evening Post* to the high-minded *World's Work*. Stoddard was born in 1883, son of a popular author and travel lecturer named John Lawson Stoddard. He went to Harvard College (Class of '05), then law school at Boston University, and made a brief attempt to settle down as a lawyer. But the legal life bored him, so he went back to Harvard and collected a Ph.D. in history. For his doctoral dissertation he wrote about the late-18th century slave revolts in what is now Haiti. A horrifying yet scholarly presented tale of atrocities and massacres, *The French Revolution in San Domingo* was a popular and critical success when published in 1914.

Stoddard suddenly found himself a big draw on the lecture circuit. Without intending to do so, he was following in his father's footsteps, and loving every minute of it.

Over the next thirty years, Stoddard wrote on many topics but, like a public speaker who modifies his talk slightly to suit different groups, always returned to the same points:

- Race is the key factor in the rise and fall of civilizations.
- Civilization is a fragile thing that can be produced only by a homogeneous people whose intelligence and character are of a high average.
- The finest and most cultured white peoples are in grave danger of being swamped by the fecund and irresponsible "colored" races.
- In America the best people are of the old, pre-Revolutionary stock that founded the nation; subsequent waves of immigration have brought ever-less-worthy types to our shores.

Is this what the public wanted to hear? Apparently so: during the 1920s and early 1930s, at least, Scribner's brought out a new Stoddard title nearly every year. To name a few: *Re-forging America*; *Social Classes in Post-War Europe*; *Racial Realities in Europe*; *The Revolt against Civilization*; *Clashing Tides of Color*. The titles alone conjure up the cultural anxiety of the years immediately after the Great War, years which also saw the publication of Spengler's *Decline of the West* and Ortega y Gasset's *Revolt of the Masses*.

But by the mid-1930s, Lothrop's career was in eclipse. Like Scott Fitzgerald at that time, Lothrop Stoddard came to be regarded as a sort of period piece, an embarrassing memory of the Jazz Age. His books went out of print, and Scribner's dropped him from its stable of authors. By the time be died in 1950, he was all but forgotten. A perfunctory obituary in the *New York Times* noted that "Mr. Stoddard had written more than a dozen books on world affairs and more recently had contributed editorials on foreign political developments to the *Washington Star.*"

No mention in that obituary of Stoddard's most popular work, *The Rising Tide of Color*, or of his most enduring legacy. That legacy was the 1924 Immigration Act, which sought to halt the racial degeneration of the U.S. by pegging national-origin quotas to the proportions of the American population as of 1890. Since non-white immigration had already been severely restricted, the practical effect of the 1924 act was that immigrants from the British Isles and northern Europe could acquire U.S. citizenship with little difficulty, while immigration from southern and eastern Europe was greatly curtailed. In arguing for the act's passage, Congressmen quoted liberally from the works of the eminent Lothrop Stoddard; the bill became law with little opposition. These national-origin quotas remained on the books till 1965, when a new immigration law abolished them.

When one reads Stoddard today, it's easy to see why he was so popular. He wrote in an engaging, authoritative, self-effacing style. The effect was like that of an unsigned newspaper editorial: Olympian opinions handed down without apparent personal bias. This kind of lofty, breezy prose was very typical of 1920s upper-middlebrow journalism, and survived for decades in the "house styles" of two bright new magazines of the era, *Time* and *The New Yorker*. In fact, it persists still, as a kind of ironical fossil, in *The New Yorker*'s "Talk of the Town" column.

Then of course, there was Stoddard's subject-matter. Questions of race and ethnicity were much in vogue in the America of the early 1920s. There was a number of reasons for this. Statistical-based tests for intelligence and aptitude were the newest thing in the educational kit. Along with pop-Darwinism and the new sub-science of eugenics, these tests encouraged people to think of humanity as a species of animal that could be improved by proper breeding — or ruined by crossing with the wrong "stocks." In the 1920s, every high school graduate knew about the Jukes and the Kallikaks, those two classic case-studies of recurring criminality and feeble-mindedness in American families. Even advertising slogans of the 1920s were rife with eugenically attuned catch-phrases, e.g., "Blood will tell!"

On top of the eugenics fad, we had the aftermath of Great War, the rise of Communism in Russia and elsewhere, the growth of motion pictures, migration of the Southern Negro to Northern cities, race riots, and the growing presence of Jews in the legal system and the press — all of which helped to excite a new wave of "nativism" during the 1910-1925 period. This was the time of the Great Red Scare, the rebirth of the Ku Klux Klan, the beginning of Prohibition, and, the election of Warren G. Harding on a platform of "return to normalcy." As Frederick Lewis Allen informed the nation as soon as the decade ended (in *Only Yesterday*), it was also a period of Hollywood sex scandals, gangsters, bobbed hair, Leopold and Loeb, Aimee Semple MacPherson, crossword puzzles, Mah Jongg, the Scopes trial, Ponzi schemes, Teapot Dome, stock-market speculation, flagpole sitting, anarchists, Bolshevists, and schemes for self-improvement that reached their apex with a little Frenchman named Emile Coué who sold a positive-thinking routine he called Autosuggestion — "Day by day in every way I am getting better and better!"

For many Americans it was a dizzying, confusing time, a time ripe for nostrum peddlers, scientific popularizers, and literate explainers. Fitzgerald explained the culture of the flapper, H. L. Mencken and Sinclair Lewis explained the hilarious vapidity of the small-town Boobus americanus, and Lothrop Stoddard dissected the vital link between race and civilization.

Nowadays, neglected as they are, Stoddard's writings constitute a kind of Rosetta Stone for curious souls trying to decipher the cultural history of 1920s America. His books and articles lay out clearly what was on the minds of educated Americans who were neither artists nor poets nor trendy cosmopolites ("bobbed-hair thinkers," in Stoddard's phrase). The kind of country-club Americans portrayed in the fiction of John P. Marquand and John O'Hara, the slightly brash burghers you see in old Peter Arno cartoons, the outspoken, opinionated souls we come across in our grandparents' diaries and correspondence — these were the people for whom Stoddard wrote and lectured. When we marvel today at the frankness with which novelists of the period expressed themselves on racial and cultural matters, when we note the snide and easy grace with which the editors of *Time* or *Vanity Fair* printed ethnic jokes that later generations would find tasteless, it helps to have a little Stoddard at hand to give us our bearings.

Knowledge of early-1920s cultural currents is key to understanding the wild philanthropic passion that impelled America's leading industrialist, Henry Ford, to devote a good part of his fortune in the dissemination of information about what he called "The World's Foremost Problem" — *The International Jew.* And it explains why a nation that had existed for a century and a half without any clear immigration policy seemed suddenly to shut the gate to all but the "most desirable" elements.

If Stoddard's stature in the 1920s is readily understandable, the reasons behind his decline in the 1930s are even clearer. His views came to be seen as not merely faddish, but bizarre as well, perhaps even insidiously evil. The racial preachments of the National Socialists in Germany often seemed to have been lifted straight from the works of Stoddard. In fact, Herr Hitler himself sometimes tossed an approving nod to Lothrop Stoddard and America's 1924 Immigration Act.

Said Chancellor Hitler in April 1933, in a speech to the German Medical Federation that was reported in *Time* magazine: "The American people were the first to draw practical and political conclusions from differences among races and from the different value of different races. Through its immigration laws it has prevented the entry of those races which seemed unwelcome to the American people ..."

But Lothrop Stoddard was no Nazi or Fascist. In fact, he had shown himself distinctly unfriendly toward the European nationalist governments of the 1930s. Here is what he had to say about Germany in 1935:

> Racialist ideas are, of course, most strikingly prominent in the Nazi Germany of today. These ideas, however, are so mixed up with an ulcerated nationalism and are so surcharged with mere emotion that the resulting compound is hard to evaluate. Ever since the war, Germany has been highly abnormal in almost every respect. She is obviously in rapid transition, and just how she will evolve is at present highly uncertain. (*Clashing Tides of Color*, p. 23)

As a social commentator, Stoddard sometimes seemed to lack imagination. No doubt his critical writings were hobbled by the idiom of middlebrow journalism, which then as now require an author to anticipate and pander to his readers' prejudices, without making too great a strain upon their erudition or thought processes. In any event, Stoddard had no positive social program for America, other than a vague wish that dysgenic breeding could somehow be discouraged, and that the old-stock Founding Father type could again be firmly in the ascendant. When he wrote for *The Saturday Evening Post* in the early 1920s, Stoddard imparted an idealized, Jeffersonian vision of a American Golden Age, circa 1750-1820, an era dominated by a yeoman aristocracy that flowered most brilliantly in New England and Virginia; an era which ended only when this aristocracy thinned itself out in westward migrations.

Hand-in-hand with this wistful naivete goes Stoddard's charming but (to modern eyes) embarrassing "Anglo-Saxon" chauvinism. Anything English, or English culture, is by definition the best there is — whether language, race, mercantile methods, or system of government. Below the English in the pecking order of mankind come the related nations and races, beginning with the Scots (Welsh and Irish are seldom referred to, but evidently follow several paces behind). Next come the Holland Dutch and the Germans, largely "Nordic" peoples who at their best are scarcely distinguishable from the Anglo-Saxon.

Stoddard's romantic Anglomania at first made it difficult at times for him to come to terms with the modern world. In this wise he was no different from such popular contemporary English historians as H. M. Trevelyan or Winston Churchill with their fusty nattering about doughty little Britain, forever girding its loins to face the foeman alone and unafraid. A pleasant fantasy, perhaps, and not too harmful so long as the enemy was a bunch of spear-chucking fuzzy-wuzzies, or Dutch farmers in the Bushveldt. By the time Trevelyan, Churchill, and Stoddard reached maturity, however, these delusions made it possible for the United Kingdom (egged on by American Anglomaniacs) to rush headlong into tragedy. Britain emerged "victorious" from the 1914-18 war at the price of two million casualties and an economic future mortgaged to the United States. Stoddard, let it be said, was one Nordicist and Anglophile who drew warranted conclusions from the bloodbath of the First World War. In the preface to *The Rising Tide of Color*, he had written: "The most disquieting feature of the present situation, however, is not the war but the peace. The white world's inability to frame a constructive settlement, the perpetuation of intestine hatreds, and the menace of fresh white civil wars complicated by the spectre of social revolution, evoke the dread thought that the late war may be merely the first stage in a cycle of ruin."

Stoddard was opinionated, forthright, courageous and — most wonderful of all! — successful as a journalist. When his star fell in the 1930s, he had independent means, as well as an detached outlook that set him apart from other scribes and solons. During the 1930s, popular journalists and writers who wanted to stay publishable learned to make the right noises about the evil Fascists and Nazis. Ernest Hemingway, Dorothy Thompson, Vincent Sheean, Quentin Reynolds, and dozens of others all profited by this course. Stoddard took the opposite tack. He began as an opponent to the nationalistic movements (Mussolini and Hitler were not, after all, "Nordics" or "Anglo-Saxons") but gradually warmed to the fascisms.

Or at least lukewarmed. One gathers Lothrop Stoddard never really liked or trusted the Fascisti or Nazis. It wasn't that they goose-stepped or spoke a foreign language; they simply didn't have anything that Stoddard could recognize as idealism. To Stoddard, Italian Fascism and German National Socialism were preeminently systems of government guided by cool pragmatism. Fascists were men who had tested democracy, capitalism, social-democratic ideals — what-have-you — and found them all wanting. "Let's try this, then," says the fascist. "Let's see if it works. If not, we'll move on to something else."

> The vital factor in Fascism is, therefore, something essentially subjective — a driving force which may not know precisely whither it is headed, yet which, wherever it goes, is always sure of itself. The goal of Fascist policy is thus, not a fixed objective, but rather a working-idea, itself evolving with the course of time.
> (*Clashing Tides of Color*, p. 140)

In the 1930s and 40s it was fashionable for Americans and Englishmen to criticize Nazi Germany by mocking the tendentious philosophizing and bombastic propaganda of the National Socialist leaders. Stoddard ignored this official balderdash. He focused instead on the nuts-and-bolts workings of the German economy — its privations, its rationing, its long-term planning — and on Hitler's new social order, in its impact on farmers, workers, women, youth, and — through the eugenics program — on generations yet to come. As a result he managed to produce a unique "primary" historical document: a report of what the early days of war were like for the average man and woman.

This book was first published in 1940 by Duell, Sloan & Pearce, a house that specialized in collections of newspaper columns. (Scribner's had dropped Stoddard in the early 1930s.) As soon as war broke out in September 1939, Stoddard proposed to a news syndicate that he go to Germany and report on social conditions in wartime Europe. His name was well known in Germany, and soon Dr. Goebbels's Propaganda Ministry was offering the eminent Herr Doktor Stoddard a guided tour of the wartime Reich.

Because Stoddard was corresponding for the American man and woman in the street rather than in the university common rooms and the Communist cells, he tended to keep his eyes focused on such things as shoe leather and food baskets. The questions he posed concerned the same sort of everyday-life minutiae that the French historian Fernand Braudel would later study when investigating European life of the 15th and 16th centuries. How did one do grocery shopping under the German ration-coupon scheme? How was clothing allocated, and what was it made of? How many ration coupons did the German Fräulein have to spend to buy a brassiere? And how did they all manage to keep morale up?

This book is the product of the newspaper dispatches that answered these questions. Rewritten in a lucid and leisurely essay form, the book is arguably Stoddard's finest and most sustained piece of journalism. It reveals the arcana of everyday life in the Third Reich during the days of the "phony war" of 1939-40. Poignantly it notes the immense sense of freedom (and abundance of food!) that Stoddard felt whenever he took the train out of wartime Germany into the still-neutral lands of Italy or Hungary. (Ah, Christmas lights! Ah, butter!)

Again and again Stoddard returns to the dearth of consumer goods in Germany during the "phony war" period. His revelations will raise some eyebrows. After all, was not Germany a rich and prosperous country at this time, about to defeat France a send the British scurrying from Dunquerque in the spring of 1940? Perhaps it was; but we learn that neither the government nor the man in the street expected quick victories. Germany was actually preparing for several years of siege warfare.

Undoubtedly the title, *Into the Darkness*, was chosen to make the book more salable. The insinuation was that Hitler Germany is a darkly sinister place. But the darkness in the title was not figurative. When crossing back into Germany, the lights in the sleeping cars had to be turned off. The only artificial lighting permitted on public transportation in Germany emanated from dim blue bulbs. More than the rationing and other restrictions, this is the element of early wartime Germany that Lothrop Stoddard found most depressing. Yet, in light of Stoddard's evident affinity for the Germans, his affectionate treatment of such peoples as the Hungarians, and above all his foreboding of "fresh white civil wars," may we not suppose that the title signified also his dread at the prospect of another terrible war among the white nations?

It would be nice to report that this, Stoddard's last published book, was greeted with glowing reviews by the American journalists and litterateurs. Actually, it was largely ignored, for reasons that we can infer from this short, mocking treatment in *Time* during early 1940:

> Dr. Lothrop Stoddard, Brookline, Mass. political lecturer and author, whose racial theories (he used to frighten the U.S. with the yellow

peril) make him *persona grata* to the Nazis, went recently to Germany as correspondent for the North American Newspaper Alliance. Last week glib Dr. Stoddard got an interview with Minister for Propaganda and Public Enlightenment Dr. Paul Joseph Goebbels ...

Time here offered the following snatch from the Goebbels interview (see pages 65-70):

"Listen! If I wanted to get the German people emotionally steamed up, I could do it in 24 hours ... We Germans do not like this war. We think it is needless and silly. The average German feels like a man with a chronic toothache — the sooner it is out, the better. And he does not need brass bands and flowers to get it over with."

Time's headline for this squib: Toothache ...

Time sneered, but Lothrop Stoddard has the last grim chuckle. The middle-brow press used to wave away Stoddard's racial concerns as delusional. But nowadays *Time* and its ilk inform, with the same breezy certitude, that the eclipse of the white, Western world is inevitable — and we should just lie back and enjoy it. Not the sort of vindication "this man Stoddard," who saw himself more the Paul Revere than the threnodist of his race, might have hoped for, of course — but today matters are long out of his hands, and in ours.

Rachel F. Dixon
New York
2000

I. THE SHADOW

ALL EUROPE IS UNDER THE SHADOW OF WAR. IT IS LIKE
an eclipse of the sun. In the warring nations the darkness is most intense, amounting to a continuous blackout. The neutral countries form a sort of twilight zone,
where life is better, yet far from normal.

In nature, an eclipse is a passing phenomenon; awe-
inspiring but soon over. Not so with the war-hidden
sun of Europe's civilization. Normal light and warmth
do not return. Ominously, the twilight zone of neutrality becomes an ever-bleaker gray, while war's blackout grows more and more intense.

I entered wartime Europe by way of Italy, making
the trip from America on the Italian liner *Rex*. It was
a strange voyage. This huge floating palace, the pride
of Italy's merchant marine, carried only a handful of
passengers. War's automatic blight on pleasure tours,
plus our State Department's ban on ordinary passports,
had dammed the travel flood to the merest trickle. So
I sailed from New York on an almost empty boat.

First Class on the *Rex* is a miracle of modern luxury.
Yet all that splendor was lavished upon precisely
twenty-five passengers including myself. Consequently
we rattled around in this magnificence like tiny peas

in a mammoth pod. A small group of tables in one
corner of the spacious dining salon; a short row of re-
clining-chairs on the long vista of the promenade deck;
a pathetic little cluster of seats in the vast ballroom
when it was time for the movies—these were the sole
evidences of community life. Even the ship's company
was little in evidence. Save for the few stewards and
deck-hands needed to look after us, the rest did not
appear. Now and then I would roam about for a long
time without seeing a soul. The effect was eery. It was
like being on a ghost ship, "Outward Bound" and
driven by unseen hands.

There was not much to be gleaned from my fellow-
passengers. Most of them were Italians, speaking little
English and full of their own affairs. A pair of American business men were equally preoccupied. For them,
the war was a confounded nuisance. The rapid-fire
speech of a Chilean diplomat bound with his family for
a European post was too much for my Spanish. The
most intriguing person aboard was a lone Japanese who
beat everybody at ping-pong but otherwise held himself
aloof.

Back aft, Tourist Class was even more cosmopolitan,
with a solitary American set among a sprinkling of
several nationalities, including a young Iraki Arab returning to Bagdad from a course at the University of
Chicago. He was a fiery nationalist deeply distrustful
of all the European Powers, especially Soviet Russia
with its possible designs on the Middle East. In both
Tourist and Third Class were a number of Germans,
mostly women but three of them men of military age.
All were obviously nervous. They had taken the gamble that the *Rex* would not be stopped by the English

at Gibraltar, Britain's key to the Mediterranean. In that event, the men knew that a concentration camp would be the end of their venturesome attempt to return to the Fatherland.

Passing the Straits of Gibraltar is always a memorable experience. This time it was especially impressive. We entered about midafternoon. The sky was full of cloud-masses shot with gleams of watery sunshine. At one moment a magnificent rainbow spanned the broad straits like a mammoth suspension-bridge. On the African shore the jagged sierras of Morocco were draped in mists. By contrast, the mountains of Spain were dappled sunlight, their brown slopes tinted with tender green where the long drought of summer had been tempered by the first autumn rains.

At length the massive outline of the Rock of Gibraltar came into view. It got nearer. We forged steadily ahead on our normal course toward the open Mediterranean beyond. Would the British let us pass? Nobody knew but the ship's officers, and they wouldn't tell. Then, when almost abreast of the Rock, our bow swerved sharply and we swung in past Europa Point. The British were going to give us the once-over!

Hastily I climbed to a 'vantage-place on the top deck to view what was to come, my Japanese fellow-passenger following suit. As the *Rex* entered Algeciras Bay we could see Gibraltar's outer harbor crowded with merchant shipping. When we got closer, I could discern by the big tricolor flags painted on their sides that most of them were Italian. Seven Italian freighters and three liners, all held for inspection. We cast anchor near the *Augustus,* a big beauty on the South American run.

As the anchor chain rattled, my fellow-passenger turned to me with a bland Oriental smile. "Very interesting," he remarked, pointing to the impounded shipping. "Do not think Japanese Government let this happen to our steamers."

We continued to view objectively happenings that did not personally concern us. Not so the bulk of the ship's company. The sight of those many impounded ships stirred every Italian aboard. Officers assumed tight-lipped impassivity and stewards shrugged deprecatingly, but sailors gathered in muttering knots while passengers became indignantly vocal, especially as a large naval tender approached us from shore. It was filled with British bluejackets and officers with white caps. I also spotted two military constables, which meant that they were after Germans.

As the tender swung alongside just beneath my 'vantage-point, a young Italian fellow-passenger strode up and joined us. Since he had already proclaimed himself an ardent Fascist, I was not surprised when he relieved his pent-up feelings with all the vigor of his seventeen years.

"Look at all our ships held in here!" he shouted. "Isn't it a shame?"

I couldn't resist a mischievous thought. "Just a little pat of the lion's paw," I put in soothingly.

The tease worked to perfection. He fairly exploded.

"Lions?" he yelled, shaking his fist. "Insolent dogs, I call them. Just you wait. This war isn't over; it's only begun. Some fine day, our Duce will give the word. Then we'll blast that old rock to smithereens and hand the fragments to our good friend Franco as a gesture of the friendship between our two Latin nations."

This speech set off a sailor who was painting nearby. He joined us, gesticulating with his brush. "I know how the English act," he growled, "I went through the Ethiopian War. Wouldn't I like to drop this paint-brush on that So-and-So's head, down there!" That So-and-So was a young British navy officer standing very erect in the tender's stern. I shudder to think what might have happened if the sailor had obeyed that impulse.

By this time most of the British officers had climbed aboard, so I went below to see what was up. The spacious entrance salon was dotted with spectators. Through the open door of the purser's office I could glimpse two Britishers going over the manifest of the ship's cargo. Just outside the door, flanked by the constables, stood our three Germans of military age—stocky men in their thirties or early forties. They stood impassive. This stoical pose was perhaps due to the fact that they had been drinking all the afternoon to quiet their nerves, so they should have been pleasantly mulled. Presently they entered the purser's office. The interview was short. Out they came, and the constables escorted them downstairs to the lower gangway.

I hurried on deck to watch the tender again. It was now dark, but by our ship's floodlights I could see some cheap suitcases aboard the tender. Soon a constable climbed down the short rope-ladder; then the three Germans; then the second constable and the British investigation officers. The Germans, clad in raincoats, huddled around their scanty baggage and lit cigarettes. As the tender chugged away, the young officer previously menaced by the paint-brush shouted up to us in crisp British accents: "You can go straight away now!"

The ordeal was over. It had lasted less than four hours. With only mail and a bit of express cargo, there was no valid reason for detaining us longer. We were lucky. Some ships with a full loading were held up for days. Anyhow, we promptly weighed anchor and were off. The twinkling lights of Gibraltar Town slipped quickly past and vanished behind Europa Point. The towering heights of the Rock loomed dimly in the sheen of the moon. Then it, too, sank from sight.

Approaching Italy, the weather turned symbolic. The last night on board we encountered a violent tempest marked by incessant lightning and crashing thunder. With the dawn a great wind came out of the north, blustering and unseasonably cold. The Bay of Genoa was smartly whitecapped as the giant *Rex* slid into the harbor and nosed cautiously up to her dock.

Historic Genoa, climbing its steep hills against a background of bare mountains, looked as impressive as ever. Yet there was a strange something in the picture which I could not at first make out. Then I realized what it was—an almost Sabbath absence of motion and bustle, though the date was neither a Sunday nor a holiday. Broad parking spaces behind the docks were virtually empty of motor cars, while the streets beyond were devoid of traffic save for trams and horse-drawn vehicles. Civilian Italy was denied gasoline. The precious fluid had been impounded for military purposes.

Friends met me at the dock, helped me through customs, and took me to the nearby railroad station in one of the few ancient taxis still permitted to run. At the station I checked my baggage as I was leaving town late that same evening. Apologetically, my friends escorted me to a tram in order to reach their suburban home some miles out. On the way I noted big letters painted on almost every deadwall. *Duce! Duce! Duce!* Such were the triple salutes to Mussolini, endlessly repeated. Less often came the Fascist motto: *Believe! Obey! Fight!* Italy being partly mobilized, I saw many soldiers.

Yet, despite all those exhortations, neither soldiers nor civilians appeared to be in a martial mood. On the contrary, they seemed preoccupied, walking for the most part in silence, huddling down into their clothes against recurrent blasts of the chill mountain wind. Once beyond the heart of the city, traffic became even thinner. The few trucks encountered were run by compressed methane gas. I could tell this by the big extra cylinders clamped along their sides. They were like exaggerated copies of the Prestolite tanks I recall from my early motoring days.

At dinner that evening my friends and their guests talked freely. "We're just getting over a bad attack of jitters," remarked my American-born hostess. "You should have been here a month and a half ago, when the war began, to realize how things were. At first we feared we were going right in, and expected French bombers over our heads any hour. You know that from our balcony we can glimpse the French coast on a clear day."

"The worst feature was the blackouts," added my host. "Thank goodness, we don't have any more of them. Wait until you get up into Germany. Then you'll know what I mean."

"The Italian people doesn't want to get into this

row," stated a professional man decisively. "We've been through two wars already—Ethiopia, Spain. That's enough fighting for a while."

"If we should intervene later," broke in a retired naval officer, "it will be strictly for Italian interests. And even then we'll get what we want first. No going in on promises. We don't forget how we got gypped at Versailles. That won't happen a second time."

"I must apologize for not serving you real coffee," said my hostess. "But this *Mokkari*, made from roasted rice, isn't so bad. You know we can't get coffee from South America any more on a barter basis and we mustn't lose any gold or foreign exchange in times like these except for imports vitally needed."

"As a matter of fact," put in a guest, "we could have a small coffee ration from what we get in from Ethiopia. But that coffee is very high grade and brings a fancy price on the world market. So the Government sells it all abroad to get more foreign exchange."

"We've been systematically learning to do without luxury imports ever since the League sanctions against us during the Ethiopian War," said my host. "You'd be surprised to learn how self-sufficient we have become."

"Autarchy," stated the retired naval officer sententiously, "is a good idea. Puts a nation on its toes. Makes more work. Stimulates invention. Of course we can't do it a hundred per cent. But the nearer we can come to it, the better."

During the railroad journey from Genoa to the German border, my social contacts were scanty. Fellow-travelers were Italians, and my knowledge of that tongue is far too sketchy for intelligent conversation. Still, I found an army officer who spoke French and a business man who knew German.

The army officer was an optimist, due largely to his faith in Mussolini. "Our Duce is a smart man," he said emphatically. "He's keeping us out of that war up north because he knows it isn't our fight. Not yet, at any rate. Should conditions change, I'm sure he's smart enough to pick the right side for us." Ideologies evidently didn't bother him. In his eyes it was just another war.

The business man was equally unconcerned with ideals but did not share the officer's optimism. "This is a crazy war," he growled. "I can't see how the leaders on either side let it happen. They ought to have had sense enough to make some compromise, knowing as they should what it will probably mean. If it goes on even two years, business everywhere will be hopelessly undermined and may be nationalized. If it lasts as long as the other war, all Europe will be in chaos. Not organized Communism. Just plain anarchy."

"Won't Italy gain commercially by staying neutral?" I inquired.

"Oh, yes," he shrugged. "We're doing new business already and we'll get more. But we'll lose all our war-profits and then some in the post-war deflation." He sighed heavily and looked out of the window at the autumn landscape flitting by.

A number of Germans boarded the train at Verona. I later found out that they were vacationists returning from a short trip to Venice. Typical Hansi tourists they were—the men with round, close-cropped heads; the women painfully plain, as the North German female of the species is apt to be.

I presently engaged one of the men in conversation. He complimented me on my German and was interested to learn that I was bound his way. "You'll find things surprisingly normal in Germany, considering it's wartime," he told me. "Though of course, coming straight from your peaceful, prosperous America, you won't like some aspects of our life. Blackouts and food-cards, for instance. Even so, I'm glad to be going home. Italy's a lovely country, but it isn't *Gemuetlich*. The Italians don't like us and make us feel it. At least, the people here in Northern Italy do. Further south, I'm told they are not so anti-German."

By this time our train had entered the region formerly called South Tyrol, annexed to Italy at the close of the World War. Despite two decades of Italianization, the basic Germanism of the region was still visible, from the chalet-like peasant farmsteads to the crenelated ruins of old castles perched high on crags, where Teutonic knights once held sway. I had known South Tyrol before 1914 when it was part of Austria, so I was interested to see what changes had taken place. Even from my car window I could see abundant evidences of Italian colonization. All the new buildings were in Italian style, and Latin faces were numerous among the crowds of Third-Class passengers who got on and off at every stop. The stations swarmed with soldiers, police, and Carabinieri in their picturesque black cutaway coats and big cocked hats. The German tourists viewed all this in heavy silence. It was clear they did not wish to discuss the painful subject.

As the train wound its way up the mountain-girt valley of the Adige, the weather grew colder. Long before we reached Bolzano, the ground was sprinkled with snow—most unusual south of the Brenner in late October. It was the first chill breath of the hardest winter in a generation, which war-torn Europe was destined to undergo. The mountains on either hand were well blanketed with white.

Bolzano (formerly Botzen) is a big town, the provincial capital and the administrative center. Here, Italianization had evidently made great strides. Large new factories had been built, manned by Italian labor. The colonists were housed in great blocks of modern tenements, forming an entire new quarter. On the walls were inscribed in giant letters: "Thanks, Duce!" There must be a big garrison, for the old Austrian barracks had been notably enlarged. They bore Mussolini's famous statement: "Frontiers are not discussed; they are defended!"

When we had reached Bolzano, the autumn dusk was falling. As we waited at the station, a gigantic sign on a nearby hill blazed suddenly forth, in electric light, the Latin word *Dux*. When the train started its long upward pull to the Brenner Pass, the snowfields on the high mountains to the north were rosy with the Alpine-glow.

The crest of the historic Brenner Pass is the frontier between Italy and Germany. It is likewise the dividing-line between peace and war. To the south lies Italy, armed and watchful but neutral and hence relatively normal. To the north lies Germany, a land absorbed in a life-and-death struggle with powerful foes. The traveler entering Germany plunges into war's grim shadow the instant he passes that mountain gateway.

I crossed the Brenner at night, so I encountered that most startling aspect of wartime Germany—the universal blackout. All the way up the Italian side of the range, towns and villages blazed with electric light furnished by abundant water-power. Also my train compartment was brilliantly illuminated. There was thus no preparation for what was soon to happen.

Shortly before reaching the frontier two members of the German border police came through the train collecting passports. Being still in Italy, they were in civilian clothes, their rank indicated solely by swastika arm bands. They were not an impressive pair. One was small and thin, with a foxy face. The other, big and burly, had a pasty complexion and eyes set too close together.

At Brennero, the Italian frontier station where Hitler and Mussolini were later to meet, the German train-crew came aboard. The new conductor's first act was to come into my compartment and pull down the window-shades. Then in came the official charged with examining your luggage and taking down your money declaration. In contrast to the border police, he was a fine figure of a man—ruddy face, blue eyes, turned-up blond mustache, and a well-fitting gray uniform. After a brief and courteous inspection he stated crisply: "Only blue light allowed." Thereupon the brilliant electric globes in my compartment were switched off, and there was left merely a tiny crescent of blue light, far smaller than the emergency bulbs in our subway trains. So scant was the illumination that it did little more than emphasize the darkness. Had it not been for a dimmed yellow bulb in the train corridor, it would have been almost impossible to make my way around.

With nothing to do but sit, I presently tired of my compartment and prowled down the corridor to find out whether anything was to be seen. To my great satisfaction I discovered that the windows to the car doors had no curtains, so I could look out. And what a sight I beheld! It was full moon, and the moonlight, reflected from new-fallen snow, made the landscape almost as bright as day. Towering mountain-peaks on either hand shot far up into the night. The tall pine and fir trees were bent beneath white loads. Now and then, tiny hamlets of Tyrolean chalets completed the impression of an endless Christmas card.

As the train thundered down from the Alpine divide it entered a widening valley with a swift-flowing little river. Houses became more frequent, hamlets grew larger. Now and then we passed a sawmill, apparently at work, since smoke and steam rose from the chimneys. Yet nowhere a single light. Only very rarely a faint gleam where some window was not entirely obscured. The landscape was as silent and deserted as though the whole countryside had been depopulated.

At Innsbruck, the first city north of the border, are freight-yards, and here I could appreciate more fully the thoroughness of German anti-air raid precautions. The engines had no headlights—only two small lanterns giving no more illumination than the oil lamps in front of our subway trains. In the freight-yards, switch-lights were painted black except for small cross-slits. Here and there, hooded lights on tall poles cast a dim blue radiance. Only on the station platform were there a few dimmed bulbs—just enough for passengers to see their way.

From Innsbruck on I was allowed to raise my window-shade, so I could sit comfortably in my compartment and view this blacked-out country at my ease. So extraordinary was the moonlit panorama that I determined to forego sleep and watch through most of the night. The sacrifice was well repaid.

As we got into the Munich metropolitan area I could judge still better the way urban blackouts are maintained. Munich is a great city, yet it was almost as dark as the countryside. The main streets and highway intersections had cross-slitted traffic lights, but since these are red and green they doubtless do not show much more from the air than does blue. Furthermore, at this late hour, there was almost no traffic beyond an occasional truck. No ray of white light anywhere, and except along the railway no hooded blues. Passing through this great darkened city, the sense of unnatural silence and emptiness became positively oppressive.

The streets of Munich presently gave way to open country once more. The mountains lay far behind, and the plateau of Upper Bavaria, powdered with snow, stretched away on either hand until lost in frosty moon-mist. The monotonous landscape made me doze. Some sixth sense must have awakened me to another interesting sight. My train was passing through the Thuringian Hills. They were clothed with magnificent pine forests, as deep-laden with new-fallen snow as those of the Tyrolean Alps. Those Thuringian forests grow in rows as regular as cornfields. The hills are belted with plantings of various heights, giving a curious patchwork effect. Where a ripe planting has been cut over, not a trace of slash remains and seedlings have been set out. Here is forestry carried to the nth degree of efficiency.

Out of the hills and into level country, I dozed off

again, not to awaken until sunrise—a pale, weak-looking late-autumn sun, for North Germany lies on the latitude of Labrador. The sun was soon hidden by clouds, while at times the train tore through banks of fog. We were well into the flat plains of Northern Germany, and a more uninteresting landscape can hardly be imagined. Houses and factories are alike built chiefly of dull yellow brick, further dulled by soft-coal smoke. The intervening stretches of countryside are equally unattractive. The soil, though carefully tended, looks thin, much of it supporting only scrub pine.

At some of the larger stations were sizable groups of soldiers, perhaps mobilized reservists waiting for troop trains. They were in field kit, from steel helmets to heavy marching boots coming halfway to the knee. Incidentally, the present German uniform is not the "field-gray" of the last war. It is a dull gray-green, unimpressive in appearance yet blending well with the landscape, which wartime uniforms should do.

Towns became more frequent, until we were obviously on the outskirts of a metropolitan area. I was nearing Berlin. Now and then the train passed extensive freight-yards. Here it was interesting to note the quantity of captured Polish rolling-stock. Like the German freight cars, they were painted dull red, but were distinguished by a stenciled Polish eagle in white with the letters PKP. In most cases there had been added the significant word DEUTSCH, meaning that the cars are now German.

At length the train slackened speed and pulled into the vast, barn-like Anhalter Bahnhof, the central station for trains from the south. I had arrived in Berlin, Germany's capital and metropolis.

II. BERLIN BLACKOUT

MY ENTRY INTO BERLIN WAS NOT A CHEERING ONE. THE train was nearly two hours late and there was no diner, so I had had nothing except the traditional cowpuncher's breakfast—a sip of water and a cigarette. The chill autumnal air made me shiver as I stepped from the train. Porters, it seemed, were scarce in wartime Germany, and I was fortunate to pre-empt one to carry my abundant hand-luggage.

My first job was to get some German money, for I hadn't a pfennig to my name. You can't legally buy Reichsmarks abroad. What the traveler does is to take out a letter of credit before he leaves his native land. While in Germany he draws on this and gets what is known as Registered Marks which are much cheaper than the official quotation of 2.4 to the dollar. I bought my letter of credit in New York at the rate of nearly five to the dollar. That meant a twenty-cent mark—a saving of almost 100 per .cent. The traveler is supposed to use this money only for living expenses, and every draft is entered on his passport as well as on his letter of credit, thus enabling the authorities to check up on what he has spent when he leaves Germany. However, the allowance is liberal, and unless his drafts indicate that he has been buying a good deal, he will have no trouble. Of course, one gets ordinary currency. The Registered Mark is merely a bookkeeping phrase.

At one of the bureaus maintained at every large railway station I drew enough cash to last me for a few days, then my porter found me one of the few taxis available. Both cab and driver were of ancient vintage, but they rattled me safely to my hotel. This was the famous Adlon, situated on Berlin's main avenue, Unter den Linden.

While unpacking I had the pleasure of a telephone call from a German named Sallett whom I had informed of my coming. I had known him when he was attached to the German Embassy in Washington. Now he was in the American Section of the Foreign Office, so I counted on him to start me right. Since the day was Sunday there was nothing officially to be done, but he asked me to meet him at lunch for a preliminary chat and to come to his home for dinner that same evening.

Before keeping my luncheon date, however, I took care to equip myself with food-cards—those precious bits of paper on which one's very life depends. Incidentally they are not cards, but blocks of coupons, reminiscent of the trading-stamps issued by some of our department stores. The clerk at the desk inscribed my name in a big book and handed me a week's supply in the shape of little blocks of coupons variously colored. Each coupon is good for so many grams of bread, butter, meat, and other edibles. Every time you eat a meal you must tear off the various coupons required for each dish, the amount being printed on the bill of fare. And the waiter must collect them when you give your order, because he in turn must hand them in to the kitchen before he can bring you your food. This has nothing to do with price. In the last analysis, each of these food-coupons is what the Germans call a *Bezugschein*—an official permit to purchase an article of a specific kind and quality. Let me illustrate: You want to buy some meat. Each of your meat coupons entitles you to so many grams. You may go into an inexpensive restaurant and get the cheapest grade of sausage or you can go into the best hotel and get a finely cooked filet mignon. The price will differ enormously, but the number of meat coupons you hand over is precisely the same.

I needed to take along my food-cards even though I had been invited to lunch. In Germany, no matter how wealthy your host may be, he has no more coupons than anyone else and so cannot furnish them for his guests. That is true of all meals in hotels or restaurants. It does not apply when the host invites you to his own home. He then has to do all the honors. This severely limits domestic hospitality. In such cases the guests are usually served fish, game, or some other delicacy for which food cards are not required.

Dr. Sallett had asked me to lunch with him at the Kaiserhof, a well-known hotel some distance down the Wilhelmstrasse. It is the Nazi social headquarters, and when prominent members of the Party come to Berlin from the provinces they usually stop there. Sallett met me in the lobby, resplendent in a gray diplomatic uniform cut with the swank which military tailors know how to attain. Being Sunday, the usual week-day crowd was lacking in the dining room. Those who were present seemed to be much of a type—vigorous men, mostly in their thirties or forties, some of them hard-faced and all with an air of assurance and authority. Nearly all of them wore the Party emblem, a button about the size of a half-dollar bearing a red swastika on a white background.

My first meal in the Third Reich was a distinct success. As might have been expected in this pre-eminent Nazi hostelry, the food was good and the service quick. The imitation coffee, an *Ersatz* made of roasted barley, was banal, but it was remedied by an excellent pony of old German brandy. Thereafter, my friend Sallett explained to me the various things I must do in order to get going without loss of time.

When we had parted until evening, I strolled back along the Wilhelmstrasse to get the feel of my new abode. I noted how the famous street had architecturally had its face lifted since I was there a decade before. Across the broad square from the Kaiserhof stood the new Chancery, while on the opposite side of the street was the equally new Ministry for Popular Enlightenment and Propaganda—an institution I was to know extremely well, since all foreign correspondents fall under its special jurisdiction. Both buildings typify the new Nazi architecture—their exteriors severely plain, whatever magnificence may be within. This is a conscious reaction from the ornate exaggerations of the old Empire style, which is frowned on as vulgar and tasteless.

Just beyond the Chancery is the rather modest old eighteenth-century palace which is Adolf Hitler's official residence. It sets well back from the street behind a high iron railing. Above its gabled roof floated a special swastika flag to denote that *Der Fuehrer* was at home. That is the way Germans always speak of him. Very rarely do they use his name. With a sort of impersonal reverence, he is *Der Fuehrer,* The Leader, in Teutonic minds.

The railing before the palace has two gates through which motor cars can enter and leave by a semicircular drive. These gates were guarded by Security Police, nicknamed *Schupos,* in green uniforms and visored black leather hats. Before the entrance to the palace itself stood two military sentries in field gray. Across the street clustered a large group of sightseers, gazing silently at their leader's residence. Even on weekdays one can always find such onlookers from dawn to dusk, after which loitering on the Wilhelmstrasse is not allowed.

The streets were well filled with Sunday strollers, and since the misting rain of the forenoon had let up, I thought it a good opportunity to get a look at the holiday crowds. I therefore walked for an hour or more up and down Unter den Linden, around the Pariser Platz, and finally back to my hotel. My outstanding impression of these wartime Berliners was a thoroughgoing impassivity. They seemed stolidly casual with expressionless faces. Almost never did I see a really animated conversation; neither was there laughter or even a smile. Twice I dropped briefly into a café. In both cases the patrons sat chatting quietly, and from snatches of talk I overheard the conversation was wholly about personal or local affairs. Not once did I catch a discussion of the war or other public matters.

Uniforms naturally abounded. Soldiers, obviously on Sunday liberty, passed and repassed, sometimes in large groups. They never sauntered but clumped along at a fair pace, their hobnailed boots clashing heavily upon the pavement. Most of them had fine physique and all looked well nourished and generally fit. Now and then I saw a Nazi storm-trooper clad in brown with a red swastika arm band. More often I encountered a black-uniformed S.S. man—the Party's *Schutz Staffeln,* or Elite Guard. Twice I passed groups of Hitler Youth, boys dressed entirely in dark blue, from cloth hat to baggy ski-trousers tucked into high boots. There was much punctilious saluting. The soldiers gave the army salute, a quick touch of the fingers to helmet or forage cap. The others gave the stiff-armed Nazi greeting.

The most interesting example of Berlin's impassive popular mood was the attitude toward the tightly closed British Embassy which is just around the corner from the Adlon. There it stands, with gilded lions and uni corns upon its portals. I had rather expected that this diplomatic seat of the arch-enemy would attract some attention, especially on a Sunday, when this part of town was thronged with outside visitors. Yet, though I watched closely for some time, I never saw a soul give the building more than a passing glance, much less point to it or demonstrate in any way.

Another surprising thing was how well dressed the people appeared. I saw many suits and overcoats which had obviously been worn a long time, but invariably they were tidy and clean. At the moment I thought this good showing was because everyone was wearing Sunday best, but I could detect little difference on subsequent days. In fact wherever I went in Germany the people dressed about the same. Nowhere did I see ragged, unkempt persons. I was told that the cheaper fabrics, made largely of wood synthetics mixed with shoddy, absorb dampness quickly, get heavy, and are hard to dry out. Nevertheless, they *look* good, though

I doubt the efficacy of their resistance to rain and cold.

One thing those clothes did lack, however, and that was style. The range of models was small, and they were obviously designed for service rather than smartness. Overcoats were mostly of the ulster type, and that goes for the women too. While I did see a considerable number of ladies who were well-dressed according to our standards, the average Berlin female, with her ulsterette or raincoat, her plain felt hat, her cotton stockings, and her low-heeled shoes, rarely warrants a second look. I may add that she uses little or no make-up and seldom has her hair waved. Such beautifying is frowned upon by strict Nazis as unpatriotic.

My first stroll indicated another thing confirmed by subsequent observation. This is that Berlin remains what it always was—a city lacking both color and the indefinable charm of antiquity. Its architecture is monotonous, and the drab effect is heightened by its misty northern climate. Most of the autumn season is cloudy with frequent light rain. Even on so-called clear days the low-hanging sun shines wanly through a veil of mist.

By this time the early autumn dusk was falling, so I returned to the Adlon. I did not dress for my evening appointment because in wartime Germany one rarely wears even a dinner jacket. A double-breasted dark suit is deemed ample for almost all occasions. My friends the Salletts lived some distance away from my hotel, but I had ordered a taxi so I was sure of transportation. The taxi situation is one of the many drawbacks to life in wartime Berlin. Because of the strict rationing of gasoline, taxis are scarce even by day and scarcer still at night. They are supposed to be used only for business or necessity, so drivers are not allowed to take you to any place of amusement, even to the opera. Neither do they cruise the streets for fares, so unless you know a regular cab stand you can almost never pick one up.

The hotel lobby was brilliantly lighted when I descended, but thick curtains had been drawn across the entrance. I slipped through them to encounter that most trying of all wartime Berlin's phenomena, the *Verdunklung,* or blackout. As I emerged through the swing-doors it hit me literally like a blow in the face. The misting rain had begun again, and it was dark as a pocket. The broad avenue of Unter den Linden was a maw of blackness. Not a street light except the cross-slitted traffic signals at the nearby corner of the Wilhelmstrasse. They were hardly needed for the few motor cars and occasional buses that crawled slowly by. Well might they drive cautiously, for their headlights were hooded save for a tiny orifice emitting a dim ray. As I stood on the sidewalk waiting for my taxi, pedestrians picked their way warily in the inky gloom, sensed rather than seen. Some of them wore phosphorescent buttons to avoid collisions with other passers-by. Others used small electric lamps to guide their steps, flashing them off quickly and always holding them pointed downward toward the ground. Any other use of a flashlight is strictly prohibited. To turn it upward to read a street sign or find a house number rates a warning shout from one of the policemen who seem to be everywhere after dark. Indeed, such action may lead to arrest and a fifty-mark fine, which at par is about twenty dollars.

I entered my taxi with some trepidation. How was the driver going to find my friend's address, avoid collisions, or even keep to the roadway on a night like this? Yet he seemed to know his business, for he forged steadily onward, with many mysterious turns and twists through the maze of unseen streets and avenues. As for me, I could not see even the houses on either hand, though I sensed their looming presence and marveled at the thought of all the life and light pent in behind numberless shrouded windows. The only visible objects were pin-point lights of approaching motor cars and occasional trams or buses which clattered past like noisy ghosts. They were lit within by tiny blue bulbs revealing shadow passengers. Wartime Berlin had indeed become a "city of dreadful night." No description can adequately convey the depressing, almost paralyzing, effect. It must be *lived* to be understood.

At length my taxi halted. The driver flashed a light which showed a couple of doorways quite close together. "It must be one of those two," he said, as I got out and paid him.

Fortunately I had with me a flashlight brought from America. It was small as a fountain pen and could be clipped into my vest pocket. The sight of it never failed to evoke envious admiration from German acquaintances. Heedless of lurking policemen, I flashed its tiny beam upward at the house number which, as usual, was perched on the tip top of a high door. It was not the right place. I tried the next door. It had no number and seemed to be disused. I tried the next house. The numbers were running the wrong way. Meanwhile the misty drizzle had increased to a smart downpour.

Feeling utterly helpless, I determined to seek information; so I pressed the button to the first floor apartment and as the latch clicked I went inside. As I walked across the hallway the apartment entrance opened and a pleasant-faced young woman stood in the doorway. I explained the situation, stating that I was a total stranger. Her face grew sympathetic, then set in a quick frown.

"You say that taxi man didn't make sure?" she exclaimed. "Ach, how stupid! The fellow ought to be reported. Wait a minute and I'll show you myself." She disappeared, returning a moment later wearing a raincoat.

I protested that I could find my way from her directions, but she would have none of it. "No, no," she insisted. "Such treatment to a newly arrived foreigner! I am bound to make up for that driver's inefficiency."

Together we sallied forth into the pattering rain. On the way she explained that my friend's apartment house, though listed as on her street, had its entrance just around the corner on another avenue. She thought that also very stupid.

Arriving as I did somewhat late, I found the others already there. To my great pleasure the chief guest was Alexander Kirk, our Chargé d'Affaires in Berlin. He is doing a fine diplomatic job in a most difficult post. Generally popular, he does not hesitate to speak plainly when he needs to. And, instead of getting offended, the Germans seem to like him all the better for it. Some weeks later, Mr. Kirk won new laurels by vetoing the usual Thanksgiving celebration of the American colony in a restaurant or hotel. He argued that, when all Germany was strictly rationed, such public feasting would be in bad taste. Instead, he invited his fellow-citizens to a private dinner at his own palatial residence in a fashionable suburb. The Germans considered that the height of tactful courtesy.

The other two guests were Herr Hewel, one of Hitler's confidential advisers, and Dr. Otto Schramm, a leading Berlin surgeon. In the course of the evening, Dr. Schramm told me about a new synthetic fat which had just been invented. Elaborate experiments were being made to produce not only a substitute for soap but also an edible compound to supplement animal fats and vegetable oils. This, he claimed, would soon remedy blockaded Germany's chief dietary danger, since it could be produced from chemical constituents abundantly available. The talk ran late. Fortunately, I was taken back to my hotel in Herr Hewel's car, which, being an official, he could still use.

Just before reaching the Adlon we encountered a column of huge army trucks going up Unter den Linden and out through the Brandenburger Tor. I was afterward told that material and ordnance, routed through Berlin, are usually moved late at night. There must have been plenty of activity on that occasion, for long after I had retired I could hear intermittent rumblings of heavy traffic whose vibrations came to me even through the Adlon's thick walls.

III. GETTING ON WITH THE JOB

I WENT TO EUROPE AS SPECIAL CORRESPONDENT OF THE North American Newspaper Alliance, a press syndicate with membership in the United States, Canada, and other parts of the world. My main field was Germany, with side-glances elsewhere in Central Europe. Since N.A.N.A. is a feature service, my job was to study conditions, do interpretive or local color articles, and get important interviews. I was not professionally interested in spot news. To do a good job I had to have an open mind; so I did my best to park my private opinions on this side of the ocean. And since my return I've tried not to pick them up again.

An objective attitude was made easier by the fact that the outbreak of the European War caught me in a place where it meant nothing except its effect on the price of sugar—Havana, Cuba.

Between a survey I was making with a Washington colleague, H. H. Stansbury, and the terrific heat I could pay scant attention to European affairs, which were badly covered in the Havana press. Everybody was absorbed in local politics. The Batista Government was getting ready to celebrate the anniversary of its revolutionary origin, the momentous date being September 4th. So Havana was all bedizened with flags and bunting, while across the harbor on Morro Castle and

Cabañas Fortress rose huge transparencies bearing the legends: BATISTA and CUARTO SETIEMBRE electrically blazing forth o'nights in giant letters of fire. Then, just before the big party, Europe had to explode! Small wonder that it hardly made a dent on Cuban thinking, except the sugar phase.

However, it made a big dent on my mind. I had already canvassed the possibility of personally covering the German situation, for which I had certain qualifications such as an intermittent knowledge of the country since childhood and a working knowledge of the language. I had also followed German events regularly in my studies of foreign affairs. Therefore as soon as I could wind up my Cuban survey, I hurried home, reaching New York late in September. Three weeks afterwards I was on the *Rex*, Europe-bound. I thus arrived on the scene of action in an objective state of mind.

To get working quickly and efficiently, three things had to be done as soon as possible. First of all, I must present my credentials and acquire the permits needed by a foreign correspondent in wartime. Then I had to establish correct and personally amicable relations with the officials with whom I would be in contact. Last but not least, I should get on really friendly terms with the outstanding members of the foreign press corps—not merely the Americans but those of the other neutral nationalities stationed in Berlin. An experienced, capable foreign correspondent is your best source of information. He usually knows more and sees clearer than a diplomat of the same caliber. This is also true of certain long-resident foreign professional or business men. Furthermore, both they and the correspondents can talk more freely to you. There are certain things which members of the diplomatic corps hesitate to discuss unreservedly with you even in the strictest "off the record."

Fortunately I was able to make a good start on all three lines the very first day after my arrival in Berlin. Monday noon found me at the Foreign Office, half-way down the Wilhelmstrasse, where I was to attend the foreign press conference held there daily at this hour. These conferences are usually held in a large oblong room, elaborately paneled. Down the middle of this chamber runs an enormously long table covered with green baize. On one side of the table sit a line of Government officials drawn from both the Foreign Office and the Propaganda Ministry. One of these men is the Government spokesman for the day, who makes announcements and answers questions either directly or through some other official who is a specialist in the particular matter. On the other side of the table cluster the foreign correspondents, representing every neutral country in Europe, plus a few Orientals and a strong contingent of Americans. The average attendance runs between fifty and seventy, including several women journalists.

Personal relations between these Government spokesmen and the foreign correspondents are generally friendly and sometimes cordial. The officials are intelligent men specially picked for the business of tactfully handling foreign journalists. The correspondents are, for the most part, old hands who know how to play the game. So the conferences, which are conducted in German, usually go off smoothly, with humorous undertones as a shrewd query is met by an equally shrewd parry. These bits of repartee are often greeted by a general burst of laughter.

After the conference that morning I was introduced to the chief officials, and I likewise met several of our American press delegation to whom I had been recommended or with whom I was previously acquainted. The officials were nearly all university men, some with doctorate degrees. Those in the American Section were well fitted for their posts. Dr. Sallett, the Foreign Office contact man for Americans, had lived in the United States for years before he entered the diplomatic service and had done postgraduate work at Harvard. Dr. Froelich, head of the Propaganda Ministry's American Bureau, has a Harvard Law School degree, while his junior colleague, Werner Asendorf, is a graduate of the University of Oregon. Both these men have American wives. The head of the entire Foreign Press Section, Dr. Boehme, is an engaging personality with a quick intelligence and cynical sense of humor, who has traveled widely in many lands including the United States. I felt from the first that here were men who knew us well and with whom one could get along harmoniously.

That same afternoon I attended another foreign press conference, this time at the Propaganda Ministry. These conferences, likewise held every week-day, deal more with special topics than with spot news. Government specialists address the correspondents on current military, naval, or economic situations, while outstanding figures are produced for inspection. For instance, when a big aerial battle was fought over the North Sea, the squadron commander and his flying aces appeared be-

fore the foreign journalists to tell their side of the story
and be questioned.

Before the inevitable blackout ended my first working day in Berlin I had been duly enrolled in the foreign press corps and had filed my application for a Press
Wireless permit. This is the correspondent's most important privilege. It enables him to file press despatches
to his newspaper or syndicate, payment guaranteed at
the other end. Furthermore, those despatches go
through uncensored. I am sure of this, both from what
I was told and from my own experience. For instance,
I filed a despatch at a small sub-station as late as 6.15
P.M., Berlin Time (12.15 noon, Eastern Standard Time)
and it appeared in all editions of the New York *Times*
next morning. This would have been impossible if
there had been even the short delay which a most
cursory check-up before putting the despatch on the
wireless would have involved.

This brings up one of the most interesting aspects
of wartime Germany—the system of handling foreign
journalists. Right at the start I was told at the Propaganda Ministry just where I stood and what I could,
and could not, write. Military and naval matters were,
of course, severely circumscribed, together with topics
such as sensational rumors obviously tending to dis-
credit the German Government and give aid and comfort to its enemies. There was a sort of gentleman's
agreement with the correspondent that he would abide
by rules laid down for his guidance. If he overstepped
the line and a despatch, when published in his home
paper, contained matter which the German authorities
considered untrue, unfair, or otherwise unprofessional,
the correspondent would be called onto the carpet and

warned to mend his ways. If the offense was flagrant he might be formally expelled from the foreign press corps, thereby losing his official status with all its attendant privileges. His professional usefulness would thus be at an end, and he might as well leave Germany even though not formally expelled.

This gentlemen's agreement system is equally obvious in the matter of interviews. When you interview an official personage you are required to submit your manuscript to the Propaganda Ministry which makes a German translation and lays it before the person interviewed for his approval. Obviously, it is necessary for the Government to see to it that its leading spokesmen are correctly quoted and that statements made to the interviewer "off the record" are not published. So it often happens that considerable changes have to be made before the final draft is O.K.'d. Once approval is given, however, there is no further check-up and the interview can be filed for the wireless in the same way as any press despatch. Technically, there is nothing to prevent your sending the original version. But naturally, if the published interview does not tally with the draft agreed upon, it will be clear that you have broken faith, and confidence in your reliability is destroyed.

The same policy applies to foreign telephone service. Most Berlin correspondents of newspapers in European neutral countries have telephone permits similar to Press Wireless for us Americans. Such permits enable the European correspondent to telephone his despatches directly from his Berlin office to his home paper. These talks may be subject to a double check—by listening in and by transcription on dictaphone records. However, even when this is done, it is seemingly to catch such

obvious indiscretions as discussion of military matters.
I never heard of a press telephone conversation being
broken into or stopped. Here again the foreign correspondent is called to account only when a despatch
published in his home paper contains something which
German officialdom considers a violation of the rules
of the game.

During my stay in Berlin, the Propaganda Ministry
evolved an ingenious method of expediting press stories
sent by mail. All such material could be turned into a
special bureau with the understanding that the manuscript would be read and mailed within twenty-four
hours unless something objectionable should be discovered. Being mailed in a special envelope, it went
through without scrutiny by the regular censors. In case
of objection, the correspondent was notified, and specific changes or eliminations were suggested. Here, as
elsewhere, objections seemed to have been rarely made
except for reasons already explained.

The foreign correspondent can go pretty far in describing current conditions and general situations. German officialdom seems to have realized that it is no use
trying to stop press stories about matters which are un-
deniably true and widely known. Let me cite one instance from my own experience. I had written a pair of
"mailers" describing in detail the many vexations and
hardships which German housewives had to endure.
They went through the Propaganda Ministry all right,
but I wanted to find out the official reaction to them.
Accordingly, I tried them out on an official who I was
sure had not read them. He scanned them carefully and
handed them back with a slightly wry smile. "American
readers will be apt to think we're in tough shape," he

said. "I really think you left out certain qualifying factors which would have made the picture less dark. However," he ended with a shrug, "what you do say is all true, and I believe you're trying to be fair. So, under our present policy, we can make no legitimate kick."

Of course, the latitude extended foreign correspondents has its practical limits. Should a correspondent unearth some unpalatable information he is more than likely to be told that such a despatch, even though true and not falling under the ordinary tabus, is displeasing to the German Government. I know of one such instance where the offender was plainly told that, if he publicized any more exceptional discoveries of this kind, he would get into serious trouble.

There seems also to be distinct discrimination between the latitude permitted the correspondents of powerful neutrals and those of the small European countries which fall more or less within Germany's orbit. More than once their press representatives said to me: "We can't write nearly as freely as you Americans. If we did, the German Government would either crack down on us directly or make strong diplomatic protests to our own Governments, who in turn might make it hot for our home papers."

Such things make it abundantly clear that, in its seemingly liberal attitude toward foreign correspondents, the German Government is animated by no idealistic motives. Its policy is severely practical. The shrewd brains which run the Propaganda Ministry have decided that it pays to treat foreign correspondents well and help them to get their despatches out with a minimum of red tape and avoidable delay. Nothing makes a newspaperman more contented than that. But that isn't the only reason. The very fact that Berlin despatches to the foreign press sometimes contain items unfavorable to Germany tends to give public opinion the idea that a Berlin date-line is relatively reliable, and this in turn aids the German Government in pushing out its foreign propaganda. Finally, there is no danger that any of those unfavorable items will leak back to the German public, because they are not allowed to be printed in any German newspaper.

Nothing can be more startling than the contrast between the respective treatments of foreign journalists and their German colleagues. The German press is rigidly controlled. Indeed, German papers print very little straight news as we understand the term. Every item published is elaborately scrutinized. I had one illuminating instance of this when I was invited by the head of a German press syndicate to contribute a short statement of my impressions of wartime Europe. Having been assured that I could write what I chose, I stated frankly that we Americans thought another long war would ruin Europe economically, no matter which side was victorious. The Propaganda Ministry promptly vetoed publication, and I was tactfully but firmly told that such a statement, though quite proper for my fellow countrymen, was deemed unsuitable for German readers.

When he travels, the foreign correspondent encounters the same condition of circumscribed freedom as he does in sending his despatches. Over most of Germany he can travel almost as freely as he could in peacetime —by train or commercial bus, of course, since gasoline rationing makes private motor trips impossible. The only apparent check on his movements is the requirement to turn in his passport when he registers at a hotel. But there are certain parts of the Reich which are rigidly barred zones. He cannot go anywhere near the West-Wall, the fortified belt of territory along the French, Belgian, and Dutch borders. He cannot visit the fortified coasts of the North Sea and the Baltic. He cannot enter German-occupied Poland—at least, he could not during my stay in Germany. He has to get special permission to enter the Protectorate of Bohemia-Moravia, and even then he is under such close surveillance that no patriotic Czech will dare come near him.

Such, briefly, are the conditions under which the foreign correspondent lives and works in wartime Germany. Within limits, he can operate quickly and efficiently. There are quite a few locked doors, and he had best not try to open them. But at least he knows where he stands, and the rules of the game are made clear to him.

IV. JUNKETING THROUGH GERMANY

AT THE VERY FIRST PRESS CONFERENCE I ATTENDED AT the Propaganda Ministry we were informed that a trip was being arranged for foreign correspondents and all who wished to go were asked to register. It was to be a three-day journey through Central Germany and the northern Rhineland. Its purpose was to observe the "Inner Front"; how the peasants and industrial workers were doing their bit to carry on the war.

"I advise you to come along," said an American colleague with whom I sat. "I can't vouch for how much they'll show us, but you'll see quite a bit of the country, and then you'll get to know a good many of the press corps. That alone should make the trip worth while for you."

Accordingly, the fourth day after my arrival in Berlin found me ready to take the road again. Noon saw about forty journalists assembled with light luggage at the Propaganda Ministry. Ours was a cosmopolitan group, drawn mostly from European lands, together with five Americans, two Japanese, and an Egyptian with crinkly hair and complexion *café au lait*. A lone Danish lady journalist, rather pretty and on the bright side of thirty, had ventured to join this phalanx of masculinity. Having observed her at several press conferences, I judged her capable of taking care of herself in any circumstances likely to arise.

We were welcomed by a bevy of officials, some of whom would accompany us. After a fulsome speech, our itinerary was read out, telling just where we were going and what we were to see and do. Before starting on a sightseeing trip, Germans apparently like to have everything worked out down to the last detail. Good staff work, yet sometimes a bit trying; since, under no circumstances, can there be the slightest deviation from the plan prescribed.

After the oratory had ended we were bidden to fall to on several platters heaped high with sandwiches, which graced the long table about which we were standing. One of the things you quickly learn in Germany is to eat whenever eatables come your way. Food restrictions and uncertainties soon develop in you a sort of psychological hunger which is never wholly out of your mind. So we did full justice to this buffet lunch.

Leaving the festive board we descended to the street, where we found awaiting us two enormous sightseeing buses into which we climbed. We Americans had kept together, so we were all seated in Bus Number One. Near me were seated a Belgian, a Dutch, and a Hungarian journalist. Swinging out by Unter den Linden and thence to Potsdam, we presently found ourselves on one of the Third Reich's famous motor roads. Mile on mile the twin ribbons of concrete stretched before us, separated always by a broad grassy strip. No crossings to look out for, since all intersecting roads and railways are taken care of by over- or underpass. Yet this magnificent highway was virtually empty of traffic. With all private motoring forbidden, official cars, army camions or commercial trucks were almost its sole occupants.

Every few miles I noted a combined restaurant and filling-station tastefully built. About mid-afternoon we stopped at one of them for another meal. Incipient hunger was assuaged with hot frankfurters and sauerkraut, cold ham, cheese, and rye bread, washed down with plenty of schnapps and beer. Before proceeding on our way we were lined up before one of the buses and had our picture taken. Group photography is a German specialty, so this was repeated on every noteworthy occasion. Subsequently, each of us received the whole collection mounted in a handsome album, as a souvenir.

As our cavalcade rolled swiftly southwestward, the afternoon waned into misty twilight, and with the universal blackout we knew that there would be no bus lights for us. To brighten our spirits, a large carton in the rear of the bus was opened, revealing a case of brandy. Our hosts were indeed missing no opportunities to create a favorable impression. An attendant went up and down the aisle pouring drinks into paper cups. Pleased to find it was a good French brand, I expressed my appreciation to one of the Propaganda Ministry officials seated across the way. He smiled jovially, then winked, nodded toward the nearby carton, and whispered: "Slip a bottle into your overcoat pocket while the going is good." Somebody started a song up ahead. The brandy was getting to work. My American seatmate slapped me on the knee. "Looks like a good junket," he chuckled somewhat cynically.

It was long after dark when our buses rolled through the blacked-out streets of Weimar and halted before

Haus Elefant. The Elephant House is the name of Weimar's splendid new hotel. I understand it was built to accommodate the tourist trade to this picturesque old town, but now there are no tourists. That evening we were given a banquet presided over by the *Gauleiter,* or Provincial Governor of Thuringia, and attended by all the local Nazi notables. I sat next to him at table and thus had a chance to chat with him.

I liked that Gauleiter. He was very much a self-made man, having started as a sailor, literally "before the mast" on a windjammer. He was also self-educated, but he exemplified Lord Bacon's dictum that much reading maketh a full man, because he had obviously digested his books. Although sincerely devoted to the Party's program and policies, he did not parrot them forth in set phrases, as many Nazis do, but interpreted them with shrewd common sense.

I did not care much, however, for the other local notables. They looked to me like German equivalents of our own ward politicians. Few of them could have amounted to much before they landed a Party job. Even more revealing were their womenfolk, who joined us in the big hotel lounge for *Ersatz* coffee and liqueurs after the banquet was over. Most of them were pretentiously dowdy. They exemplified better than anything I had yet seen the fact that National Socialism is not merely a political and economic upheaval but a social revolution as well. To a very large extent it has brought the lower middle class into power. To be sure, one finds quite a few aristocrats and intellectuals in the Nazi regime. Furthermore, there are plenty of Nazis sprung from peasant or worker stock, some of whom, like the Weimar Gauleiter, would rise in any society. Yet the lower middle class seems to be inordinately in evidence. One does not notice this so much in Berlin, because the ablest elements in the Party tend to gravitate to the seat of power. In the provinces the *Spiessbürgertum* comes much more to the front.

With our heavy schedule, we rose early and descended to an amazing breakfast for wartime Germany. I could hardly believe my eyes when they feasted themselves on plenteous eggs and butter unlimited. We were the guests of the Propaganda Ministry, so for us food restrictions were politely waived. One luxury, however, we did not get—real coffee. That tabu was seemingly unbreakable.

With the inner man thus fortified we climbed into our buses, toured Weimar briefly to glimpse its historic sights, and took to the highroad once more. Just outside of town we were delayed by a long caravan of army trucks, crammed with everything from supplies and field kitchens to troops and machine-guns. Flanked by convoys of sputtering motorcycles, they thundered endlessly past. Everything was slate-gray.

All that morning we motored through the hills and valleys of Thuringia, a charming countryside dotted with mellow villages and clean little towns. Peasants and townsfolk alike looked well-fed and warmly clad. The many children who waved to our passing were rosy-cheeked and smiling. The day was unseasonably cold. Snow powdered even the lower hills.

Shortly after noon we reached the Wartburg. For nearly two hours we were herded through the historic place like holiday trippers while we were shown every last detail down to the exact spot on the wall where Martin Luther's inkstand is supposed to have missed the devil. I got distinctly bored. I wasn't in Germany for sightseeing, and I knew the Wartburg of old. I wanted to be shown peasants, farms, dairies, cold-storage plants—the rural sector of that "Inner Front" we had heard so much about. But apparently we weren't going to be shown.

I said as much to one of our official guides. He assured me that I would see peasants that very evening. It was all nicely arranged. So we rolled through country growing ever more hilly until darkness overtook us on the slopes of the Sauerland Mountains. Soon we arrived at what had originally been a large farmstead, now transformed into an inn. As we sat down to a bounteous country supper, in walked our peasants. They were the real articles, all right: sturdy, weatherbeaten men, washed and dressed up for the occasion yet still exhaling a faint aroma of livestock. A couple of them were assigned to each table, and I was fortunate enough to have a fine old fellow for my right-hand neighbor. In rural Germany they have a habit of sandwiching schnapps and beer, which makes a potent combination, and we soon got on famously. After several rounds, my companion waxed garrulous and began to air his views on several subjects, including the war. Before he had got far, however, a young servingman bent down and muttered in his ear: "Gaffer, you've had a lot to drink. Bridle your tongue!" Thereafter he kept to safer topics.

In mid-evening we left our bucolic partners and motored on to a fine new winter-sports hotel perched on the summit of the range, where we were to spend the night. Here winter had already come, though it was only the beginning of November. The ground was well covered with snow, and more was falling, whipped by a biting wind.

Next morning we were again up bright and early, and after another "off the record" breakfast our buses plowed through snow-clogged mountain roads which wound downwards through fine forests until we emerged from the mountains and struck out into the Westphalian plains. Quaint timbered-brick farmsteads and villages gave place to industrial towns until we were fairly into Germany's "black country," the industrial ganglion of the Rhineland, dotted with factories and murky with coal smoke. Snow had long since been left behind. The autumn day, as usual, was cloudy with spits of rain.

We grazed the outskirts of Cologne but got only a distant glimpse of its twin-towered cathedral. Our destination was Duesseldorf, where we were promised the most interesting feature of the trip. This was a luncheon with the workers at the big Henkel Soap Products factory. We were to hobnob with them at their noon hour, share their food, and generally get acquainted. After the meal we and the workers were to be addressed by none other than Dr. Robert Ley, head of the Labor Front, the organization which welds all the workers of the Third Reich into a gigantic whole. A sort of Nazi One Big Union.

With Teutonic punctuality, our buses drew up before the Henkel factory at precisely the appointed hour. After a brief reception by the managerial staff we repaired to the dining hall, an enormous place capable of holding over a thousand people. The workers, about equally divided between men and women, were already pouring in. They were in their work clothes; the men in dark overalls, the women mostly in smocks. They had evidently washed up for lunch, for all looked neat and clean. Besides, a soap factory ought not to be a very dirty place.

These working folk looked fairly healthy, though few of them had much color and many had pasty complexions. They seemed cheerful and smiled readily. I even noted some surreptitious sky-larking between the young men and girls. However, it should be remembered that these were Rhinelanders, folk temperamentally freer and gayer than the stiff, dour Prussians to the eastward.

We journalists were mixed thoroughly with the workers. I sat at a table accommodating some twenty of them. Opposite me were three men: one a nondescript type, the second a hulking blond giant, the third a slim, darkish, handsome fellow who looked like a Frenchman. At my left hand sat a plain-featured woman in middle life; at my right, a chunky little blonde girl in her late teens.

Hardly were we seated before a bevy of waitresses swept through the hall bearing large trays laden with plates of thick potato soup. The next course consisted of pork, red cabbage, and mixed vegetables, served in miniature platters with separate compartments. Slabs of rye bread went with the soup. It certainly was a hearty lunch, and well cooked. The meat gravy was good, and there was plenty of it. I could not finish all that was set before me.

My neighbors were obviously hungry and attended so strictly to the business of eating that conversation languished until toward the end of the meal. The girl beside me smilingly accepted one of my proffered cigarettes. Before I had time to invite the men across the table, each had produced a packet of his own and lit up. I then began asking a few tactful questions. They told me that this was an average luncheon, that they were working longer hours than before the war but were paid a bit extra for overtime, that part of the plant was being diverted to munitions, and that comparatively few men from the factory had as yet been called to the colors since so many of them were skilled workers. This was about all the information I got, since they were bent on asking me questions about America.

Suddenly a gong sounded and all eyes turned toward the center of the hall, where a rotund figure in a blue uniform had mounted one of the tables and was bowing smilingly to left and right in response to a growing ripple of applause. He was the great Dr. Ley. His rotund countenance was wreathed in smiles as he acknowledged the greeting. Then he began speaking in a loud, rasping voice, addressing the assembled workers as "Soldiers of the Inner Front" and assuring them that their labors were as praiseworthy and vital to the conduct of the war as were deeds of valor on the battlefield. He then launched into a diatribe against England and its allegedly diabolical attempt to starve out the German people, including women and children, by the hunger blockade. A lurid picture of the terrible starvation years of the last war was followed by comforting reassurances that the Government had rendered such privations in the present struggle impossible because of careful preparations and methodical planning. Foodcards might be annoying, but there was enough to go around and everyone, rich or poor, was assured of his or her rightful share. "This time," he shouted, "we all eat out of the same dish!" He closed with an eloquent appeal to stand beside their inspired Fuehrer until complete and lasting victory had been won.

It was a rousing speech, and it seemed to strike home. Those working folk listened with rapt attention, at the high points breaking into applause which was clearly spontaneous. Dr. Ley is obviously a good psychologist. He knows his audience. Certainly he was onto his job that day as head of the Labor Front.

When the speech was over and the workers had returned to their labors we correspondents were introduced to Dr. Ley and were then shown around the factory buildings in the usual detail. Needless to say, we did not see the munitions section to which my luncheon companion had casually alluded.

It was mid-afternoon when we reached our hotel, one of the best in the city. With nothing officially scheduled until dinnertime, a number of us strolled about town. One of my acquaintances had a severe head cold and needed to buy some handkerchiefs. He could not buy ordinary cotton or linen ones, because that required a local clothing card. However, he finally found some expensive silk handkerchiefs which were "card-free," because they were *Luxuswaren*—luxury goods.

The dinner that night turned out to be a big banquet, with an excellent menu and vintage wines. Again the local Nazi notables were present, and they averaged better in appearance than those at Weimar. All but the Gauleiter. He was a distinctly sinister-looking type; hard-faced, with a cruel eye and a still crueler mouth. A sadist, if I ever saw one. I can imagine how unpopular he must be among the good-natured, kindly Duesseldorfers.

The banquet was a lengthy affair, interspersed with

speeches. Parenthetically, the German method of sandwiching food and speech seems to me a good idea; much better than our way of gobbling the entire menu and then sitting back to endure a long series of orations in a state of mingled repletion and boredom.

From the banquet room we descended to the blacked-out street where, by the aid of electric torches, we got into our darkened buses and went some distance to witness a special entertainment given in our honor by the local organizations of *Kraft durch Freude*—Strength Through Joy. Later on I shall describe this characteristic institution of the Third Reich in some detail. Enough to say here that it is an elaborate system designed to brighten the lives of the working classes in various ways.

The program that evening, put on entirely by "local talent," included choruses, group-gymnastics, and vaudeville turns, most of the latter being pretty amateurish. The high spot in the program was a military band, which was really thrilling in its spirit and fire.

Next morning we could take things easy, since our train back to Berlin did not leave until noon. I therefore ordered breakfast served in my room, and received not merely eggs but a whole platter of cold meats as well. The Propaganda Ministry was evidently determined to make our trip enjoyable to the very end!

Our homeward journey was uneventful. We had a special car, but the stern realities of life were brought back to us when we went into the diner and had once more to use our food-cards to obtain a meager and expensive lunch. The train did not reach Berlin until after dark. It was a misty evening. When I emerged from the station, I literally could not see my hand before my face. Not a taxi was to be had, and I was far from my hotel, so I would have to go by subway. The Berlin subway system is a complicated network which needs some knowing before you can find your way about, and I had quite forgotten the combination, especially as several new lines had been built since I was last there years before. Fortunately a colleague was going my way and came to my rescue.

As I walked up the flights of steps from the subway, leaving behind me a brilliantly lighted station redolent of modernity's inventive genius, and barged into primeval darkness, it seemed to me symbolic of what this war was doing to European civilization. This, I reflected, was no local blackout. It stretched like a vast pall over three great nations and might soon spread to other lands as well. "Where, and when, and how would it end?" I reflected as I picked my way through the gloom and finally stumbled into the lobby of the Adlon.

V. THIS DETESTED WAR

THE GERMANS DETEST THIS WAR. THAT WAS THE EVER-deepening impression I got throughout my stay in the Third Reich. Wherever I went, it was the same story. Public opinion in Berlin about the war tallied with what I found in my travels through West-Central Germany as far as the Rhineland and the North Sea Coast, and through South Germany to Vienna. This attitude is shared by Nazis and non-Nazis. On this point there is no difference between them.

Yet we should clearly understand the reason for this agreement. It is not founded on moral opposition to war as such. In the Third Reich, pacifism is akin to treason. Such genuine pacifists as may still exist there outside of concentration camps are so carefully camouflaged that, like Arctic hares in winter, they cannot be detected against the landscape.

German aversion to the present war, therefore, though general and genuine, is due to strictly practical reasons. What maddens the Germans is that they are obliged to fight desperately in order to keep what they now hold. During the past three years they have marched with giant strides toward the realization of one of their oldest dreams—the domination of Central Europe. Long before Hitler was even heard of, *Mittel-Europa* was a phrase to conjure with. Rightly or wrongly, most Germans believe that hegemony over mid-Europe is necessary for their national future. As often happens in such cases, they have "rationalized" their desire until they have come to think it their just due. So whatever is done to achieve this goal seems to Germans quite right and proper.

Embattled Poland was the last local obstacle to *Mittel-Europa*. By a series of amazing diplomatic victories, Adolf Hitler had taken all the other hurdles without firing a shot. This led the average German to believe that the Fuehrer would complete the process without recourse to arms. Like Al Smith, he said: "Look at the record!" In German eyes, the Anglo-French guarantee to Poland was wholly uncalled-for. Why, they asked, should Britain and France stick their noses into what was none of their business? Most Germans did not believe that the Western Powers would risk a general war over Poland. The German people was thus psychologically unprepared for what actually happened.

When they found themselves suddenly plunged into a decisive struggle with the Western Powers, Germans were torn between two emotions: disgust at what they considered a stupidly needless war, and fear for the consequences which it might involve. All sorts of persons I talked with stigmatized the war as a tragic blunder. Some of them went so far as to criticize their Government for having acted too precipitately. They thought the war could have been avoided by cleverer diplomacy. But those very persons approved of the end sought, no matter how sharply they disapproved of the means. Even ardent Nazis, who claimed that Hitler had taken the only possible course and who professed perfect confidence in ultimate victory, revealed the same underlying mood of regretful irritation. "Think of it," they would explain, "here we were busy making over our country, and now we have to lay aside most of our fine reconstruction plans to go and fight it out with those damned Englishmen!"

In this respect, Germany's attitude can perhaps best be compared to that of the big winner in a poker game who was just raking in the chips when somebody kicked over the table.

Yet, needless or not, the great war was here! That was the grim reality which suddenly confronted the German people. And they seem to have been literally stunned. At first they just couldn't believe it was true. From all I could gather, their attitude during the first month or so was that of a man in a nightmare who tries to wake up and find it is only a bad dream. The amazingly quick military decision in Poland produced, not so much popular jubilation over the victories themselves, but rather a belief that Poland's rapid collapse would cause Britain and France to accept the situation, and that the war in the West would therefore soon be over.

That was the prevailing mood when I entered Germany toward the end of October, 1939. Almost everyone I talked to, from hotel waiters and chambermaids to chance acquaintances in restaurants and cafés, asked me if I didn't think the war would end soon. And they didn't need any tactful prodding. They usually raised the question themselves early in the conversation.

Another irksome feature in German eyes was that, as time passed and nothing much happened in a military way, the war tended to become a bore. No one could get very excited over intermittent land skir-

mishes, a few airplane dog-fights, or an occasional sub-
marine exploit. Meanwhile the numberless irritations
of a strictly rationed life went steadily on. People in the
cities hadn't any too much to eat, and they had to fuss
with their multitudinous food-cards every time they
bought a meal or went marketing. They certainly had
none too much to wear, yet to get that little they must
go through the rigamarole of clothing-cards and *Bezug-
scheine*. Practically everything could be bought only in
limited amounts, and many things could not be bought
at all. Social life had been disrupted or distorted by the
general blackout. While as yet there was little acute
suffering, everyday life was full of minor irritants and
nothing was quite normal.

The result of all this was a depressing mental atmosphere. People were obviously uneasy, dully unhappy,
and uncertain about the future. At first I thought this
indicated really bad morale and I began to wonder
whether the German people might not soon crack under the strain.

Presently, however, I revised my opinion. For one
thing, I recalled from past experience that Germans
have always been complainers. They seem to enjoy having what the English call a "grouse"—with Berliners
perhaps the biggest grousers of the lot. The Germans
have a slang word for this sort of thing. They call it
meckering, which means the ill-natured bleating of a
billy-goat. Indeed, a long-term American resident of
Berlin told me that he considered *meckering* a healthy
sign; it is when the German says nothing that you must
look out for trouble.

Another thing I noted was that, with every passing
week, the Germans were putting aside their wishful

thinking for a quick peace and were mentally accepting the stern reality that they were in for what would probably be a long and bitter struggle. Despite surface appearances, therefore, it became clear to me that the German people was not in what the French call a "defeatist" mood. Not once did I hear a single German, high or low, rich or poor, suggest even in the most confidential talk that the Reich should throw up the sponge and accept peace terms in accordance with British and French war aims. To give up Poland, Czechoslovakia, and Austria, for example, seems to most Germans quite impossible. By gaining control over those lands, the Germans believe they have got what they have long wanted—an unshakable economic and political supremacy in Central Europe. Since Britain and France challenge that supremacy and seek to overthrow it, the attack must be met and broken, no matter how long the job may last or how painful it may become. That, in a nutshell, was the basic popular mood which I saw ripen and harden under my eyes.

England was regarded as the arch-enemy. There seemed to be almost no hostility towards the French, who were looked upon as Britain's cat's-paws and dupes. Popular hostility toward Britain, however, grew visibly more intense from day to day. In part, this was undoubtedly due to the violent diatribes in the press and in public utterances of official spokesmen; in part it was a natural and inevitable reaction against the country which was held responsible for all the discomforts of the wartime present and the dangers of the future. But, during my stay in Germany, this anti-British trend seemed to be a dour anger rather than flaming emotion. People did not go around shouting *Gott strafe England!*

as was done in the last war; neither was anything written similar to Lissauer's *Hymn of Hate*. Popular hysteria was notably absent.

Indeed, the whole war-psychology of the German people today seems to be quite different from that of a quarter-century ago. Kaiser Wilhelm loved military glitter and trappings; his army was the Empire's Exhibit A, and writers like Bernhardi glorified war as a healthful exercise to keep a people fit or even as a "biological necessity." So, when real war came in 1914, the Germans went into it with jubilation. And, for the first year or two, they kept up this hysterically romantic mood.

You find nothing like that spirit in Germany today. Bitter memories of the last war and the chronic misfortunes which ensued have cured the present generation of the war-heroics in which their fathers so liberally indulged. To be sure, the average German seems ready to fight and die for what he believes to be his rightful place in the world. However, he doesn't sentimentalize over it. He's usually hard-boiled on the subject. It's just a dirty chore that, if needs be, must be done.

That seemed to suit the Nazi Government, which made no attempt to whip up popular emotion by either military or Party displays. During all the months I was in Berlin or other cities, I never saw any of those big parades with blaring bands and dress uniforms which we are apt to associate with wartime. The only marching soldiers I saw were occasional platoons of infantry going to change guard where sentries were posted. And the German soldier, in his lead-colored steel helmet, his slate-green clothes, and his clumping high boots, is a severely practical person. I should think it would be hard for the most sentimental Teuton to work up much of a thrill over this matter-of-fact fighting man.

Another noteworthy point is that the Government made no attempt to ease the people into the war by tactful stages. Quite the reverse. Nazi spokesmen tell you frankly that they cracked down hard from the start and made things just about as tough as the civilian population could bear. Indeed, they say that severe rationing of food and clothing from the very beginning was done not merely to avert present waste and ensure future supplies; it was done also to make people realize that they were in a life-and-death struggle for which no sacrifice was too great.

This was stiff medicine for a people as stunned, depressed, and jittery as the Germans certainly were during the first two months of the war. I do not recall any other Government which has prescribed a course of treatment so drastic, under similar circumstances. Flag-waving and assorted heroics are the orthodox formula. I was therefore deeply interested to discuss this original method with the man who carried it out. He was no less a person than Dr. Paul Joseph Goebbels, head of the vast propaganda machine which is perhaps the most outstanding feature of the Third Reich.

This lithe, brunet Rhinelander, with his agile mind, cynical humor, and telling gestures, is an excellent person to interview. He is mentally on his toes every instant, and he is full of what the journalist calls "good lines." He got one of them off early in our conversation when he stigmatized the British blockade of Germany by exclaiming: "It's high time that forty million people stopped dictating to eighty million when they should have a cup of coffee!" As Dr. Goebbels warmed to his subject, his words flowed with the smoothness of a well-oiled machine.

"Mr. Minister," I began, broaching the subject uppermost in my mind, "the thing that strikes me most since I've been in Germany this time is the great difference between the popular mood now and in the last war. No hurrahs, parades, bands, and flowers like in 1914."

"That's right," he shot back quickly, "and the reason is very simple. In 1914 the German people didn't know what it was all about. They had no clear war aim. Some French iron mines! A bit of Belgium! *Gott strafe England!* Slogans and phrases! That's no way to wage a war. And our rulers then couldn't make them understand. They were an aristocratic caste, out of touch with the people."

"And now?" I put in.

"Now?" he countered. "We National Socialists are men of the people. We know how our fellow-citizens think and how to make them understand. But, really, the British have done it for us. They've given us our war aim by forcing the war on us."

"Meaning what?" I asked.

"Meaning this," he replied. "We made it clear to the British that we didn't want to disturb their empire. We carefully kept our hands off sore spots like India and Ireland. Why, we even offered to give them a military guarantee of their empire's integrity. But we made it clear that, in return, they were to keep their hands off our sphere of interest—Central Europe. Well, they wouldn't have it that way. They're trying to crush us. So, this time, every German knows what it's all about."

"And that's why they're so quiet about it?" I asked.

"Exactly," nodded Dr. Goebbels with a quick smile. "We Germans don't like this war. We think it's needless —silly. But, since England feels that way, we see it's got to be gone through with. The average German feels like a man with a chronic toothache—the sooner it's out, the better. And he doesn't need brass bands and flowers to get it over with. That's where our aristocrats went wrong last time. They forgot old Bismarck's saying that hurrah-patriotism isn't like pickled herring that you can put up in barrels and store away for years. Listen! If I wanted to get the German people emotionally steamed up, I could do it in twenty-four hours. But they don't need it—they don't want it."

"Then, psychologically—" I began.

Dr. Goebbels cut in with a sweeping gesture. "Psychologically," he answered, "we are way ahead. Last time, I admit, it was very different. Then, at the crucial moment, both France and England produced great men —Clemenceau and Lloyd George, both men of the people. If we on our side could have produced a Bismarck or a Hitler, we should have won. This time, we have the right men and the others haven't. We National Socialists understand profoundly that it is the human being who counts—not just material resources. England is socially unsound. She is a colossus with feet of clay. Furthermore, England has a negative, defensive war aim. This time, it's the British who talk in vague phrases like 'aggression.' What does it mean to Tommy in the trenches to tell him he's fighting 'aggressors'?"

"Would you mind enlarging on that a bit, Mr. Minister?" I asked.

"Certainly not," he answered. "The more you examine British war aims, the more negative they appear.

The English admit they have nothing tangible to get out of this war but that they have a lot to lose. We, on the other hand, have very little to lose and a lot to win. Here we Germans are—eighty million of us, all together. And right next to us is our sphere of influence in Central Europe—everything under one roof. Sooner or later, we massed Germans are bound to get what we need. The British, on the contrary, are spread all over the map. They draw their resources from the four corners of the earth. Their empire is too dispersed, too artificial. They're bound to lose in the long run."

"Then the British Empire—" I began.

"Please understand," broke in Dr. Goebbels. "We had no designs upon it. We showed this clearly when we made the naval treaty with England limiting our fleet to one-third their size. In face of that fact, any responsible German who might have meditated an attack upon the British Empire would have been guilty of criminal madness. It is only now, when England forces us to a life-and-death struggle, that we hit back in every possible manner. All we asked was that England regard us, too, as a great nation with its own special sphere. After all, nations should be treated on their merits, for what they are. Live and let live was our motto toward England. It is the British who would not have it that way."

"The English," I remarked, "seem to believe that this is a struggle between democracy and dictatorship."

"Dictatorship!" shot back Dr. Goebbels scornfully. "Isn't the National Socialist Party essentially the German people? Aren't its leaders men of the people? How silly to imagine that this can be what the English call dictatorship! What we today have in Germany is not a dictatorship but rather a political discipline forced upon us by the pressure of circumstances. However, since we have it, why shouldn't we take advantage of the fact?"

"Just what do you mean by that, Mr. Minister?" I queried.

"I'll give you an example," answered Dr. Goebbels. "Take the difference between the way we and the English handle radio. We don't let our people listen to foreign broadcasts; the English do. Why should we permit our people to be disturbed by foreign propaganda? Of course we broadcast in English, and the English people are legally permitted to listen in. I understand lots of them do. And can you imagine what is one of the chief discussions about it across the Channel? It is, whether our German announcer has an Oxford or a Cambridge accent! In my opinion, when a people in the midst of a life-and-death struggle indulge in such frivolous arguments, it doesn't look well for them."

"Then, Mr. Minister," I asked, "you don't think there is much likelihood that history will repeat itself?"

Dr. Goebbels' dark eyes lighted. "History never repeats itself," he exclaimed with a sweeping gesture. "History is like a spiral—and we believe that, since the last war, we have made an ascending turn while Britain has made a descending one. Today, we have a national unity, discipline, and leadership vastly superior to that of 1914, and even more superior to anything which England has as yet produced. The rightful claims of the German people were thwarted a generation ago. They cannot be denied a second time."

So saying, the world-famous Minister of Popular Enlightenment and Propaganda rose briskly from his chair and gave me a vigorous handshake. One last look at the slim, dynamic figure and his spacious office hung with historic portraits, and the interview was over. I had got "the dope," all right, from headquarters. And the more one studies the text of that interview, the more revealing it becomes—in many ways! It certainly was propaganda of the Goebbels brand.

VI. VIENNA AND BRATISLAVA

ABOUT A FORTNIGHT AFTER MY ARRIVAL IN GERMANY I
had an opportunity to secure two worth-while interviews away from Berlin. The first was with General
Loehr, Commander-in-Chief of the Air-Arm at Vienna.
The second was with Father Joseph Tiso, newly elected
President of the equally new Slovak Republic, at his
capital, Bratislava. Neither had as yet been interviewed
by an American journalist.

Since I was to be the guest of the Air Ministry, an
army transport plane had been placed at my disposal.
Accordingly, I motored out to Berlin's main airport, accompanied by a major of the Air-Arm who was to be
with me on the journey. A pleasant-faced Hanoverian in
his mid-forties, he proved to be an agreeable companion.

The tri-motored, slate-gray plane took off on schedule, and we soon rose above the ground-haze into the
clear air of a crisp autumn morning. Flying at about
2,000 feet, we skimmed swiftly over the flat plains of
North Germany—an endless patchwork of forest and
farmland, interspersed with lakes and dotted with villages or towns. The sky was cloudless until we approached the Bohemian Mountains, when we encountered a billowing wave of white pouring like a giant
cataract onto the Saxon plain. Rising steeply above this
cloud-sea, we lost sight of earth during most of our

flight over Bohemia. Only now and then did I catch a glimpse of the Protectorate through a rift in the white veil. I had a quick sight of Prague. Its palace-citadel looked like a toy castle. The river Moldau was a silvery ribbon winding across the landscape.

As we neared the hilly border between Bohemia and Austria, the cloud-belt beneath us was again unbroken, though a few mountain summits rose like dark islets above a white sea. On the outskirts of Vienna the clouds thinned and the pilot could see his way to a smooth landing. Greeted cordially by airport officials, the Major and I motored to our hotel, a quaint hostelry named the Erzherzog Karl, on the Kaerntner Strasse. We were in the heart of old Vienna, a city I am always glad to see. I knew it in its glory before the Great War, when it was the capital of the vanished Habsburg Empire. I knew it again in the dark post-war days, when hunger and despair stalked its shabby streets. Now I was to see it in a new guise—demoted to a provincial center of the Third Reich.

Curious to sense the feel of the place, I wandered about town all that afternoon and evening, sizing up the street crowds, revisiting old haunts, and dropping into an occasional café. In their general appearance the people looked similar to those in Berlin. I saw no ragged or starving persons, neither was I accosted by beggars. But the old Viennese spirit was gone. The mental atmosphere was one of tired resignation to whatever might be in store.

However, the Viennese did not have the stiff stolidity of the Berliners. They still smiled easily and entered quickly into friendly conversation. The most notable difference was in the women, who have retained some of their former *chic* despite the cramping limitations of hard times and clothing-cards. My biggest surprise was when I saw perfectly respectable women and girls in a leading café casually take out their lipsticks and freshen their make-up.

Bright and early next morning the Major and I went to the *Hauptkommando,* a huge, dingy old building rising to the height of seven stories. Here I met the military censor who was to pass on my interviews and give me permission to get them on the wireless for transmission to America. He was a tall, slender man, obviously Austrian, as were the other officers to whom I was introduced. The necessary formalities having been completed, I motored to Air Headquarters not far away, where General Loehr awaited me.

The General received me in a large office equipped with an exceedingly long conference table. This came in handy for a panoramic series of air photographs which stretched its entire length. With these the General illustrated his story of the great air attack which he had commanded during the Polish campaign. In vigorous middle life, with graying-dark hair and an agreeable voice, he is typically Austrian in both appearance and manner. An airman since youth, his recent exploits in Poland are the climax of a brilliant professional career.

With soldierly promptness, General Loehr wasted no time starting the interview. His dynamic forefinger swept over the photographic panorama that lay on the conference table. "Picture to yourself," said he, "a thousand troop trains jammed along a sixty-kilometer stretch of railway under mass-attack by bombing planes." Taken from a great height, the photos were in miniature, but with a magnifying glass I could spot the trains, singly or in bunches along the right-of-way, or filling sidings and freight-yards. Now and then I noted squadrons of bombers at lower altitudes than the photographing plane and could spot their work by puffs of smoke where bombs exploded with deadly accuracy over the double-track railroad line.

The General went on to describe the terrific disorganization wrought by this mass air attack upon the Polish army retreating from the Posen front to form a new line before Warsaw—soldiers leaping to the tracks from troop trains and losing their formations; horses and guns forced from freight cars, with no unloading platforms. This harassed army was still full of fight and tried to attack, but it so lacked co-ordination that the bravest efforts were vain. To make matters worse, the telephone and telegraph lines, which in Poland follow railroads rather than highways, were likewise shattered by bombing, so communication was destroyed. Loehr also showed me aerial glimpses of the countryside dotted with Polish soldiery breaking up into small groups.

Asked to give what he considered the reasons for his quick victory over the Polish air force which preceded the bombing of the army, just related, Loehr replied substantially as follows: The German air force had as its primary aim the destruction of Polish air power—if possible on the ground. So the very first day of the war all practicable airfields were assailed. On that fateful first of September the weather was very bad for flying. This made the task a hard one, but the Poles were not expecting a general air attack in such weather and were thus caught unprepared. Loehr attributed much of his success to blind-flying excellence, which he claimed was a German specialty. Caught unprepared, the Polish airfields were terribly mauled. To give one instance, twenty-five planes in one hangar at Cracow were destroyed by a single bomb. This first attack was followed by a second that same day. Again the Poles were unprepared, because they did not think the German bombers could reload and refuel so soon. They were thus caught salvaging their damaged planes and fighting airfield fires.

This initial German success was not without its price. Loehr frankly admitted heavy losses in these first attacks—losses which might have been troublesome if they had kept up. But the vast damage the Germans inflicted had so weakened the Polish air force that, only two days after war broke out, it was incapable of further concerted action, and Germany had obtained command of the air. Thereafter Polish air activity was limited to sporadic counterattacks by small squadrons or single planes. Only after the Polish air power was thus broken did the German Air-Arm turn its attention to the railways and ground forces.

Loehr stated that in this campaign Germany's initial air preponderance was not so great as commonly imagined abroad. At the start, he had only about one-third numerical advantage. This was less than the Allied lead over the Germans on the West Front during the World War, where the Allies never attained real command of the air. The General closed the interview with expressions of polite regret that he could not invite me to the luncheon he had planned for me, because he had been suddenly ordered to fly for a conference at Berlin.

I spent the afternoon writing out my interview and transcribing it in semi-code for the wireless—a technical job which always takes some time. The obliging censor passed it with a couple of minor changes, and I saw the interview safely on its way across the ocean, returning to my hotel just in time to meet friends with whom I was to spend the evening. We dined at *The Three Hussars,* a cozy little restaurant long famous for its food and wines. The wines were still up to par, but the food had sadly deteriorated from the old days. In fat-short wartime Germany, really good cooking is as unlikely as bricks made without straw.

During dinner we discussed the local situation. Both my host and his wife were members of the Party and thus enthusiastically in favor of *Anschluss.* They admitted, however, that Austria's inclusion into the Third Reich had produced many economic difficulties. Much of Vienna's local industry had been luxury products for foreign markets. This had greatly suffered since annexation, owing to several factors such as difficulty of obtaining raw materials through lack of foreign exchange, competing German lines, and the boycott of German goods (now extended to Austrian goods) in foreign lands, notably in the United States. He himself had suffered through the closing of a factory of which he had been manager. Controlled by German interests, it had been closed after Anschluss as uneconomical. Things had been pretty bad until the outbreak of war, when the increase of employment on war work coupled with army mobilization had relieved the labor situation. He believed that, on the long pull, Austria would benefit economically by Anschluss, but she was going through a trying transition period.

That evening we went to one of the best-known music halls, where we saw a typical Viennese program,

full of skits and jokes—many of them sharp knocks at
current conditions. I expressed my surprise and said I
did not think such latitude would be tolerated in Berlin. My hostess laughingly assured me that the Viennese
must have their satirical jokes. It was an historic tradi-
tion, and the German authorities had been persuaded
that they had best not sit on this characteristic Austrian
safety-valve.

Another surprising matter was the number of officers
and soldiers sitting together in gay parties throughout
the audience. I had already noted instances of this in
North Germany, but not to the same extent. Recalling
as I did the rigid caste lines in both the old Imperial
Army and the small professional *Reichswehr* established
after the World War, it took me some time to get used
to these evidences of social fraternization. The new
trend is due to two causes. In the first place, it is part
of the Nazi philosophy to break down class and caste dis-
tinctions, and weld the whole nation into a conscious
Gemeinschaft—an almost mystical communion, as contrasted with the rest of the world. In such a socialized
nationhood, the traditional caste barriers, first between
officers and soldiers, secondly between army and civilians, are obviously out of line. The present German
army is undoubtedly more of a *Volksheer*—a People's
Army, than it ever was before. This new tendency is
also furthered by the fact that with better education,
specialization, and technical training of the rank-and-
file, officers and men are more nearly on the same plane.
The old Imperial Army, unmechanized and made up
so largely of peasant lads commanded by Junker
squires, was a vastly different institution.

Yet, despite all social changes, military discipline and

authority do not seem to have suffered. No matter how friendly men and officers may be off duty, the heel-clicking and stiff saluting on duty are as punctilious as they ever were in the old days.

Next morning, the Major and I set off by military car to get my interview with the new Slovak President. The little Republic of Slovakia, so recently carved from the former Czechoslovakia, is technically an independent state, though actually it is a German Protectorate. The fiction of sovereignty is carried out in every detail. The Major and I had both sent our passports to the Slovak Consulate in Vienna to obtain visas for our one-day trip in a "foreign" land.

The fine weather of the past two days had given place to heavy clouds and spitting rain. Once out of Vienna, there was little to see except marsh and sodden fields as we motored down the Danube valley. To pass the time, I entered into conversation with our military chauffeur, who was an unusual type—a man with an air of good breeding enhanced by slender hands and dark, well-cut features. I was surprised to learn that he was a German from the Caucasus, one of the few survivors of a flourishing colony established there long ago under the Czars but wiped out by the Bolsheviks in the Russian Revolution. Escaping as a boy, he had wandered in many countries, returning at last to the ancestral Fatherland which he had never previously seen. Incidentally, it is curious how often one encounters in Germany such persons come home from the Teutonic *diaspora*. Besides Austrian Adolf Hitler, four of the top-flight Nazi leaders were born abroad—Wilhelm Bohle in Britain, Alfred Rosenberg in Russia, Rudolf Hess in Egypt, and Walther Darré in the Argentine.

From Vienna to Bratislava is only an hour's quick run by motor car. For a national capital, Bratislava is most unhandily situated. It lies on the north bank of the Danube. On the south bank stretches the German Reich, while a few miles downstream is the Hungarian border. Bratislava is thus wedged narrowly between two foreign nations. Still, it's the only city in Slovakia, so there's no second choice. The rest of the little country is a jumble of mountains inhabited by a primitive and pious peasantry. When I called on the Minister of Foreign Affairs that same afternoon, his office windows looked out across the river directly at alien soil. Certainly a unique situation.

We arrived at the international bridge about noon. The usual formalities of passport and customs inspection were gone through with on the German side, plus money control. Although we were to be out of the Reich only a few hours, we had to leave our marks behind and thus quit German soil with no money except a little loose change. Fortunately we were to be the guests of the German Minister, so we did not have to go to the bother of getting Slovak currency. Incidentally, it was lucky we made the trip when we did. That very night Adolf Hitler was to have his narrow escape from being blown up by the bomb explosion in Munich which killed or wounded so many of his old companions-in-arms. Thereafter, for some days, I understand that every frontier of the Reich was almost hermetically sealed.

Crossing the massive bridge over the muddy Danube, our car came to a halt at the Slovak customs control. This did not take long, and we were soon motoring through the town on our way to the German Military

Mission, where we were to check in. The people on the streets of Bratislava were distinctly Slavic in type, with broad faces and high cheekbones. Slovakia has a small army of its own, so I saw a few soldiers. They still wore the regulation Czechoslovak uniform, which is so like the American that they looked strangely similar to our own doughboys. All the business signs were in Slovak. The street signs were in both Slovak and German.

The Germans were apparently trying to avoid publicly ruffling Slovak sensibilities. The iron hand seems to be covered by a well-padded glove. Their Military Mission is inconspicuously tucked away in a modest villa on a side street; so is the Legation, to which we soon drove in order to meet the Reich's diplomatic representative. In fact, it is too small to house the Minister and his numerous family. He is therefore obliged to live at Bratislava's one hotel.

The Minister is a clever man, as he has to be to fill so responsible a post. He is also a jovial soul, as I soon discovered when we began to swap jokes. Before long we adjourned to the hotel for lunch. That meal was an eye-opener to me. Slovakia is a neutral land which grows a surplus of foodstuffs, so rationing is unknown. What a joy it was to tuck into a Wiener Schnitzel with sour cream gravy, backed by vegetables with a good butter base! A momentary fly in the ointment appeared when a message was brought to our table that President Tiso might be unable to see me as arranged because he was closeted with Parliamentary leaders putting the last licks on Slovakia's new legal code. My face must have shown some dismay, but the Minister put a reassuring hand on my arm. "Don't worry," he smiled, "I'll get right on the phone and persuade him." Soon he was back. As he sat down, he remarked with a sly wink: "He's persuaded."

Accordingly, late afternoon found me hurrying from a call on the Foreign Minister to keep my rendezvous with Slovakia's clerical President. The newspapermen in Berlin had already told me that the reverend gentleman was a pretty tough political operator—more holy than righteous, as the saying goes. So I was curious.

The interview took place under conditions typical of this *al fresco* republic. Since the President's official residence is not yet ready, his temporary office is on the second floor of an apartment house. Two stolid Slovak sentries at the house entrance alone marked it off from other buildings in the block. In response to our summons a small boy opened the house door. I climbed a flight of stone stairs, rang a bell, and was promptly ushered into the Presence.

The President was equally informal but by no means so unimpressive. Father Tiso is a big man—big head, broad face, broad shoulders, massive body, and legs like tree trunks. A typical peasant even in his black clerical garb, he is visibly rooted in the soil.

The many persons of Slovak origin in my native land naturally came to mind, so my first question was what message he had for them. The answer came quickly in a deep rich voice: "Tell my Slovak brothers in the United States that all goes well here; that we have peace again now that the Polish War is over; that order prevails, and that our new state will work out its national evolution by its own inner strength. I beg the Slovaks in America not to believe the many rumors I know to be current there about our situation. They simply aren't true."

"You mean, Mr. President," I queried, "reports that Slovakia is merely a puppet state of the Reich?"

Father Tiso smiled calmly. "How long have you been in this country?" he asked in turn.

"About six hours," I admitted rather ruefully.

"All right," he shot back quickly. "Stay here a week and travel through Slovakia. Then you'll learn the answer yourself."

That seemed to settle that, so I tried a new tack. "How do Slovakia's aims and ideals differ from the former Czechoslovakia, of which it formed a part?"

"Our aim," began President Tiso deliberately, "is the perfecting of Slovak nationality. Czechoslovakia was founded on the fiction of a Czechoslovak nation without the hyphen—that precious hyphen which we were promised from the first as an equal member of a dual nation. The Czechs gave us nothing to say. They claimed we were merely backward Czechs, whereas there are deep cultural differences between us. We have our own history, language, art, music, folk-songs. For centuries we defended this cultural heritage against foreign rulers. And on those deep-laid foundations we propose to build our own national life."

"What sort of life?" I countered. "Let's take the practical angle. Will your economic development be individualistic business, peasant equality, or national socialism?"

Again the President replied slowly. "It is true that today we are mainly a land of peasants. But the rapid increase of our population makes the development of industry an urgent necessity. However, we intend that industry shall serve the good of the whole nation—not merely its own good. So I may say that our economic aim is our special type of national socialism based on Christian principles and practices. We know that capital must be allowed to earn a fair return. But we intend that the worker shall have a fair livelihood, with security against unemployment and unmerited poverty. The Government will interfere in industry to correct—but not to direct."

I turned to politics. "Isn't it true," I asked, "that you have some non-Slovak national minorities, especially Hungarians and Germans? How will you handle them?"

"We assure them cultural liberty," said the President. "They will have the right to their own language, education, and Parliamentary representation proportionate to their electoral voting strength."

"Well, what about the Slovak majority?" I queried. "How does it stand politically?"

"There is only one Slovak party in Parliament," answered President Tiso. "This is the National Party, until recently headed by our revered leader, the late Father Hlinka. In the recent elections, the Slovaks were unanimous, and the next elections will be five years hence. There is nothing in the Constitution to prevent the formation of new parties. But there aren't any others just now."

So saying, this clerical President rose to indicate that he must return to his task of building a nation. "A clever man," I thought to myself. "He knows all the words."

When I left the presidential apartment, night had fallen. But, in neutral Bratislava, night was normal. There was no blackout. How gay I felt to walk, even in a chill rain, along well-lighted streets with cheery shop-window displays and glimpses of folk dining or drinking comfortably in restaurants and cafés! You learn to prize the simplest amenities of peacetime when you have lost them for a while, even though that apparent peace may cloak an iron repression.

VII. IRON RATIONS

No intelligent foreigner can be in Germany a week without asking himself: "How do these people stand it?" When he has been there a month, he says: "How long can they stand it?" After three months, his verdict will probably be: "I guess they'll stand it a long time." Those, at any rate, were my reactions. And, from conversations with many foreign residents in Germany, I believe they are typical ones. Let me explain how this mental evolution came about.

Germany is today a fortress under siege by the British naval blockade. Even where the Reich has apparently unhampered sally-ports through neutral neighbors, its freedom is relative; for the neutrals in turn feel the pressure of British sea-power in whatever may aid England's arch-enemy. In the World War, Germany collapsed through this strangling grip. To avoid a similar fate, the Nazi Government has developed an amazingly elaborate system of rationing which extends to the smallest details.

The foreign visitor to wartime Germany encounters this all-pervading system the instant he crosses the border, when the frontier inspector hands him a few bread, meat, and butter coupons nicely calculated to avert hunger till he reaches his destination. Thereafter he receives full sets of coupons (collectively termed "food-cards") enabling him to buy specified amounts of eatables. As already related, the quality depends on the prices he is willing to pay; also he can purchase certain high-priced luxuries, such as game which (with the exception of venison) is card-free. But, no matter how great his wealth, he cannot get more coupons than are legally allotted him. Except under special circumstances, he gets the same treatment as the average citizen of the Reich. Germans or foreigners, they all "eat out of the same [official] dish."

Offhand, one would be apt to think that such severe restrictions would produce a thriving bootleg trade. As a matter of fact, underhand trading does exist. But it is relatively small and very much undercover, because German law punishes the buyer equally with the seller, and sentences can be imposed up to ten years at hard labor. For most persons, therefore, the risk is too great.

Legal differences in rationing there are. These, however, are based, not on wealth or influence, but on age and occupation. Infants and small children get special foods to safeguard their health and growth. At the other end of the scale are two favored classes known as "heavy" and "heaviest" workers—persons engaged in specially strenuous or hazardous labor. These classifications are prized almost more than higher wages in laboring circles. The most appreciated favor handed us newspaper correspondents by the Propaganda Ministry was when it had us classified as *heavy workers*. Thereby we were entitled to draw an extra food-card allotment amounting to nearly fifty per cent above normal.

What, you may ask, is normal? The answer is that the allotment varies somewhat from month to month; and, interestingly enough, it tends to rise. For various reasons, the Government determined to start in with wartime restrictions as severe as the people could presumably stand without immediate injury to their health and without arousing too much discontent. The official calculation was that slight additions to the allotment from time to time would produce marked improvement in popular morale. This was certainly true, as I myself can testify. I shall not soon forget how much brighter the world looked when my microscopic butter ration was increased by nearly a pat a day. The difference totaled only a few ounces per month, but the psychological effect was great indeed.

Here is a table of the principal items of rationed foodstuffs for the month of December, 1939. The reader can easily translate them into ounces by remembering that 1,000 grams equals 2.2 pounds. Normal rations which could be bought per head, per week, were:

Item	Grams
Meat	500
Butter	125
Lard	62.5
Margarine	80
Marmalade	100
Sugar	250
Cheese	62.5
Eggs	1 (egg)

Bread, flour, and other grain products are likewise rationed, but the allotments are so large that the rationing is chiefly to avoid waste. Nobody except a tremendous eater could begin to consume his bread ration while I was in Germany. That is because the Reich is amply supplied in this respect, due to abundant harvests in recent years with consequent large carry-overs. Potatoes and vegetables generally are unrationed. So are fruits, though these are scarce and of mediocre quality, judged by American standards. Tropical fruits, even oranges, tangerines, and lemons, are rarely seen. I understand that most of these come from Southern Italy. Mondays and Fridays are fish days. Wartime Germany's fish supply now comes mainly from the Baltic, which is not in the active war zone.

It takes only a glance at the table just given to spot the weak point in Germany's food supply—edible fats. This danger point has long been realized, and the Government has done its best to remedy the deficiency, both by increasing domestic production and by imports from abroad. Despite these efforts, however, Germany's domestic fat production averaged only 56 per cent of her consumption in the years just before the war. In anticipation of the war danger, the Nazi Government has undoubtedly laid up large emergency fat reserves. As far back as the autumn of 1938, Hermann Goering announced at the annual Party Congress at Nuremberg that the Reich had a 7½ months' fat supply in storage, while trade statistics indicate that this figure should be even larger today. Germany can, and does, import much fat, together with meat and dairy products, from its Continental neighbors. This trade is, of course, not stopped by the British blockade. Still, the fat shortage remains; and in a long war it will be apt to get more acute.

Certainly, the present regulation diet is out of balance. There is an obvious deficiency, not only of fats, but also of foods rich in protein, mineral salts, and vitamins, such as fruit, green vegetables, and dairy products, especially milk and eggs. The present diet contains far too much starch, as the writer can emphatically testify, since he gained twelve pounds during a stay in Germany of less than four months, although his weight had not varied half that much in years. And he met many other persons, both foreigners and Germans, who were having similar experiences. When healthy, well-balanced individuals react that way, there must be something wrong with the dietary picture. Unless remedied, it cannot fail to produce bad results on the general population in the long run.

However, if the food ration can be kept at its present level, the bad results will be so gradual that they should not notably lower the average German's strength and efficiency until after a long lapse of time. When the war broke out the German people were reasonably healthy. Yet this health standard had been maintained on a diet which, in American eyes, must seem meager and monotonous. For many years, most Germans have been restricted in their consumption of fats and dairy products. The war is thus not a sudden change from plenty to scarcity, but a relatively slight intensification of chronic shortages. I discussed food conditions with working-men, and they said that, if they could get their full food-card allotments, they fared about the same as before the war. These statements checked with what competent foreign observers told me. The winter diet of the working classes has always been potatoes, bread, and cabbage, together with some fish, less meat, and even less fats. They hadn't the money to buy anything better. It is the upper and middle classes who have been hit hardest by war rationing, and it is among them that you hear the loudest complaints.

Those upper and middle class folk certainly *mecker* vociferously over the food situation, but their complaints are mingled with a somewhat sour sense of humor. Here is a typical food joke which was current in winter Berlin: "Recipe for a good meal: Take your meat card. Wrap it in your egg card, and fry it in your butter or fat card until brown. Then take your potato card, cover with your flour card, and cook over your coal card until done. For dessert, stir up your milk and sugar cards; then dunk in your coffee card. After this, wash your hands with your soap card, drying them with your cloth card. That should make you feel fine!"

These complaints, however, are for the most part mere emotional kicks at hard conditions which cannot be helped. They do not imply condemnation of the rationing system, as such. The German people have poignant memories of the terrible starvation years during the World War, and they are willing to undergo almost anything rather than see mass-starvation come back again. The Government claims that it has devised a starvation-proof system including not merely the food-cards but also the complete "rationalization" of agriculture, with fixed prices all the way from producer to consumer. Before the farmer starts his spring planting, he knows that everything he raises will be bought at a figure which should normally enable him to make a slight profit. At the other end of the scale, when the housewife goes to market, she knows that the storekeeper cannot charge her more than the Government permits. The food regulations today in force assure to the poorest German the basic necessities of life while the richest cannot get much more than his share. So long as the German people believe that the system will enable them to keep above the hunger-line, there seems to be scant likelihood of a popular revolt over food alone.

What the system means was explained by Walther Darré, Minister of Agriculture and in supreme charge of the food situation, when he said to me: "Our food-cards constitute merely the last link in an economic chain which we were forging long before the war. This chain extends from farm grower to consumer, with stable prices all along the line. The food-card is the final act of the whole carefully-worked-out process, ensuring to each citizen his share of food, no matter what the size of his income. In the World War, food-cards were a sign of want. They were started only when a dangerous scarcity already existed. This time, food-cards, started the very first day of the war, are a symbol of strength."

Herr Darré's statement has a two-fold significance. It shows both the economic advantages of wartime rationing and its steadying effect on the popular state of mind. This second aspect is perhaps the more important. In the World War, the old Imperial German Government did practically nothing to control food conditions during the first two years of the struggle. The result was a vast deal of hoarding, profiteering, and a general skyrocketing of prices. Rich families laid in big stocks while poor men went hungry. These obvious injustices did more than anything else to rouse popular resentment and promote revolutionary unrest. It is well known that civilian morale broke down long before that of the soldiers at the front. Also, this civilian breakdown ultimately infected the armies in the field. The

Nazi leaders are keenly aware of all this and are determined that it shall not happen again.

Nevertheless, the task is great and the struggle complex. Another sector of the gigantic battle against the British blockade is the clothing situation. The Government tackled this problem as promptly as it did the question of food. From the very start, clothes were strictly rationed. At first, this was done by the *Bezugschein* method. As already explained, a *Bezugschein* is an official permit enabling the holder to purchase a specific article. Accordingly, if a man or woman needed an addition to the wardrobe, he or she had to go to the Permit station established in their particular neighborhood and state the case. The officials in charge, being themselves local people, usually had a good idea of the applicant's honesty and reliability. With a good reputation, permission was generally granted at once, though the applicant often had to wait in line a long time before his turn came. In doubtful or suspicious cases, however, the applicant was told to return with his old coat, suit, shoes, even shirt or underwear, to prove it was really worn out. In extreme cases his house might even be searched to make sure he was not trying to hoard.

This makeshift system obviously involved great loss of time, caused many hardships, and produced much popular irritation. It also did not give a sufficiently clear picture of popular needs. With characteristic German thoroughness, the Government made a searching study of the problem. Its answer was the clothing cards issued in the late autumn of 1939. There are different cards for men, women, boys, and girls. Thereby the Government intends to regulate both production and consumption in an efficient and predictable way.

The woman's clothing card was issued first, and I still recall the impression it made on me when I puzzled over the announcement of it which was published in the morning papers. To me, its complexities seemed almost like an exercise in higher mathematics. Like the food-cards, it is based on the coupon method. The left-hand side of the clothing card contains a list of articles available, together with the number of coupons required for permission to purchase each article; for, as already explained in relation to food-cards, they are really little Permits which have nothing to do with price. The quality of the article purchased depends on the buyer's pocketbook.

The right-hand side of the clothing card contains the precious coupons—and here American women readers of this book are due for a shock. There are only one hundred of these coupons, popularly known as "points," and they must last the feminine holder of the card for an entire twelve-month, starting from November. A hundred points may sound like quite a lot, but just wait until we note how fast they can go and how little they mean! One handkerchief takes one point. A brassière takes four points; a set of "undies" 12; a slip 15; and so on up to a warm winter suit, which sets the lady back no less than 45 points—almost one-half of her whole clothing allowance for the year.

The most poignant item is hosiery. On her card the German woman is allowed a "normal" ration of four pair of stockings per year—each pair taking four points. If she insists, she can get an additional two pair; but in that case she is penalized by having to give up eight points apiece for her temerity.

A paternal Government sees to it that she shall not

rush frantically out to the nearest store and get all her clothing ration at once. The points are "staggered." One-third of the total are available immediately; but the next ten can't be used before January 1st; then twenty on March 1st; and other twenties in May and August respectively. Clothing cards are personal. They cannot be transferred, and coupons detached from the card have no value. Any attempt at cheating is punished by a 100-point fine, which leaves the culprit unable to buy anything for a whole year!

The meticulous way in which this system has been worked out shows in the smallest details. Even thread and darning-yarn are exactly rationed. There is a wide difference between various kinds of textiles; woolen articles, which are admittedly scarce, call for nearly twice as many points as do articles of the same sort but made of different materials. An attempt is likewise made to differentiate between articles of such prime necessity that they are worn by rich and poor alike, and those worn chiefly by persons in comfortable circumstances. The former articles take less points than the latter, though the differential is not great.

Men are even more drastically rationed than their womenfolk. *Meinherr* must part with 8 of his 100 points for each pair of socks, 27 to 35 points for a full-length set of underwear, and a devastating 60 points for a business suit. No wonder that he was pleased last Christmastide when the Government announced a "present" in the shape of its gracious permission to buy a card-free necktie. Milady was simultaneously gratified by the right to purchase a pair of stockings without losing any of her points.

It should be noted that these cards do not cover a

number of important items such as overcoats or cloaks, boots and shoes, bedclothing, and household linen. Clothing for infants and very young children is likewise not covered by the card system, though boys and girls have cards similar to those issued to adults. All cardless items must be obtained by the Permit method previously described.

To any American above our poverty-line, the severity of this clothes rationing will presumably seem little short of appalling. It certainly appalled many Germans with whom I discussed the matter. This was especially true of the women, some of whom threw up their hands in despair at the grim prospect while others asserted vehemently that feminine discontent would reach such proportions that the Government would be forced to relent before they reached the rags-and-tatters stage. Ardent Nazis tended to minimize the hardships—at least, in my presence. They reminded me that Germans are thrifty souls who wear their best clothes sparingly, with second- or even third-best apparel for ordinary use. Thus, most persons are apt to have a clothing reserve which can be stretched over this emergency period. Nazi ladies laughingly predicted that next summer's hosiery would all be in brown shades—the brown of sun-tanned bare legs. Still, I detected a melancholy ring to their most patriotic sallies.

Resident foreigners are issued the same clothing cards as Germans. Transients have none, the assumption being that they need none for a short stay. The wise foreigner will equip himself in advance with everything needful. I certainly did, down even to shoe polish, having been informed that, owing to lack of grease, the *Ersatz* mixtures now used in the Reich were hard on leather. I thus personally suffered no inconvenience, though I was continually haunted by the thought that I might lose something or that my shirts might not stand the wear of wartime German laundries. But woe to the traveler who enters Germany short on clothing! He cannot buy even a pocket handkerchief by ordinary methods. I saw some harrowing sights during my stay in the Reich. One instance was that of an American lady who arrived at the Adlon from Southern Italy minus her baggage, which had gone astray. She had nothing with her but the lightest summer shoes. The rain and chill of autumn soon gave her such a heavy cold that she could not go out until she had proper footwear. She had to enlist the good offices of the American Embassy to have a special *Bezugschein* issued to her without delay.

Restrictions on food and clothing are merely the outstanding aspects of everyday life in Germany, which is Spartan throughout. Possession of cards is no guarantee that the articles covered by them can always be bought. In the big cities, especially, many temporary shortages occur, due chiefly to faulty transportation or distribution. Shopping involves much delay, especially through having to stand in line before being waited on. Articles technically card-free are effectively rationed because they must all be bought in small quantities; so even persons with plenty of money can never get much ahead of their immediate needs. Also, one is never sure of being able to buy anything, because it may suddenly be temporarily or even permanently sold out. To a foreigner, this sort of existence soon becomes maddening. So he is apt to fancy that it must be equally unendurable to Germans, and he may therefore conclude that they cannot stand it much longer.

Such generalizations, however, are unsound. The Germans have been through a lengthy and bitter schooling in adversity. They have not known a really normal life since the World War broke out in July, 1914. That fateful summertide was twenty-six years ago. For more than a quarter-century the Germans have experienced about every sort of vicissitude—war, inflation, an unsound boom, deflation, civil strife, the Nazi Revolution, and now war again. No German man or woman under twenty-six years of age was even born into what we would call a normal national life or has had any personal experience of it unless they have been abroad. No German under forty has more than childhood recollections of the "good old times."

This historical background should always be kept in mind if we are to judge correctly German reactions to their surroundings. We see here a people so accustomed to do without things or to get them only with difficulty and in limited amounts that they are used to it. Therefore Germans take lightly or never think about many matters which, to Americans especially, are irritations and grievances. We thus encounter two standards of living and attitudes toward daily life which differ from each other so profoundly that they cannot easily be compared.

In this connection we should remember another point —the factor of war psychology. Nearly all Germans have come to feel that they are in for a life-and-death struggle. They believe that defeat in this war would spell something like the destruction of their nationhood. They therefore bear cheerfully, through patriotic emotion, privations which, to the resident foreigner with nothing at stake, are personally meaningless and therefore exasperating.

I cannot illustrate this matter better than by citing a conversation I had one day with a German acquaintance. In the course of our chat I remarked how much I missed coffee. "I used to be quite a coffee drinker too," he answered, "and at first I also found it hard. But I realized that, by doing without coffee imports, we Germans strengthen our economic situation and thereby help beat the English. You know, that thought was so satisfying that it overcame my desire for coffee. So now I am not only reconciled to our *Ersatz* but I actually enjoy drinking it and have no wish to go back to real coffee, even if I were given a supply." From similar remarks heard on many occasions, I am sure that he was sincere and that he typified an important aspect of the national state of mind.

VIII. A BERLIN LADY GOES TO MARKET

IF WE ARE REALLY TO UNDERSTAND CONDITIONS IN strange lands, it's well to get down to cases. So let me tell the tale of the housewife in wartime Germany. She is a composite lady, the combined result of several studies I made into the daily life of families living in Berlin. Two of them had kept house in America. In that way I got intelligent comparisons between German and American standards.

All these families are financially well-off; able to pay for everything they really need. I chose such families deliberately, because I wanted to eliminate the factor of financial worry from the picture. What I tried to find out was how, and to what extent, the everyday life of these Berlin homes is affected by wartime conditions.

On the day in question our composite lady sallies forth to do her marketing in the middle of the forenoon. This is her regular market day, and she should have started earlier, but couldn't because of home work due to lack of servants. She goes at once to a nearby grocery. Of course she is a regular customer there, as she is with her butcher and other tradespeople. That is the only way she can cope with the food-card situation.

Let's follow her in and take a look around the place. The first thing that strikes our American eye is the meagerness of the stock. In part, this impression is due to the fact that there are no canned goods on display. They are all being kept off the market until green vegetables and autumn fruits are exhausted. Then the Government will release canned goods for public sale to bridge the gap until the next fruit and vegetable crops are available. We should also understand that, in Germany, grocery stores are more specialized than ours. They sell chiefly staple food and dairy products, together with lines such as jams and jellies, condiments, smoked meats, and light table wines. Still, the stock is not large and the store is a small place, though with several clerks—all women.

As she enters the store, Milady catches the eye of the head clerk and gets immediate service. That's a bit of good luck, for the woman is much quicker than the others, which means a saving of precious time. As soon as she reaches the counter, Milady opens a pocketbook containing several compartments, each bulging with folded papers of various colors. These are food-cards—sheets of paper about a foot square, on which are printed many coupons that can be torn or cut off, stamped, or punched, as the case requires.

Let us assume that this lady shops for a good-sized family—say, herself, husband, and four children. Each of these six individuals needs seven food cards; so Milady has to carry forty-two cards with her whenever she goes to market. I may add that she has still other cards at home—clothing cards for each member of the family, and special milk cards if any of her children are young. But, as Kipling would say, that is another story.

Let's take a look at those cards as Milady unfolds them and lays them on the counter. That's what everybody has to do in Germany before one can even start buying anything. The saleswoman has to make sure the customer hasn't exceeded her quota, while the customer has to find out if what she wants is in stock that day. In big cities like Berlin there are, as I have said, many temporary shortages of foodstuffs. In the smaller towns there is no such trouble.

The cards are now spread out. First the bread card. This covers not only baked bread but also flour of various kinds. No difficulty here; the bread ration is ample. Secondly the sugar card, which includes jams, jellies, etc. Again no trouble. Thanks to a big sugar-beet crop, this is well taken care of. Now the meat card. This is chiefly for the butcher; but Milady happens to want a bit of sausage and smoked ham, so she uses it in the grocery store. The saleswoman informs her that she is getting the last of the ham, because it has been decreed a luxury, so farmers have been ordered not to smoke any more for the delicatessen trade.

Now the fat card. Here we run into a sore spot. Germany is short on fats; so butter, margarine, and lard are very strictly rationed. However, Milady does pretty well here, because she has three young children, who rate much more fats than do adults. Incidentally, they get some chocolate, reserved for child consumption. Next comes the soap card—another sore point which we will investigate when Milady gets home. Now the adult milk card. Grown-ups rate only skimmed milk, which, to my American taste, is an unpleasant substance that I never use. Neither, apparently, do Germans except for cooking or sparingly in their imitation coffee or tea. Last comes a card entitled *Naermittel*, best translated by our word "victuals." It's a sort of catch-all, covering a wide variety of rationed items ranging from macaroni and noodles to packaged cereals, *Ersatz* tea and coffee, and certain kinds of game.

We can now understand what a prolonged huddle Milady goes into with the saleswoman. Each food-card has to be taken up separately, since quotas vary for adults, half-grown children and small children. When a quota is calculated to the last gram, that particular card is punched, stamped, or snipped, and another card is investigated. The varied rations are jotted down on a slip of paper for adding up when the list is completed. As before stated, all this rigamarole has nothing to do with price. It's just a preliminary canter to find out how much bread, butter, lard, sugar, or other foodstuffs the buyer is *entitled* to. Only when that has been ascertained are the actual prices of the goods figured out and written down on another slip.

Let's try to translate those prices into our money. After considerable investigation, I reckon the purchasing power of German currency to Germans at a trifle over four Reichsmarks to the dollar, thus making the Reichsmark roughly equivalent to our quarter. On that basis, staple groceries average only a trifle higher than they do in America. Some items, especially bread, are cheaper. Fats are distinctly higher. Butter, for instance, is over fifty cents a pound. However, German housewives have the satisfaction of knowing that these prices are fixed by law and cannot be raised except by a new official edict.

By this time Milady's purchases have been duly assembled on the counter. Only when strictly necessary are they sparingly wrapped in paper, because paper is scarce. String is even scarcer, so it is seldom used. Instead of paper bags, the goods are placed in containers which look like sections of fish-nets. These mesh bags must be furnished by the customer, who is supposed likewise to carry away the purchases under a general "cash and carry" rule. However, should they be too heavy and bulky, the store will usually oblige a regular customer by sending along one of the women clerks, if she can find a moment to spare.

The most notable aspect of Berlin marketing is the time it takes. Often, a bill of goods coming to only a few dollars will keep saleswoman and customer engrossed for a full hour. When our synthetic lady leaves the shop, the business is over so far as she is concerned. Not so with the grocery store. Those coupons from Milady's food-cards go to swell multicolored piles which have to be sorted out, pasted on big sheets of paper, and fully accounted for before they are turned over to the food-control authorities. These jigsaw-puzzle economics are usually done after business hours and sometimes last far into the night.

However, our Berlin lady is too busy with her own affairs to think about the extra work she has made for grocery clerks. Laden with her fish-net bags, she deposits them at her apartment and hurries off to do more marketing at a nearby butcher's shop. Luck is with her when she notes a good line of meats on display, for meat distribution is uncertain. Luck is with her again when she points to a badge worn in her coat lapel and marches to the counter ahead of a line of waiting customers. That badge shows she is the mother of at least four offspring. She is thus *Kinderreich*—rich in children. A *Kinderreich* matron has many privileges, among them the right to immediate attention at any store; the theory being that she should be helped to save time for her family duties in every way. It certainly comes in handy this morning, for Milady is very anxious to get home, where she is already long overdue.

Her meat purchases are soon made—veal cutlet at 45 cents a pound, and some pork chops at 30 cents. Then a quick dash to the vegetable market a couple of blocks away where she doesn't need food-cards. But of the limited oranges and lemons there aren't any for sale today.

At last Milady can go home. She is anxious to see how the washing is progressing and how her younger children are getting on. Both those worries are due to a crowning ill—lack of a servant.

"Ah!" the reader may exclaim, "here is one familiar feature in wartime Berlin." In the larger sense, however, you'd be wrong. While Germany had a shortage of competent servants even before the war, wartime conditions have intensified this shortage into an acute famine. It is no longer a question of money. No matter how good wages one may be willing to pay, servants are often unobtainable at any price.

Here's how it happened. The instant war broke out, the Government "froze" domestic service. No servant could thenceforth leave her employer except for self-evident reasons like non-payment of wages or genuine mistreatment. Neither could the servant demand a raise. That regulation prevented "servant-stealing" by wealthier employers and a consequent skyrocketing of wage scales.

This was fine if you happened to have a city-bred servant or one that was middle-aged. However, Berlin servants, particularly the general-housework variety, are apt to be young women from the country. Of course the

Government had them all ticketed. So, when mobilization called the young peasants to the colors, their sisters were summoned back from domestic service to remedy a labor shortage on the farms.

Let us suppose that our Berlin lady's general-housework maid was thus taken away from her a couple of months after war broke out. She went promptly to an official employment agency to see what could be done. The woman in charge smiled at her sadly. "My dear lady," she remarked, "we already have so many cases like yours ahead of you that I can't give you much hope." So there was our good housewife, left single-handed with a sizeable apartment, a hard-working professional or business husband, and four children to care for. Certainly a tough break for a well-to-do woman who has always had competent servants.

However, since our Berlin lady is a German, she has presumably had a thorough domestic training before her marriage, that being the custom even for girls of wealthy families. So she knows how, not merely to superintend her household, but actually to do the work herself. Furthermore, since she has young children, she has first call on whatever domestic service there is to be had. That is another of her *Kinderreich* privileges. So we may assume that, by the time our story opens, she has been able to get the temporary services of a part-time woman to come in, say, a couple of days a week to do the washing and heavy cleaning.

Furthermore, being *Kinderreich,* she is almost sure that her servant problem will be solved with the spring. Next April 1st, multitudes of young girls will graduate from school. Those girls are thereupon subject to a year's *Dienst,* which means National Service. On the one hand, they can go into *Hilfsdienst,* which usually means domestic service in a family with young children. That is where our Berlin lady comes in. She is virtually certain to get one of those girl recruits. For city girls, especially, such tasks may be more congenial than *Arbeitsdienst,* which means work on the farm.

There are no exemptions from this compulsory service. Rich or poor, all are alike subject. During my stay in Berlin, I dined one night with some aristocratic and wealthy Germans who introduced me to their charming daughter, just returned from getting in the potato crop on a farm a hundred miles from Berlin.

As far as the servant problem is concerned, our Berlin lady's first war-winter will presumably be the hardest, and if she is a strong, healthy young matron she probably won't be much the worse for it. Still, it isn't easy. She has to be up early and get breakfast for six. The husband is at the office all day, while the older children take their lunches with them and don't get back from school until mid-afternoon. Her younger children are the hardest problem. They can't be left alone, so Milady is tied to her home except on the days when her part-time servant is there. Those are the precious hours she takes for marketing and other necessary shopping. She gives the youngsters an airing when she can, but the little tots do lack outdoor exercise.

Let us now see what Milady does when she gets home from market and takes her purchases to the kitchen. That kitchen will almost certainly have a gas or electric stove and other modern conveniences. But it will probably lack American specialties like an electric icer or a washing-machine. And right there we touch upon another very sore point in wartime Germany's domestic life. That point is soap.

We have already noted how short Germany is in butter, lard, and kindred products. But this shortage goes beyond edible fats. It applies to soap-products as well. Nowhere are Germans more strictly rationed. Each person gets only one cake of toilet soap per month. The precious object is about as large as what we call a guest-cake size, and it has to do the individual not only for face and hands but for the bath as well.

The same strict rationing applies to laundry soap and powder. Furthermore, the fat content of both is so low that, though it takes the dirt out, the clothes are apt to look a bit gray. And bleaches must be used sparingly, since they tend to wear out clothes. That is why most families have their washing done at home instead of sending it out to commercial laundries. Incidentally, when the washing is done, the sudsy water is not thrown away. It is carefully saved for washing floors or other heavy cleaning.

Let us assume that Milady finds the washing going well and that the little ones haven't got into too much mischief during her absence. It's now about time for her to get lunch. The children's meal brings up the interesting point of juvenile milk. Only children get "whole" milk in Germany today. They are issued special milk cards and are rationed according to age. Infants up to three years get one liter per day—a trifle over a quart. Children between three and six years get half a liter, and those between seven and fourteen one-quarter liter—half a pint. Thereafter they are considered adults and can have only skimmed milk. Those juvenile milk quotas seem pretty stiff, but they are the winter ration. I understand that they are substantially increased when the cows are turned out to grass in the spring. I may add that I have tasted children's milk and found it good—fully equal to what we in America know as Grade B.

When luncheon is over, disposal of the scraps introduces us to another notable feature in wartime Germany's domestic economy. Every family is in duty bound not to waste anything. So each German kitchen has a covered pail into which goes all garbage that can be served to pigs. This pail is taken downstairs and dumped into a large container which is collected every day. Meat bones are usually taken by the children to school as a little patriotic chore.

What we in America call "trash" must be carefully segregated into the following categories: (1) newspapers, magazines, or other clean paper; (2) rags; (3) bottles; (4) old metal; (5) broken furniture or about anything else that is thrown away. City collectors come around for this segregated trash at regular intervals. There are no private junk dealers. An all-seeing paternal state attends to even this petty salvage. Wartime Germany overlooks no details.

IX. THE BATTLE OF THE LAND

"THE PEASANT IS THE LIFE-SPRING OF OUR REICH AND our race." Thus did Walther Darré, Minister of Agriculture and Food Supply, concisely state the Nazi attitude toward the land and those who work it. *Blut und Boden!* "Blood and Soil!" That is one of National Socialism's key slogans. Nowhere has this revolutionary regime undertaken more daring and original experiments than upon the land itself. Of that I was aware when I came to Germany, so I was anxious to study this challenging phase of German life by first-hand observation.

The Minister was more than willing to assist. This big, energetic, good-looking man is one of the most interesting personalities among the Nazi leaders. As his name indicates, he descends from Huguenot ancestors who came to Germany three centuries ago. Furthermore, as I have stated, he was born in the Argentine. The son of a wealthy German resident, he spent his early life in South America. He is well qualified for his job, since he is an expert on agriculture and stockbreeding.

I have already quoted Dr. Darré on the food-card system now in operation. However, in our conversations, he repeatedly emphasized that this was merely part of a much larger organic whole which far transcended the war. Here is how he summarized National Socialism's agricultural aim and policy: "When we came to power in 1933, one of our chief endeavors was to save German agriculture from impending ruin. However, our agricultural program went far beyond mere economic considerations. It was based on the idea that no nation can truly prosper without a sound rural population. It is not enough that the farmers shall be tolerably well-off; they should also be aware of their place in the national life and be able to fulfill it. Here are the three big factors in the problem: First, to assure an ample food supply; second, to safeguard the future by a healthy population increase; third, to develop a distinctive national culture deeply rooted in the soil. This ideal logically implies an aim which goes far beyond what is usually known as an agrarian policy."

These factors were dealt with by three important pieces of legislation passed shortly after the Nazis came to power. They were: (1) The National Food Estate; (2) The Hereditary Farmlands Law; (3) The Market Control Statute.

The Food Estate is a gigantic quasi-public corporation embracing in its membership not only all persons immediately on the land but also everyone connected with the production and distribution of foodstuffs. Large landowners, small peasants, agricultural laborers, millers, bakers, canners, middlemen, right down to local butchers and grocers—they are one and all included in this huge vertical trust. The aim is to bring all these group interests, previously working largely at cross-purposes, into a harmonious, co-ordinated whole, concerned especially with problems of production and distribution.

The Market Control Statute links all this with the consumer. The aim here is a thoroughgoing, balanced economic structure based on the principle known as the "just price." Everybody is supposed to make a profit, but none are to be out of line with the others. Furthermore, the ultimate consumer is to be protected from profiteering.

The Hereditary Farmlands Law revives the old Teutonic concept that the landowner is intimately linked to the land. It is officially stated that "The idea engendered by Roman law that land was so much merchandise to be bought and sold at will is profoundly repugnant to German feelings. To us, soil is something sacred; the peasant and his land belong inseparably together." Emphasis is thus laid on the *Bauer*, imperfectly translated by our word *peasant*. The German *Bauer* is an independent landowner, self-respecting and proud of the name. We can best visualize him as like the old English yeoman.

This is the class which National Socialism seeks to foster by making peasant holdings hereditary; keeping the farm in the family, and keeping it intact by having it descend through the oldest son. That was the old Teutonic method, which still prevails by custom in parts of Germany. Over 700,000 of these hereditary farm holdings have now been established. They cannot be sold or mortgaged; neither can a creditor seize the crop for the owner's personal debt. To qualify as a hereditary peasant, however, a man must be of German blood and be able to manage his property. Title to the land is thus not absolute; it is rather functional in character.

This type of peasant is most numerous in Northwestern Germany. In the eastern provinces, great estates predominate. In Southern Germany, on the contrary, where farms have customarily been divided among all the children, holdings tend to be too small. The Nazis consider either extreme economically and socially unsound. They therefore seek to split up the big estates into moderate-sized peasant farmsteads, and combine small parcels into normal units. They are not trying to rush things, but considerable progress has been made along both lines.

As usual, the Nazis have tried to enlist psychology in their agricultural endeavors. The *Bauer's* traditional pride is flattered in many ways. He is extolled as the Third Reich's "nobility of the soil"; the vital wellspring of national life. Everything is done to encourage his corporate spirit, from reviving costumes and folkdances to an annual Peasant Congress and a gigantic festival on the historic Bueckeberg. The Nazis frankly admit that mere planning and regulation from above, no matter how efficient, will not attain the desired goal —a flourishing agriculture which will feed the whole nation. Not unless the rural population is inspired to do its utmost will the experiment succeed. It is this psychological aspect which Nazi spokesmen have in mind when they speak of the *Inner Front.* As Darré told me: "We saw from the first that we could not reach our goal through state action alone. We needed the help of the organized farmers to put it over."

Such was the theory. How was it working out in practice? "See for yourself," said Dr. Darré. He thereupon proposed that I make an investigation trip through what he considered the most instructive region—rural Westphalia and Oldenburg. There I would see in successful operation an agricultural system and way of life basically unchanged since the Middle Ages. It was upon this system, adapted to modern conditions, that the National Socialist Government had framed its land laws, which it intends ultimately to extend throughout the Reich. I would thus see a sort of working model for a hoped-for future.

A few days after this conversation I left Berlin for the projected tour, accompanied by one of the Minister's right-hand men. He was Dr. Friedrich Sohn, a leading agronomist who had also studied agricultural conditions in America and had done special work in the Brookings Institution at Washington. He could thus compare German and American agriculture in a most useful way. As usual, an elaborate schedule had been drawn up for a comprehensive survey, with many stops to visit farms, large and small, and ample time to chat with the owners, look over their livestock, and examine methods of cultivation. A shy man, Dr. Sohn handed me the typewritten schedule rather anxiously. "This means that we'll be going every day from dawn till after dark," he said with a deprecating smile. I assured him that was all right with me, as I wanted to make the most of this trip. This cheered him up no end. Germans really like hard work, and they seem always delighted when a foreigner is willing to hit the same pace.

We left Berlin by train just after lunch and journeyed westward via Hanover to Minden, where we were to spend the first night. We arrived after dark. The railway station is some distance from the town itself, so we had to rustle our bags through the misting rain to a waiting tram almost tiny enough to pose for a model of the famous Toonerville Trolley. On our way, we nearly ran over a drunk who had chosen the space between the rails for his couch. The motorman heaved the sleeper impatiently to the roadside and kept on, reporting the incident to a policeman on post as we entered town.

We stopped at a little hotel decorated in the plush splendor of the 1870's. They dine early in the provinces, so when we got to the dining-room it was almost empty except for one large *Stammtisch* in a far corner. About that table sat a dozen big, blond men smoking fat cigars and drinking from generous steins of beer. Our meal confirmed what I had already heard about the less stringent food regulations in the small towns. It was a meatless day, but I rejoiced to see egg dishes on the menu. I hastened to order fried eggs, "sunny side up," and got two big beauties. The fresh yolks beamed at me from the blue-bordered plate. Those were the first eggs I had seen in Germany since the Press junket; but those had been rather "off the record" while these were evidently a matter of course. I was still more astonished to see a nice piece of fried ham nestling beside the eggs, while the next instant my waiter placed a pat of butter on the table, with no request for my food-card. I looked inquiringly at Dr. Sohn. "Out here they don't bother much about such matters," he smiled.

After dinner, the head of the local *Bauernschaft*, or Peasants' Organization, came to pay his respects and talk over the trip planned for the next day. Like most of these officials, he was an obvious countryman. The *Bauernschaft* is really run by "dirt farmers."

We breakfasted early and entered the motor car ordered for us just as the late autumn dawn was breaking. It was a small sedan, through the windows of which I caught charming glimpses of historic Minden with its crooked streets and gabled houses. The day was cold and cloudy. By the time we had reached our first scheduled stop, I was somewhat chilled. This was the town of Enger, where we were to do a bit of sightseeing—but with a practical purpose. Here is the burial place of Widukind, the legendary Saxon chieftain who for so long withstood the might of Charlemagne. The Nazis have glorified Widukind as a popular hero, defending primitive Germanism and the old gods against Karl the Great who is described as a Latinized Teuton seeking to impose upon the Saxons the yoke of a revived Roman Empire and an equally alien Roman faith. That, at least, is the thesis of the handsome little booklet given me when I visited the new Widukind Memorial, half museum and half shrine. The booklet also states that, long after the Saxon nobles had lost heart and given up the fight, the tribal masses stood by their patriot hero to the death. Perchance the intent is to suggest a primeval *Fuehrer?*

We were now well into rural Westphalia, and our investigations had begun. But before relating details, let me sketch in the background. The districts I was to visit all lie in what is undoubtedly the most Teutonic part of Germany. From Westphalia northward to the North Sea Coast and the Holstein peninsula to the Danish border stretches the region which can perhaps best be called *Old Saxon-Land*. This region should not be confused with the modern province of Saxony, which is far to the southward and has no historical connection. What I refer to as Old Saxon-Land is the primeval home of those Teutonic tribes some of whom migrated oversea and conquered Britain. It is interesting to note that the old blood still shows in the present population.

A large proportion of the peasantry have long heads and faces, ruddy blond complexions, and frames which, though tall and muscular, are seldom rotund or thick-set. Such persons could very easily pass for English rural types. Some of them, indeed, with different clothes and haircuts, would look quite like old-stock Americans.

For the American visitor, the general aspect of this region has a familiar look. In other parts of Germany the rural population lives in villages. Old Saxon-Land, however, is throughout a country of detached farms. Each family lives on its own holding, entirely separate from its neighbors. This, indeed, typifies the traditional spirit of the folk. The Old Saxons have been, and for the most part still are, independent land-holders. There are relatively few large estates held by noblemen. The region is predominantly inhabited by a landowning peasantry.

Within itself, this peasantry varies considerably in economic and social standing. At the top stand large farms of two hundred acres or more, while the smallest holdings are only a few acres. Most of the large farms are worked, not by temporary hired labor, but by tenant farmers. The relations of these tenants to their proprietors are highly personal and are regulated by contracts and customs going back to ancient times. Some tenant holdings have been in the same family for generations.

The agricultural system and way of life in Old Saxon-Land cannot be understood unless we realize that these people, no matter what the size of their holdings, all feel themselves to be *fellow-peasants*. Even the wealthy owner of many acres and proprietor to several tenants is very much of a dirt farmer. He probably has been away to school and possesses a good education. Nevertheless, he works with his hands, wears farm clothes and wooden shoes, and is just as close to the soil as anyone else. He has no wish to be a nobleman or even a "squire" in the English sense. However, he has a deep though unobtrusive pride in himself and his place in the world. With good reason, too; for in many cases his forebears have been leaders in the local community since time immemorial. One big farm I visited, which had been in the same family for over five centuries, had been continuously cultivated with scant change in boundaries ever since the year 960 A.D.—more than a hundred years before the Norman Conquest of England!

The quiet dignity and mellow beauty of these old farmsteads must be seen to be appreciated. They consist of a number of buildings ranged about a courtyard, whence their German name of *Hof*. They are always built of timbered red brick, though the timber patterns differ from one district to another. As you enter the courtyard, you have directly in front of you the main building—an impressive structure with high-pitched roof running down to within a few feet of the ground. This building is very long; sometimes well over a hundred feet. It houses both the master-farmer and his animals. When you enter the great doorway you find cows and horses stalled on either side. Only the malodorous pigs are today usually relegated to other quarters, though formerly they lived there too.

At the rear of the farmstead are the family living-quarters. In olden days there was no partition between, so the master-farmer could survey his livestock directly from his great bed and watch the work going on. Today, the living-quarters are walled off from the barn itself, though with handy access through one or more doors. Back of the living-quarters lies a moderate-sized pleasure garden, filled with shrubs and flowerbeds, and usually walled in by high hedges. Here the family take their ease on summer evenings.

The smaller farmsteads are built on precisely the same lines as the great *Hofs*, though everything is on a lesser scale. In the old tenant farmsteads conditions are decidedly primitive. The living-quarters are not merely under the same roof; they are right in with the animals. Yet even here I found no filth or squalor. The air might be pungent with the smell of cows and horses, but the rooms were always neat and clean.

Maier Johann awaited me as my motor car drove in through the outer gate of the farmstead and stopped in the middle of the wide courtyard. The yard was surrounded by buildings of timbered brick. Indeed, the yard itself was paved with brick, liberally coated with sticky black soil tracked in by wagons, men, and animals. My host stood in the great doorway of his *Hof*, his ancestral abode.

Maier Johann is a wealthy man, as wealth is reckoned in those parts. He owns over two hundred acres of rich land, most of it under crops though with some pasture and woodland. His ancestors have owned it for nearly eight hundred years. From the first glance it is clear that he is a good manager. Everything is well kept up.

The front of the *Hof* is a sight in itself. From the high-pitched roof to the ground, this front is elaborately carved, and those old carvings are painted in many colors. From them you learn that the present *Hof* was built in the year 1757. There is a curious mixture of pious Christian texts and symbols coming down from heathen times—sun, moon, stars, the signs of fertility, and black ravens for good luck. On the massive oak timbers of the doorway, wide and high enough for hay wagons to drive in, are carved and painted the Norse Trees of Life, together with symbolic serpents to guard the humans and animals dwelling inside from evil spirits that might seek to intrude.

My host is a *Maier*. That is not a family name. It denotes his rank, and has the same significance as the original meaning of our word "mayor"—leading man in a community. The farmstead is thus a *Maierhof*. But he is not merely a *Maier*, he is a *Sattelmaier*. That means a leading man on a fully-caparisoned horse; in short, a man-at-arms, who ranked next to a knight in Feudal times. It is the very tip-top of the peasant hierarchy. Only a few *Sattelmaiers* are to be found in this countryside.

When a *Sattelmaier* dies, the bells in the parish church toll for an hour in a special way. The coffin containing the deceased is taken to the church in a wagon lined with straw and drawn by six horses. Behind the wagon paces the dead man's favorite steed, led by the oldest of his tenant farmers. During the funeral service, the horse looks in through the open church door, and he also inspects the grave while his master is laid to rest. On such occasions the whole countryside turns out to pay final honors.

These curious ceremonies have not been described merely to make a quaint story; they typify the spirit of this conservative yet virile folk. The proudest *Sattel-*

maier is neither nobleman nor squire. He is a peasant—
a master-peasant, if you will, yet still a peasant—the first
among basic equals.

Of this, Maier Johann was a good example. He knew
I was coming to see him, but he had made no attempt
to "dress up." So he met me clad in an old hunting-cap,
heavy farm clothes, and wooden shoes flecked with mud
from work about the stables. A tall, fair man, ruddy
from a life spent in the open, he led me through the
doorway into the long barnlike *Hof,* lined with cow-
stalls on one side and horse-stalls on the other. The
brick floor was partly covered by a pile of hay from the
loft above and heaps of green fodder. The loft flooring
was supported by massive oak beams two feet thick,
hand-hewn and dark with age.

At the far end of the barn was a wooden partition,
walling off the living-quarters. Into these we passed
through a low door, and I found myself in a hall
stretching the width of the *Hof.* This hall contained
several pieces of massive furniture, obviously family
heirlooms and elaborately carved. The doors and wainscoting were carved in similar fashion.

On the walls hung several portraits of army officers.
My host explained. "This," said he, pointing to the
framed sketch of a bearded man in a hussar uniform,
"is an ancestor of mine who was killed in the Danish
War of the 1860's." He pointed again: "Here is a relative who fell before Paris in 1871." Again: "This is my
uncle, killed in the World War." He made no mention
of an excellent likeness of himself in officer's field-gray.
The earlier portraits were especially interesting to anyone who recalls the caste spirit of the old Prussian
Army. They revealed perhaps better than aught else

the peculiar social status of the *Sattelmaier*—a master-peasant who was nevertheless eligible to a commission alongside noblemen and gentlemen.

One other portrait hung on the wall: a painting of a very old man with shrewd blue eyes twinkling behind features withered like a red apple. My host smiled almost tenderly. "A *Heuerling,*" he answered my unspoken question. "One of our tenant farmers. He died last winter at the age of ninety-four."

Maier Johann was the only *Sattelmaier* I visited. But he was merely a somewhat wealthier and more prominent specimen of a generalized type. The other master-peasants with whom I stopped were very similar in appearance and character, and their homes were much the same. All of them appeared to be capable, practical men, naturally intelligent and with a fair measure of education; yet never "citified" and always in closest touch with the earth which nourished them. Their homes were free from pretentiousness or cheap modernity; their farms were models of careful husbandry—a good, sound breed.

As might be expected, their hospitality was as ample as it was unaffected. Most of all do I remember the country breakfasts—those European "second breakfasts" which are eaten in the middle of the forenoon. Picture me seated in an old room with carved wainscoting and beamed ceiling, heated by a tall tiled stove. Around a long table sit big brawny men and buxom women, eating heartily of the food with which the board is laden. Those viands may sound simple to American readers in our fortunate land of plenty, but to me, fresh from strictly rationed Berlin, they were luxuries indeed. In Berlin my butter ration was about an ounce per day;

here was a stack of butter nearly as big as your head! Platters of smoked Westphalian ham and varied sausages, flanked by piles of rye bread and pumpernickel. Best of all, a big platter of hard-boiled eggs fresh from the nest. No food-cards for the folk who produce Germany's food!

The one thing lacking was coffee, for no one in Germany has coffee except invalids, wounded men in hospital, and soldiers at the front. But there were cups of strong meat bouillon, and later on small yet potent glasses of schnapps or brandy to wash down the meal. Then German cigars, mild and quite good, were passed around, and we sat back to chat amid a haze of blue tobacco smoke.

It was hard to leave those cordial hosts and their kindly hospitality. Always with regret did I quit the cozy living-room, walk down the long vista of the barn, climb into my waiting car, and wave farewells until the motor had passed out of the *Hof* gates and taken once more to the road.

One of the outstanding features of the agricultural system of northwestern Germany is the tenant farmer. In that region he is called a *Heuerling*. This is the German variant of our old English word "hireling." With us, the word has come to have a bad meaning. It signifies a man who has sold himself into some unworthy or criminal service. In German, however, it means simply a hired man, and in Northwestern Germany it applies especially to a peculiar sort of tenancy.

The *Heuerling* is not a casual or seasonal agricultural laborer. In Northwest Germany, landless, floating farm labor is little in evidence. Only since the outbreak of the present war with the consequent enrollment of many young peasants as soldiers has such labor been much needed. For centuries, the *Heuerling* has supplied the basic answer. The nearest thing we have to him in America is the "hired man" in rural New England, who is usually a farm fixture, often for life.

The New England hired man, however, is ordinarily a bachelor, living under the same roof with his employer and virtually part of the immediate family. The *Heuerling* has a house of his own, together with a small tract of land which he can work in his spare time. His home is a miniature farmstead. Like the spacious *Hof* of the proprietor, it shelters family and animals under one roof—and in the closest proximity. Those animals are supplied to him by the proprietor as part of the tenancy contract—at least one milch cow and several pigs, to say nothing of poultry. The *Heuerling* also gets a cash wage. In return for all this he is bound to give the master-peasant who employs him most of his time. A large farm of two hundred acres may have five or six of these tenant households within its borders.

I suppose that this system, like every other, has its share of abuses. But from all the evidence I could gather, it seems to work satisfactorily. In the first place, the system is very ancient, and tenancies are made in accordance with long-established custom and precedent. Even more important, there is no class distinction involved. As already remarked, all these folk feel themselves to be fellow-peasants, and they actually work side by side. Their basic social equality is revealed by the way they always speak to one another in the second person singular—the German *Du,* which implies close familiarity. Another favorable sign is the way these tenancies are cherished. Some tenant farmsteads I visited had been in the same family for generations. Certainly, all the *Heuerlings* I met and talked with appeared to be upstanding men—simple and good-natured, if you will, yet not a type to be browbeaten or ill-used. The whole system is intensely personal in its relationships. In fact, it is quite feudal, still infused with the spirit of medieval times.

The best example of the quaintly feudal loyalty which the *Heuerling* entertains toward his master-peasant employer is one which came to my attention during a visit to a certain large farmstead. The owner had died suddenly about a year before, leaving a widow, a son only sixteen years old, and a still younger daughter. The management of the farm was immediately taken over by the most capable of the *Heuerlings* in conjunction with the widow, and this joint regency was working so successfully that there seemed to be no danger that the farm would run down before the heir was old enough to take matters into his own hands.

The most vivid recollection I have of a *Heuerling's* home is one I visited late one afternoon. Darkness had already fallen as my motor struggled up a muddy, rutty lane and finally stopped before a small farmstead redolent of age. The gatelike doorway opened to our knock and I found myself in a curious house-barn interior where a cow gazed tranquilly from its stall into a tiny kitchen across the way, and where chickens roosted in surprising places. This strange household was dimly lit by a few oil lamps which threw a mellow sheen on beams and walls nearly three centuries old.

The *Heuerling*, a hale old man and his equally hale

wife, greeted me without the slightest trace of self-consciousness. I had come at a good moment, he said, for he had something interesting to show me—the pig he had long been fattening and which he had slaughtered that very morning. Visibly swelling with pride, he led me to the rear of the house, and I mentally agreed that his pride was justified, for it was certainly a mammoth porker. As the great carcass, immaculately dressed, swung gently from a beam in the ceiling, it bulked enormous in the dim light. I was told it weighed nearly five hundred pounds, and I do not think the man exaggerated.

Such, briefly, is the old *Heuerling* system, and the homes and human types it produces. It is interesting to note that the German Government is actively fostering this system and seeks to extend it further afield, with such modifications as new circumstances call for. Wherever a large or middle-sized farm needs more regular labor, the Government offers to loan the proprietor about two-fifths of the cost of building a *Heuerling* house, the loan to be repaid over a considerable term of years. Such houses as I saw were not of the old type. They were severely practical two-story affairs, with no room for animals, though with ample cellar space for storing vegetables and preserves. Built solidly of brick, tile, and concrete, they appear to be fireproof throughout. Except for a small kitchen-garden plot they have no land attached to them, but I am told that the proprietor is bound to furnish certain amounts of meat and other foodstuffs. Rental contracts run for a year. The terms vary according to the kind of employment. One man whose home I inspected was a professional milker, brought down from Friesland. He naturally has no time for anything but his cows, so his contract calls for an almost wholly cash wage.

This young man and his sturdy little wife were undisguisedly proud of the new home they had just furnished. The furniture, though plain, looked of good quality. They told me that most of it had been paid for out of the 1,000-Mark ($400) loan which the Government will make to any healthy young couple at the time of their marriage. It is to be repaid in small installments, but one-fourth of it is canceled every time a baby is born. So a prolific couple should not have to repay very much.

The Government seeks in every way to tie these new settlers to the land and make them into *Heuerlings* of the old school. One of the most striking inducements which it offers is a sort of long-service bonus. After a man has served satisfactorily for five successive years, the Government offers to make him a gift of from 600 to 800 Marks if he will sign a five-year contract with his employer. Although these attempts to extend and modernize an age-old system have been inaugurated too recently to yield much evidence as to their success, they constitute an interesting experiment in agricultural labor relations.

How are the Nazis faring in their Battle of the Land? That is a complex question, hard to answer. Personally, I examined in detail only one sector of the "agricultural front," and was presumably shown the best of that. However, we have some definite information, and I supplemented this by discussions with Germans and qualified foreign students of the problem.

The Third Reich does not seem to be in any immediate danger of actual starvation from the British blockade. At present rations, there is enough grain, meat, potatoes, and other stock vegetables including beet sugar to last for at least two years.* The German grain crop for 1938 was 27,430,000 tons—about 2,000,000 tons over normal consumption. The amount of the grain reserve is secret; but it is known to be very large. Estimates range from twelve to eighteen months. Also, Germany can import grain in quantity from Hungary and other parts of Central Europe; possibly also from Russia, especially as time goes on.

The last German potato crop was 56,300,000 tons, of which less than one-third is needed for human consumption, despite the wartime shift to a potato diet. The balance goes chiefly for feeding pigs and distillation into alcohol, used largely for commercial purposes and for mixing with motor fuels. There is an abundance of sugar beets, likewise an excellent animal feed. Cabbage, turnips, and other vegetables are all in satisfactory shape.

Germany has a growing number of hogs—a vital source of fat as well as of meat. Hogs do well on a diet of sugar beets and potatoes. The last hog census for Greater Germany showed 28,613,000 porkers, an increase of no less than 53 per cent over December, 1938. Cattle herds number almost 20,000,000. Even under the worst conditions, that should furnish a lot of milk, and

---

* This was written on the basis of what I could learn in Germany down to my departure in January, 1940. I have since had information that the record cold during the winter months froze and spoiled vast amounts of stored potatoes and other vegetables. This point and its possible effects are discussed in Chapter XXII.

of meat at the present ration—one pound per week per person.

That is the bright side of the picture, from the German point of view. But we have already discussed the dark side—a crucial lack of fats and other shortages which result in an unbalanced diet injurious to health and strength over a period of time. The German people is today on iron rations. They cannot be notably reduced without disaster. Can they be maintained for years at their present level?

The answer to that question depends on certain long-range factors, especially the efficiency of the present agricultural system and the temper of the farming population. The Nazi regime has established a highly complex economic structure with fixed prices all along the line. Agriculture has been basically socialized. To be sure, the peasant owns his land and has been protected against heavy loss, but he is no longer a free agent. He must grow what he is told and sell at established rates. He is virtually tied to the soil and his initiative is narrowly circumscribed. Economic security has been coupled with rigid state control.

For the first few years of the Nazi regime, the peasant probably gained on balance. But with the introduction of the Four Year Plan toward the close of 1936, agriculture ceased to be the White-Haired Boy. An intensive rearmament program coupled with colossal reconstruction projects had first call on both capital and labor. This imposed serious handicaps upon agriculture, which the war tends to intensify. One of these is a farm-labor shortage. At the annual Peasant Congress in December, 1938, Minister Darré admitted that there were 400,000 fewer workers on the land than when the Nazis came to power, and the deficit is probably much larger than that figure. Furthermore, we must remember that this is only part of a general shortage of labor in every phase of Germany's economic life. The Government is striving to overcome this by compulsory labor service for young men and women, and it has promised that 1,000,000 Poles would be imported to work on German farms. It remains to be seen how efficient such amateur or conscript labor will be as compared with seasoned farm workers.

Recently the Government raised the prices of milk and butter as avowed incentives to the farming population. No such disturbance of its nicely balanced price system would have been made if the need for such action had not been urgent.

The Battle of the Land thus goes forward. What the outcome will be, only time can tell.

X. THE LABOR FRONT

THE THIRD REICH'S WHOLE ECONOMIC LIFE IS WHAT
Nazis frankly call a *Wehrwirtschaft*—an economy run
on military lines. That is why they use military terms
to describe its various activities. Having observed the
Battle of the Land, let us now survey the industrial
sector, known as the Labor Front.

Before attempting this survey, however, one point
should be emphatically made which applies not only
here but also in subsequent chapters dealing with institutional aspects of the Third Reich. In each case a well-
rounded presentation would have involved prolonged
first-hand investigation and extensive research. This was
obviously impossible during a three months' stay in
Germany. The best I could do was a limited amount
of personal observation plus discussions with officials
and a study of available data. These were checked as far
as possible with qualified foreign students and observers, but I am aware that the results are not conclusive. Nazi spokesmen present the official case with in-
adequate rebuttal or full disclosure of the other side of
the story. The upshot is a more or less unbalanced
treatment which can be legitimately criticized.

All this I know and deplore. But I could see no practical alternative. To have confined myself solely to my
own observations and impressions would have meant a

series of fragmentary sketches which would have been intelligible only to readers who already had considerable knowledge of the subjects touched upon. These subjects are so little known to the general public in America that most readers would presumably have obtained neither a connected picture of wartime Germany nor a background against which matters specifically treated could be viewed.

One of the first acts of the Nazi regime was to dissolve the old labor unions and merge them into a single organization under state control. This, however, was not a mere Nazi "One Big Union." Precisely as the Nazis did in agriculture, so they here co-ordinated everybody connected with industry into a huge vertical trust. The lowliest workingman and the biggest manufacturer became (at least technically) fellow-members of the new Labor Front. And the white-collar workers were likewise in the same boat.

Here, as elsewhere, we note the underlying principle of the Third Reich—the classless State mobilized for collective aims in accordance with the slogan: *Gemeinnutz vor Eigennutz*—"The common weal above individual advantage." In short, everything and everybody subordinated to the advancement of a regime which is in some respects a cross between modern Guild Socialism and the craft guilds of the Middle Ages. The feudal note is clear. Employers are termed "leaders"; employees became "followers" or "retainers." Both are adjured to cherish mutual loyalty and duty. Their personal dignity is emphasized by "Courts of Honor." Strikes, lockouts, and arbitrary "hire-and-fire" are alike prohibited. The final arbiters in this curious set-up are "Trustees of Labor," who can discipline or discharge anyone, even "leaders." Needless to say, these Trustees are Party members. They see to it that the whole Labor Front functions efficiently in full accordance with the general policies laid down by the Nazi Government.

Such is the theory. How has it worked out in practice?

First let us try to visualize the Labor Front. This huge organization, embracing the entire structure of German industry, has nearly 30,000,000 members. Membership is compulsory. So are the dues, individually moderate but aggregating a vast fund, expended as the leadership sees fit. The leader is, of course, Dr. Robert Ley, whom we saw haranguing the Duesseldorf workers. A florid, dynamic man with compelling gray eyes, he apparently cannot modulate his voice, for my ear-drums literally ached after a long conversation I had with him.

On the whole, we can say of the Labor Front what we said of the Food Estate—it worked out most advantageously for its members during the early years of the Nazi regime. Its outstanding success was the triumph over mass unemployment. When the Nazis came to power in 1933, Germany had 7,000,000 unemployed. In proportion to total populations, this was worse than in the lowest depth of our depression at about the same time. The drastic measures of the Nazi regime, repellant though they are to our ideals, not only rapidly did away with unemployment but presently brought about a growing labor shortage. Germany was working full-time. Real wages did not make so good a showing. They had risen only slightly; so the individual workingman was financially not much better off than he had been in 1933—*if* he then had a job. However, all the former unemployed now did have jobs. Also, the Nazi apologists were careful to point out to me, the workers had gained certain advantages, such as the Strength through Joy benefits, which we will examine later on.

The year 1937 is a turning-point in the status of German labor. By that time the famous Four Year Plan had got well into its stride. The Third Reich had embarked upon an aggressive foreign policy which made war at least likely, if not certain. *Wehrwirtschaft* thus became a genuine war-economy. To prepare for all contingencies, labor and capital were regimented as ruthlessly as was agriculture. The results were as grim as they were inevitable. In the summer of 1938, a Government decree obligated all able-bodied men and women for short-term service to meet "nationally urgent tasks." Almost at the same time, another decree fixed maximum wages and salaries. Labor was not only tied to its present jobs but could be taken from them and sent anywhere the Government might think fit. The principle of the eight-hour day was discarded for a ten-hour day, with a maximum of fourteen hours in exceptional cases. Restrictions on the labor of women and children were also relaxed.

When the war actually came a year later, this draconic program was pushed to its logical conclusion. In wartime Germany today, labor is everywhere working at the limit of its capacity. Indeed, the limit of human endurance seems to have been overstepped. Although such matters cannot there be discussed in print, Germany is full of rumors concerning a falling-off of production in many lines. The main reasons seems to be sheer overstrain, but there is doubtless a considerable amount of calculated "ca' canny."

We here come to the highly controversial subject of popular discontent against the Nazi regime. Even shirking by workingmen is treated as "sabotage" and may be punished by death; so no German admits opposition to anything unless he has full confidence in the one to whom he speaks. Resident journalists sometimes have good lines of information; but even they seldom get specific for fear of betraying German informants into a concentration camp or worse. It is thus very difficult for the temporary observer to assess accurately the amount of opposition which today exists.

The nearest I came to first-hand acquaintance with militant unrest was one evening when a journalistic colleague took me to a beer hall in a poor quarter east of Alexanderplatz. The clientele looked sordid and semi-criminal. My colleague introduced me to one hard-looking citizen who, when asked how he stood politically, answered sourly: "Sure I'm a Nazi—oh, yeah? Phuuugh!" He made that last remark by breathing hard against the back of his hand pressed against his lips, which resulted in a loud "Bronx cheer." Also he made no effort to lower his voice; so his words were overheard by sitters at nearby tables—who grinned appreciatively.

However, I hesitate to generalize from this incident and a few other matters along the same line, any more than I would be apt to deduce an impending revolution in America from frequenting tough joints around Union Square, New York. I do think that genuine unrest exists in Germany today—far more than any Nazi spokesman would care to admit. But I do not believe that it is either as widespread or as deep-seated as we in America are led to believe. Many of the older trades-unionists have presumably never reconciled themselves to the new order of things, yet I found scant evidence that the younger generation shared their idealistic attitude.

The reason for this lack of idealistic roots to such militant opposition as exists is because Nazism has offered the workers certain popular appeals—some psychological, others tangible, still others evoked by the old lure of "bread and circuses."

In the first place, the Labor Front promised workingmen greater security and self-respect. The employing class under both the Empire and the Weimar Republic tended to be arrogant, hard-handed plutocrats. A Statute which stressed the dignity of labor, set up Courts of Honor, and was run by State Trustees who often cracked down on big industrialists might give the average workingman an emotional glow that partly offset low wages and strict regimentation. This was especially true in the first years of the Nazi regime.

Furthermore, the Labor Front has done something to improve working conditions along the most advanced lines. This phase of its activities is known as *Schoenheit der Arbeit*—"The Beautification of Labor." A minority of employers had voluntarily begun the movement under the Weimar Republic and even under the Empire, replacing ugly, dreary factories by more cheerful and more healthful surroundings. However, too many of the old type remained, depressing the worker by dirt, smoke, bad lighting, worse plumbing, and no fit place for luncheon or rest periods. Few owners of such factories seem to have had the vision or the money to realize that the worker's efficiency would be notably heightened by cleaner and cheerier surroundings.

The Labor Front swept away many such abuses. Employers were compelled to clean house, and were lent part of the money needed to do so. Factories were either remodeled or scrapped while new ones were erected, scientifically built to give the workers a maximum of light and air. These new factories were set in park-like grounds, wherein workers could spend their rest periods or on which they could look while working instead of having to gaze at a blank wall or a sordid shed. Tasteful rest-rooms, lunch-rooms where hot meals are served, up-to-date washroom facilities—these are the new order of the day. I can vouch for these matters, because I ate good (if simple) meals and inspected the other improvements in several factories during my stay in Germany. Especially was I minutely shown the locker-rooms, swimming-pools, shower-baths, and toilets. Coming from plumbing-conscious America, I found few novelties. But their eager pride in such matters made me realize how recent they must have been. Of course I was shown the best. I do not know their percentage to the total number of factories.

One interesting feature was the competitions between factories for model championships. I recall one factory which had gained that honor the summer previous. A special swastika banner symbolized the triumph—and it must be re-earned each year if it is not to go elsewhere. I was shown photographs of the presentation ceremonies, and of the subsequent jollification when all hands, from executives down, went off in chartered buses to a picnic at a nearby amusement place.

An even more important, and certainly a more publicized method of winning the masses to National Socialism is that known as *Kraft durch Freude*—"Strength

through Joy." This is the most gigantic scheme of
organized, state-directed entertainment that the world
has ever seen. It includes a wide variety of activities,
from "highbrow" art and music to popular amusement,
travel, and sport. Every member of the Labor Front
can participate, from high-paid executives to day laborers; from women secretaries to servant girls. Conversely,
no one outside the Labor Front can share its benefits.

The theory behind the experiment is thus explained
by Dr. Ley: "Work entails physical and nervous strain
liable to leave a feeling of bodily and mental exhaustion
which cannot be eradicated by merely going to rest.
Mind and body require new nourishment. Since during
the hours of labor a maximum of effort and attention
is demanded of the worker, it is essential that during
his leisure hours the best of everything should be
offered him in the shape of spiritual, intellectual, and
physical recreation, in order to maintain, or if necessary
restore, the joy of life and work." As he put it to me:
"The more work we give men to do, the more enjoyment we must give them too."

With typical German thoroughness, every form of
recreation has been organized. When we read of palatial
"K.d.F." liners gliding through Norwegian fjords or
special trains discharging thousands of trippers at sea
beaches or inland beauty spots, we are apt to think of
K.d.F. as a glorified tourist agency. These long vacations
are, however, only high spots for relatively small numbers of workers in a program which goes on in every
industrial locality throughout the year. The smallest
town is apt to have its little amateur K.d.F. orchestra,
gymnasium, sports field, and hiking club.

To the individualist Anglo-Saxon, all this regimented

"leisure to order" may not sound particularly attractive. "To order" it certainly is, and the Nazis make no bones about it. K.d.F. is not merely a privilege; it is a duty as well. Says Dr. Ley: "We do not intend to leave it to the individual to decide whether he desires, or does not desire, a holiday. It has become compulsory." Again, even here, we detect the military note. One of Dr. Ley's best-known publications is a pamphlet entitled: "A People *Conquers* Joy." However, these aspects are not specifically Nazi; they reflect the average German's faith in organization and his acquiescence in state direction and control. There seems to be no doubt that *Kraft durch Freude* is generally popular and that it is prized as the outstanding benefit which the industrial masses have gained from the Nazi regime.

XI. THE ARMY OF THE SPADE

ONE COLD WINTER MORNING I APPROACHED AN EXTENSIVE building on the outskirts of Berlin. Near the entrance I observed a large banner stretched upon the wall. It was red with a central circle of white, within which was a symbolic black spade from whose short handle sprouted twin wheat-ears. Below the banner was inscribed this saying by Frederick the Great: "Whoever makes two stalks of grain to grow where formerly there was only one, can claim to have done more for his nation than a military genius who has won a great battle."

That was my introduction to a study of the National Labor Service—what Germans call *Arbeitsdienst*. It is an outstanding feature of the Third Reich, variously interpreted by foreign observers. You hear good words for it, especially as it is applied to young men. But its extension to Germany's young womanhood is by no means so favorably regarded.

The Nazis did not invent the idea. It grew up spontaneously during the Weimar Republic, when various organizations established camps for unemployed youths to take them off the streets and put them to useful work, especially in the country on land-reclamation and forest projects. When the full tide of economic depression hit Germany, the Weimar regime tried to co-ordinate these groups into an officially controlled organization. Membership, however, was voluntary. The aim was a temporary one, to cope with an economic emergency. In both spirit and method, this first Labor Service closely resembled the C.C.C. organization set up under our "New Deal." However, it was not so unified or efficiently run as ours.

When the Nazis came to power in 1933, they took over this rather dubious experiment and soon transformed it along characteristic lines. In fact, they were already operating a small labor service corps of their own, commanded by Colonel Konstantin Hierl, who was destined to develop the movement to its present scope. This soldierly-looking man, with close-clipped mustache and precise mouth, seems to be one of those efficient organizers whom National Socialism has produced.

In describing the National Labor Service, two things should be kept in mind. First, what we have already stressed with other Nazi innovations—the wide distinction between theory and practice. The picture which Nazi spokesmen paint for you may be very far indeed from what is actually in operation. Sometimes they admit this; but they then point out that their regime is only seven years old and has functioned during a period of growing stress and strain culminating in a great foreign war. Under such exceptional circumstances they claim that the fair-minded foreign investigator should keep this in mind, and should neither condemn the idea itself nor deny its feasibility in more favorable times.

A second point to be remembered is the unfavorable trend in the working of Nazi institutions which set in with their ruthless concentration on the Four Year

Plan for national self-sufficiency under the imminent threat of war, and which has been further accentuated since the outbreak of war itself. This is notably true of the National Labor Service. In the early years of the Nazi regime, it resembled the ideal far more closely than it has done in recent years or than it does today.

With these qualifications, let's take a look at the theoretical set-up, as it is described to you at Labor Service Headquarters and set forth in its abundant propagandist literature.

The plan for this National Labor Service combines severely practical aims with high ideals. Become compulsory and universal, it took the entire annual "class" of twenty-year-old youths and set them to productive tasks designed to conserve and expand Germany's natural resources, especially her food supply.

The idealistic side of the story is thus expressed by Colonel Hierl: "The Labor Service restores the soul-contact between work and the worker, destroyed by a materialistic philosophy." The ideal is emphasized in the Service motto: *Arbeit Edelt*—"Work Ennobles." Members of the Service are termed "Soldiers of Labor." Collectively, it is known as *The Army of the Spade*. This army numbers approximately 400,000, normally housed in about 2,000 camps scattered throughout Germany.

The Labor Service is designed to accomplish "national tasks" useful to the German people as a whole. By this is meant such matters as drainage projects, reclamation of waste or marginal lands, reforestation, and similar works which otherwise would be done neither by private nor public enterprise because normal wages and working conditions would make it too expensive.

The Labor Army is not intended to compete with ordinary labor.

These young labor soldiers are not supposed to be "sweated" in their tasks, since that would tend to make them hate the very labor which they are taught to honor. The idea is not to overstrain them. Neither are speed and material efficiency deemed primary considerations. When I was shown the tools used by the Labor Service, it was carefully explained to me that all of them must be such as are merely helpful adjuncts to manual labor. Spades, axes, mattocks, and many other implements were there, some specially invented as the result of practical experience. But they were all *tools*, subordinate to the laborer himself. The Labor Service does not officially favor the use of mechanism like tractors, where man is a mere guider of the machine. The psychology aspect of work done by the Labor Service is thereby emphasized.

There is certainly enough to be done. Labor Service surveys estimate that there is work of this sort for 500,000 men for twenty years. At Berlin headquarters all this is graphically set forth on an immense wall-map, where at a glance you can see both what is planned and what has already been done. The war has interrupted many if not most pending projects, but much has been completed, particularly important drainage works along the Baltic and North Sea coasts, together with moorland reclamations in various regions.

According to official statements, Labor Service detachments rarely exceed two hundred men. In peacetime, they are usually housed in wooden barracks much like our C.C.C. camps. The dormitories are furnished with mattress beds, and each man has his individual locker, chair, and small table. The camp-unit centers in a larger barrack containing a big combined dining and social room, together with kitchen, larder, and officers' quarters.

The normal, peacetime working day is spent as follows:

Reveille in summer at 5.00 A.M.; in winter at 6.00 A.M. Ten minutes of setting-up exercises follow. Then an hour for washing, dressing, bed-making, clean-up, and early breakfast. Then flag parade and orders for the day.

The day's work takes up seven hours, including time taken for marching to and from work, and thirty minutes for breakfast. Dinner in summer is served at 1.30 P.M.; in winter at 2.30. An hour's rest is normally taken after dinner. The afternoons are devoted to bodily and mental training. Sports, games, and marching exercises take place on alternate days and last one hour. After that, daily instruction is given in home politics, German history, current affairs, and subjects of special interest to the Labor Service. Needless to say, all lessons are intensely propagandist and serve to implant the Nazi point of view.

Supper is served at 7.00 P.M. After that, the evening hours of leisure begin, spent according to individual inclination except twice weekly, when all join in community singing, attendance at lectures, or seeing motion pictures—further bits of propaganda. Camp tattoo and lights-out end the day at 10.00 P.M.

Such is the official program of the labor school through which more than 2,000,000 young men have passed in the last seven years. Of course it is designed primarily to make loyal Nazis, and it has undoubtedly played a large part in molding the thought and out-look of the younger generation. Nevertheless, from what I could gather, the Labor Service has been popular with both the men themselves and the general popula-tion. I was told by Germans and foreigners alike that, in parades or Party demonstrations, the Labor Bat-talions, in their warm earth-brown uniforms and with their gleaming spades, were always greeted by loud ap-plause.

What I have been describing is the peacetime scene. Today, one rarely sees those brown-uniformed youths, either at work or on parade. An omnivorous war-machine has caught up these disciplined labor forces and has drafted them for military tasks. Most of them are now concentrated either behind the West-Wall or in Poland. I was told that, in the Polish campaign, the Labor Battalions were invaluable. Going in right be-hind the troops, they did yeoman service in clean-up operations. Naturally, under stress of war, the normal peacetime schedule of work and life I depicted has given place to a sterner and more strenuous regimen. To all intents and purposes, those boys are "in the army now."

I heard few criticisms of the Labor Service for young men even in quarters strongly anti-Nazi in most re-spects. However, I encountered much criticism of the young women's branch of the service, in some instances rising to severe condemnation. In Nazi eyes, since a national labor service should be truly universal, Ger-many's young womanhood is logically included in the general scheme. In practice, however, labor service for women was not generalized until the outbreak of the present war. At first, service was voluntary, and the number enrolled annually did not average much over 15,000.

The basic idea behind the Women's Labor Service is the same as that for their brothers. Girls of all social classes live and work together, learning the value and dignity of labor—and of course becoming ardent Nazis in the process. Their surroundings and the types of work they do, however, differ markedly from those of their brothers in the Army of the Spade.

Though these girls wear a brown uniform, it is of feminine cut, quite like that of our Girl Scouts. Beyond flag drill, there are few military features, the goal being to turn out housewives and mothers; not potential female soldiers. The camps are relatively small, averaging thirty-five girls. They also tend to be less barrack-like in aspect, and camp life is concerned largely with domestic training in all its branches.

Outside of their camp curriculum, Labor Service girls have various duties. Some of these are in the line of social service. Many girls are assigned to help over-worked mothers by tending their children. To this end, some camps are established near industrial areas to aid the wives of factory workers. Such camps sometimes run kindergartens. Country children are similarly looked after by Service girls, especially in harvest time when the peasant mothers must be away in the fields.

However, Labor Service girls have been increasingly assigned directly and almost exclusively to regular farm work. Every morning they leave camp for farmsteads in the neighborhood, doing whatever the peasant or his wife may direct and returning to camp only toward nightfall. All that time they are entirely without supervision by their camp guardians and are in a rough, hard environment, associating with peasants who are apt to be coarse and uncouth, and who frequently may be drunken and immoral. I was told of distressing instances where girls had been overworked, ill-treated, insulted, and even seduced, so that they returned to their homes with child. Those are the dark aspects which seem to be inevitable in a system like this.

Yet it is precisely this phase of the Women's Labor Service which the war has greatly accentuated. Since the outbreak of war, national service for young women is being so rapidly extended that it may soon become well-nigh universal in fact as well as in name. Shortly after hostilities broke out, 60,000 girls were mustered for the Labor Corps, in addition to 40,000 already in service. New barracks were hastily built to accommodate these recruits, and I understand that girl conscription has proceeded as fast as they could be effectively mobilized. Most of them were frankly destined for farm work as replacements for peasants called to the colors.

All this is merely part of the general process which has turned the Third Reich into a vast Modern Sparta, wherein every able-bodied man or woman, youth or maiden, is part of a gigantic war-machine. We have already noted the decree giving the Government authority to send anyone anywhere on any sort of duty.

The implications of this decree are limitless. I recall a chat I had with a man in Bremen on this very point. I asked whether the virtual paralysis of that great port-city by the British blockade would not result in widespread unemployment and a difficult local situation. The man looked at me in genuine surprise.

"Of course not," he answered. "If, say, half the people here have no local work to do, they'll just be shifted elsewhere to other jobs. You understand," he concluded, "we Germans are all soldiers today, no matter whether we are in or out of uniform."

That is the spirit you encounter everywhere in this New Sparta.

XII. HITLER YOUTH

DURING THE AUTUMN AND WINTER MONTHS SPENT IN Berlin I would occasionally see groups of boys on the streets clad in simple blue uniforms. Once or twice they had their arms filled with old newspapers—a patriotic chore to which they had been assigned. More often I would see them helping extract contributions for the Winter-Help, a charity collection scheme that I will later describe.

Those are perhaps the only glimpses the casual foreign visitor gets of the extraordinary system whereby National Socialism is molding the rising generation according to its imperious will. Like many other things in the Third Reich, what you see on the surface is only a small part of what lies behind. Outwardly, Nazi Germany even in wartime does not look startlingly different from the Germany of former days. The same ordered neatness and cleanliness prevail, and you may live there a long time without having a single dramatic incident occur before your eyes. All this is apt to fool you, until you dig below that impeccable surface. Then you begin to learn and to understand the radical transformation of life and thought that is taking place.

These blue-clad boys, between 10 and 14 years old, represent the first link in a chain of evolution which begins with the unformed child and ends with the uniformed man, indelibly stamped with the Nazi brand. Their official title is *Jungvolk*—best translated as *Hitler Youngsters*. Like everything else in the Third Reich, they are organized from basic groups of ten right up to National Headquarters. However, their duties and training are elementary, as befits their tender years. The system does not get into full swing until these boys enter the *Hitler Youth,* where they remain until their nineteenth year. Thence they go into the National Labor Service, which we have already described. After that comes military service, which lasts at least two years more. Such is the arduous apprenticeship which the male German must undergo.

The German girl passes through a formative period similar in character and of about the same length. From 10 to 14 she is a *Young-Maiden;* after that she is a *Hitler Maid* until she is 21. During the latter years of her Maid-hood she is apt to be enrolled in the young women's branch of the Labor Service, but of course she has no military service to undergo.

The combined male and female membership of the Hitler Youth in all its stages aggregates a total of well over 7,000,000, highly organized in every respect. That, I imagine, is the largest single youth organization in the world.

Adolf Hitler always stressed the necessity for any proselyting movement to gain and retain a firm hold on the rising generation. At the very start of his movement he organized a small youth group, though this was shattered like every other phase of his first effort after the disastrous Beer-Hall Putsch of 1923. However, with the re-founding of the Party two years later, a youth section was promptly started and made rapid headway under a series of able leaders, of whom Baldur von Schirach is the most famous. Before an interview could be arranged for me, the leader of the Hitler Youth had made his dramatic gesture of volunteering for army service and promptly departed for the Western Front.

To gain youth's allegiance, the Nazi regime has evolved a system which enlists the interest and loyalty of the rising generation. Its core is the local *Home*—a well-appointed boys' clubhouse where the youngster meets his fellows in an atmosphere of comradeship supervised by carefully chosen leaders. Every Wednesday, the boys and girls gather in their respective Homes for their regular Home-Evening. The leader conducts the meeting according to a program prepared in advance at National Headquarters. Throughout Germany, the same songs are sung and the same subjects discussed. Then the radio is switched on, and all listen to a program entitled "Young Germany's Hour," which begins at 8.15 P.M. and is broadcast by all stations. On some other week-day evening the youngsters gather a second time for a program devoted to games and sports. It is interesting to note that there is no military drill or use of arms in these physical exercises. Unlike the *Balilla* and *Sons of the Wolf*, the corresponding youth units of Fascist Italy, there are no miniature rifles or other warlike paraphernalia. The Nazis believe that imposing military training at this early age would be a psychological mistake.

To develop loyalty and maintain interest in their organization, a whole round of activities and special events has been devised. On New Year's Day the Supreme Youth Leader makes an address to all his followers over the radio. In late January Young Germany honors the memory of its symbolic martyr, a fifteen-year-old Hitler Youth named Herbert Norkus, murdered by Communists during the years of strife before the Nazis came to power. From February to April a series of competitions takes place to determine who among them possess those qualities of leadership which qualify them to be appointed to minor offices in the organization. The Fuehrer's birthday, April 20th, is a great celebration, on which Hitler Youngsters who have attained their fourteenth year pass into the ranks of Hitler Youth. On May 1st, winners of special competitions throughout Germany are received by the Fuehrer himself. From June to August millions of Hitler boys and girls go vacationing in their Youth Camps or on hiking tours, and nationwide sport competitions take place. The highlight of this period is the annual Party Day at Nuremberg, when chosen detachments of Hitler Youth of both sexes travel thither from the remotest parts of the Reich to parade proudly before the Fuehrer and receive the applause of assembled Nazidom. This is also the day when those youths who have completed their eighteenth year formally graduate into the adult ranks of the Party. The autumn months are enlivened by various activities, especially participation in the Winter Help charity drives. It is easy to see how this continuous round of stimulating, pleasurable activities tends to center interest and loyalty around the organizational *Home* and all that it signifies.

How has all this modified the individual boy's and girl's relations to those other aspects of life—family, church, and school? Complex adjustments are inevitable, for we must remember that, however pleasurable they may be, Hitler Youth activities are *duties* which must be complied with and with which no one may interfere. In the first years of the Nazi regime I am told that this sudden shift of youthful loyalties provoked frequent domestic conflicts and caused many personal tragedies. Great numbers of non-Nazi parents were recalcitrant at seeing their children placed in an atmosphere which sapped their authority and tended to make boys and girls flout the teachings of their elders. The traditional German family is patriarchal, and many fathers objected to the claims of the Youth Home on personal grounds even when they had no strong objections to the Nazi regime as such. In many cases, this conflict of loyalties went so far that boys and girls denounced their own parents to the authorities for what the children had been taught to consider unpatriotic speech or conduct.

Today, I understand that such extreme conflicts are rare. The Nazi regime broke parental resistance as systematically as it did opposition of every kind; so the most rebellious fathers and mothers have been weeded out by concentration camps or lesser penalties. The average parent now accepts the situation as inevitable, even if he or she does not at heart wholly approve. Indeed, I was told by foreign observers that a large proportion of German parents, including of course all Party members, now assent willingly to an institution which teaches their children good personal habits, promotes their health, and brightens their young lives in many ways.

Far more serious has been the conflict with the churches. Both the Protestant and Roman Catholic confessions possessed strong youth organizations. The Nazi Government, in accordance with its policy of all-round co-ordination, insisted that these confessional groups be merged in the Hitler Youth. This raised a storm of protest from pious church folk, who deemed the Youth Homes, with their absence of denominational teaching, little short of godless, while priests and pastors encouraged and backed the protests of their parishioners. Here, again, very many distressing incidents took place. Protestant opposition has apparently lessened with the years, though a recalcitrant minority still exists. The Roman Church, however, has maintained its traditional objection to membership of its young people in non-Catholic organizations. This is one of the main reasons for the deep-going conflict between the Roman Church and the Nazi State which has existed from the start and which is by no means settled.

The uncompromising Nazi attitude is set forth in the following official statement: "The socialist conception of the Third Reich demands of each individual the unconditional subordination of his individual being to the socialist expression of his people. This socialist existence has one form of expression as far as the youth of Germany is concerned: namely, the Hitler Youth. Every youth association outside the Hitler Youth transgresses against the spirit of the community which is the spirit of the State."

That policy has been carried out by a combination of legal action and official pressure which most Roman Catholic parents have been unable to resist. The result has been the liquidation not only of the Catholic youth organizations but of most of the parochial schools as well. But I was told that a vast deal of suppressed heartburning persists.

The Nazification of the public schools presented no

such difficulties because they formed part of the State itself. The Nazis have made few formal changes in the educational system they inherited from the previous regime, but its spirit and emphasis have been profoundly altered.

Bernhard Rust, Reich Minister of Education, thus characterizes the former system: "Although the intellectual capacities of young persons had been excellently trained and although they were thoroughly qualified for their vocations in after-life, the importance of knowledge for knowledge's sake had been over-estimated, whilst physical education and the training of the will had been neglected. . . . Furthermore, excessive importance had been attached to the individual as such. It was almost forgotten that each individual is at the same time a member of a racial community, and that it is only in that capacity that he can perfect his powers to their fullest extent, while it is his duty to work for the community good."

Dr. Rust then continues his argument for the Nazi idea of education by asserting: "All forms of instruction have *one* aim—the shaping of *the National Socialist human*. But each form has its special tasks. The school is, in the main, determined by the fact that it educates by means of lessons. . . . In the past there has been a tendency towards cramming into pupils' heads every new addition to learning, but restrictions are now imposed upon that tendency. It is not necessary to teach everything that is interesting or otherwise worth knowing."

Dr. Rust's somewhat restrictive view of formal education is in exact accordance with Adolf Hitler's dictum, when he wrote in *Mein Kampf* that one should "not cumber the brain with a lot of useless knowledge, ninety-five per cent of which it has no use for and hence proceeds to jettison." In the same volume, Hitler also proposed "to cut down instruction so that it deals solely with essentials."

Among those essentials, the Third Reich emphasizes Nazi ideas and bodily development through sport. We have already seen several ways in which these aims are furthered, but even in the restricted sphere of the school they occupy a prominent part in the curriculum. The amount of time there devoted to the acquirement of what we may call book-learning is relatively less than that of former days.

Emphasis on bodily development has undoubtedly produced some good results. No foreign visitor to the Third Reich can fail to note the high average level of health and strength in the rising generation. At the same time, some foreign investigators have criticized the new system as being out of balance.

One of the most interesting of these criticisms is contained in the report of a British educational mission which visited Germany in 1937. Its report raises the query whether athleticism is not being fostered at the expense of mental development. Noting signs of nervous strain among German school children and members of the Hitler Youth, taught to regard the body as a machine which must be kept at the highest pitch of efficiency whilst the mind must at the same time be attuned to maximum receptivity to Nazi ideas, these British educators were led to wonder whether the ultimate outcome might not be "Mens *insana* in corpore sano!"

This joint emphasis upon athletics and Nazi ideology

reaches its height in certain special institutions which the Third Reich has added to the regular educational system. These are the Adolf Hitler Schools and the National-Socialist-Order Castles.

The Hitler Schools are designed to train what Nazis term "a new aristocracy" from whose ranks shall be drawn the future leaders of the Third Reich. In their choosing, the wealth or social position of parents is supposed to play no part. The candidates are selected from twelve-year-old boys, physically perfect and of sound Germanic stock, who have shown special aptitude in school and in the Hitler Youth. It goes without saying that the one indispensable aptitude is a record of unflagging zeal for Nazi ideas.

Those selected youngsters are a favored group. According to the plan, they are to pass six years in fine educational institutions where they receive every advantage, entirely at Government expense. Thereafter they are scheduled to pass into the regular Labor Service and do their military duty. After those tasks come three years of civilian life, earning their living or starting a profession in the ordinary way.

Then, at the age of twenty-five, they are to reassemble. By a second process of selection, the most eligible thousand (from the Party viewpoint) are picked for the Nazi Order of Knighthood—the post-graduate School of Leadership. In stately castles reminiscent of the medieval fortresses of the Teutonic Knights, they will pass four years of intensive training, wherein physical and ideological attainments are brought to the highest pitch of perfection. This elite thousand will then graduate, to take up their lifework of guiding and governing the Third Reich.

The reader will note that I have spoken of this grandiose conception in the future tense. That is because it was started only two years before the war, which has at least temporarily shelved the daring experiment. As far as I could learn, the Hitler Schools are closed. I visited one in Northern Oldenburg. It was architecturally impressive—but it was occupied by soldiers. The castles are likewise empty, the knights having all gone into military service.

Like about everything else in the Third Reich, its youth system is dependent upon the outcome of the life-and-death struggle wherein it is engaged.

XIII. WOMEN OF THE THIRD REICH

THE LEADER OF THE WOMEN'S WING OF THE NAZI REGIME is Frau Gertrud Scholtz-Klink, who set forth that aspect of the Third Reich in an interview she gave me. This conversation came as the climax to several studies I had made of various women's activities under the guidance of purposeful lady subordinates. Those manifold activities are managed by the *Reichsfrauenfuehrung,* a compound word which means the Directing Center of German Women's organizations. The combined membership of these societies totals fully 16,000,000. From this central point in Berlin, directive guidance reaches out to every portion of the Reich.

It was a bitter mid-winter afternoon when I hopped from my taxi and scurried for the entrance of national headquarters, an extensive building situated in Berlin's West End. The air was full of driving snow whipped by a high wind. I was glad to find shelter in the warm entrance hall, though I could scarcely make my way through a litter of hand luggage and a crowd of women bundled up as though for a trip to the Arctic regions. I was later informed that they were a party of trained nurses and social workers bound for Poland where they would care for a convoy of German-speaking immigrants being repatriated from the Russian-occupied zone. Mute testimony, this, of the multifarious activities of the *Reichsfrauenfuehrung*, alike in peace and in war.

A dynamic lady, whose mother is an American, Dr. Marta Unger soon appeared and guided me up stairs and through corridors to her chief's outer office. Presently we were admitted to the inner sanctum, a pleasant reception-room, tastefully furnished. As we entered, the famous women's leader stood awaiting us.

Frau Scholtz-Klink was rather a surprise to me. I had often seen pictures of her, but they were not good likenesses. She must photograph badly, for they all made her out to be a serious, aloof person well into middle life. When you actually meet her, the first impression she makes on you is one of youthful energy. She was then just thirty-six. A compact woman of medium height, she walks to meet you with an easy, swinging gait and gives you a firm handshake. She is quite informal and as she warms to her subject, her face lights up beneath its crown of abundant blonde hair wound about her head in Marguerite braids. She never gets too serious and laughs easily.

I started the conversation by telling her some of the organizational activities I had seen, and asked her what was the basic idea on which they were conducted. Unhesitatingly, she answered: "Encouraging initiative. You can't just command women. You should give them guiding principles of action. Then, within this framework, let them function with the thought that they themselves are the creators and fulfillers of those ideas."

This rather surprised me, and I told her so, remarking that in America there is a widespread impression that woman's position is less free in National Socialist Germany than it was under the Weimar Republic, and that this is especially true regarding women's professional opportunities and political rights.

Frau Scholtz-Klink smiled, nodded understandingly, and came back with the quick retort: "That depends on what you mean by political rights. We believe that anyone, man or woman, thinks politically who puts the people's welfare ahead of personal advantage. What does it matter if five or six women are members of Parliament, as was the case in the Weimar regime? We think it vastly more important that, today, sixteen million women are enrolled in our organization and that half a million women leaders have a weighty voice in everything which concerns women and children, from the Central Government and the Party down to the smallest village."

"How about professional opportunities," I put in. "Are German women still in the universities and in lines like higher scientific work?"

"They certainly are," she replied, "and we are glad to see them there. It is true that when we first came to power seven years ago, some National Socialists were opposed to this because they had been prejudiced by the exaggerately feminist types of women who were so prominent under the Weimar Republic. Today, however, this prejudice has practically vanished. If occasionally we run across some man with an anti-feminist chip on his shoulder, we just laugh about him and consider him a funny old has-been out of touch with the times."

"That's interesting," I ventured.

"But it's easy to understand," rejoined Frau Scholtz-Klink, "when you recall our basic attitude and policy. Unlike many women's organizations elsewhere, we don't fight for what is often called 'women's rights.' Instead, we work hand-in-hand with our menfolk for common aims and purposes. We think that rivalry and hostility between the sexes are as foolish and mutually harmful as they are scientifically unsound. Men and women have somewhat different capacities, but these should always be regarded as complementing and supplementing each other—organic parts of a larger and essentially harmonious whole."

"Then woman's part in the Third Reich, while consciously feminine, is not feminist?" was my next query.

"Precisely," she nodded. "We consider it absolutely vital that members of a woman's organization always remain womanly and do not lose touch with their male colleagues. How long do you think I could stand it if I were shut up here with several hundred woman all the time? Why, I wouldn't stay here three days! No, no, I can assure you our organization isn't run like a nunnery. We foregather frequently with our masculine collaborators in informal meetings where we chat and joke together over our weightiest problems."

"Tell me a bit more about your organization," I suggested.

Frau Scholtz-Klink thought for a moment; then proceeded: "We National Socialist women didn't start out with any cut-and-dried program or preconceived theories. When we came to power seven years ago, our country was in terrible shape and we had very little to work with. So we began in the simplest way, busying ourselves with immediate human needs. All the elaborate structure you see today has been a natural evolution—a spontaneous growth."

"How about your outstanding personalities?" I inquired.

Smilingly she shook her head. "We distinctly play down the personalities," she deprecated. "In our opinion, thinking of person implies that one is not thinking of principle. Take me, for example. I assure you that I really don't care whether, fifty years hence, when our present goal has been splendidly attained, people remember just who it was that started the ball rolling and helped it on its way."

"What are your relations with women's organizations in other lands?" I queried.

"We are not internationalists as the term is often used abroad," Frau Scholtz-Klink answered. "We concern ourselves primarily with our own problems. Of course we are only too glad to be in contact with women from other countries. Indeed, we have a fine guest-house here in Berlin where women visitors can come and stay as long as they like, seeing and studying all we do. If they approve, so much the better. We have no patents. In this sense, therefore, I believe we have a most effective women's organization. But we have not yet seen our way clear to joining the International Women's Council."

Behind that official statement of the viewpoint of Nazi womanhood lies one of the most interesting stories in the evolution of the Third Reich.

Under the old Empire, conservative views prevailed in the field of domestic relations. The man was very much the head of his family. Woman fulfilled her traditional role of wife and mother. Kaiser Wilhelm described woman's sphere as bounded by the "Three K's," *Kinder, Kueche, Kirche*—children, kitchen, church.

Most of his subjects apparently agreed with him. Some sharp dissent there was, and it was not legally repressed. But these dissenters were a relatively small minority.

When the Empire perished, domestic relations were in a turmoil. Liberal and radical ideas on woman's status became common, all markedly individualistic in character. Women were given the ballot and went actively into politics. Advanced feminist types appeared, intent on developing their personalities and seeking careers outside the home. The "emancipated" woman seemed to be setting the tone.

These radical trends might have survived in an atmosphere of political stability and economic prosperity. But the times were neither stable nor prosperous. When the world depression hit Germany at the close of the 1920's, conditions became desperate. In this chaotic atmosphere, National Socialism waxed strong and finally prevailed.

One of the first tasks of the Nazi revolution was to sweep away all the new ideas concerning domestic relations. Adolf Hitler had pronounced views on the subject. In one of his campaign pronouncements he stated: "There is no fight for man which is not also a fight for woman, and no fight for woman which is not also a fight for man. We know no men's rights or women's rights. We recognize only one right for both sexes: a right which is also a duty—to live, work, and fight together for the nation."

In this forthright attitude, Hitler apparently had a large section of German women on his side. From the very start of the Nazi movement, women took a prominent part and were numbered among the Fuehrer's most devoted followers. These women declared they wanted neither "equality" nor "women's rights." What they were after was a home. For the mass of German women, "emancipation" had meant little except hard work at meager wages, and the idea went completely sour with them when economic depression made countless unemployed men dependent upon their womenfolk. Thus, any program which promised confidently to change this abnormal situation could count on enthusiastic support from many women as well as from men.

That was just what National Socialism did promise with its pledge to re-establish the traditional order of domestic relations. It painted an alluring picture of a regime of manly men and womanly women—the manly men as provider and fighter; the womanly woman as wife, mother, and guardian of the domestic hearth.

According to Nazi economic theory, woman's natural career is marriage. By following the delusive path of Liberal-Marxist materialism, said Hitler, woman herself had been the chief victim. Having invaded business, industry, and the professions, women threw men out of jobs and became their competitors instead of their helpmeets and companions. In so doing, women not only robbed themselves of their crowning happiness (a home and children) but also became largely responsible for the economic crisis which ultimately left women financially worse off than before. When both men and women turned into producers, there were not enough consumers left to consume what they produced.

That was the Nazi theory. And it caught on like wildfire. Nazi women orators denounced the Weimar regime as having degraded German womanhood into "parasites, pacifists, and prostitutes." It was these feminine zealots who converted their sisters wholesale. The

"Woman's Front" of the Nazi movement soon became one of its most influential branches. And the interesting point is that it was run by the women themselves.

The activities of this Woman's Front are complex and far-reaching. They overlap into many fields which we have already surveyed, such as the feminine sectors of the Labor Service and the Hitler Youth, together with phases of the great social-service enterprise known as NSV, which we will describe in the next chapter.

Its earliest enterprise was the *Muetterdienst,* or Mothers' Service—a network of adult schools giving courses of instruction in infant care, general hygiene, home nursing, cooking, sewing, and the beautification of the home itself. Permanent quarters are established in all cities and large towns, while itinerant teachers conduct courses in villages and the remotest country-side. The system has now reached throughout the Reich, and several million women have passed through this domestic education—an intensive course with classes limited to twenty-five persons, since instruction takes the form, not of theoretical lectures, but of practical teaching by actual demonstration in which the pupils take part. Alongside these courses for housewives are others for prospective brides.

Most foreign observers agreed that this domestic education has helped many German women to be better wives and mothers. I myself investigated the large Mother School established in *Wedding,* a Berlin suburb inhabited by working folk. This institution also serves as a sort of normal school where teachers are trained. I met and talked with the members of the current class, drawn from all parts of Germany. They appeared to be earnest, capable young women, well chosen for their future jobs.

Another major field of service is in industry, where trained "confidence women" actually work in factories, stores, and offices employing much female labor. These women are thus in personal touch with working conditions. Naturally, such women are the best sort of propagandists for the Party and its ideas. Still other fields of activity might be described if space permitted in a general survey like this. At least half a million women are actively engaged in these various lines of endeavor.

This, of course, is the answer which Frau Scholtz-Klink and her colleagues make to the charge that National Socialism has driven women out of public life. They claim that it has changed the nature of those activities to more fruitful channels. As a matter of fact, the whole economic trend in the Third Reich, by transforming mass unemployment into an acute labor shortage, has driven women into all sorts of activities outside the home circle—which is certainly not what Hitler promised his feminine followers. It is estimated that nearly 12,000,000 women were gainfully employed in the Reich when war broke out, and that figure will undoubtedly be vastly exceeded as men are continually mobilized for war service. Yet, in these new developments, it is probable that the Nazi attitude and policy will remain basically unaltered.

XIV. BEHIND THE WINTER-HELP

As the damp chill of the north european autumn deepens into dark, cold winter, there appear increasingly the manifold activities of the *Winterhilf*—in plain English, the Winter-Help. Once a fortnight, every city, town, and village in the Reich seethes with brown-shirted Storm Troopers carrying red-painted cannisters. These are the Winter-Help collection-boxes. The Brown-Shirts go everywhere. You cannot sit in a restaurant or beer-hall but what, sooner or later, a pair of them will work through the place, rattling their cannisters ostentatiously in the faces of customers. And I never saw a German formally refuse to drop in his mite, even though the contribution might have been less than the equivalent of one American cent.

During these periodic money-raising campaigns, all sorts of dodges are employed. On busy street-corners comedians, singers, musicians, sailors, gather a crowd by some amusing skit, at the close of which the Brown-Shirts collect. People buy tiny badges to show they have contributed—badges good only for that particular campaign. One time they may be an artificial flower; next time a miniature dagger, and so forth. The Winter-Help campaign series reaches its climax shortly before Christmas in the so-called Day of National Solidarity. On that notable occasion the Big Guns of the Nazi

Party sally forth with their collection-boxes to do their bit. I am told that it is considered quite an honor to drop an offering into the cannister wielded by so redoubtable a personage as, say, Hermann Goering.

These collection-box campaigns have been going on every winter since the Nazis came to power. So has another picturesque feature—the Winter-Help Lottery. The sale of these lottery tickets is not restricted to certain periods; it goes on continuously through the entire autumn and winter season. They are sold by men in rather attractive uniforms with red-banded caps and dove-gray capes. Like the Brown-Shirts, these lottery-vendors cover every public place, even the best hotels. The tickets are enclosed in tightly sealed orange envelopes stacked in rows on a little tray. The vendor approaches you, salutes politely, and offers his wares. Should you wish to buy, you pick an envelope at random and pay him fifty pfennigs—half a Reichsmark, which is worth somewhat over ten cents. Unlike his Brown-Shirt colleagues, the vendor is not insistent and the public does not feel constrained to buy.

There's a good feature about this Winter-Help Lottery—you know right away if you *haven't* won. So purchasers promptly tear open the envelope and take out their folded ticket. Nearly always they are confronted with a large blue *Nicht,* which means "No" and shows they haven't a chance. Needless to say, that's what I drew when I tried my luck. But plenty of persons seem to play the lottery often. In gay restaurants it's quite a game for a whole group of diners to buy envelopes and greet each loser with peals of laughter—the vendor standing by and enjoying the fun.

However, buyers aren't always losers. In the first

place, out of the 6,000,000 tickets which form a series there are nearly 350,000 which carry small prizes called "premiums" ranging from 1 to 100 Marks. These minor premiums are paid by the vendor on the spot. Above these come the "prizes," which range all the way up to a 5,000-Mark Grand Prize. However, those prizes are not paid offhand. What you get is the *right* to a prize-winning number in the lottery drawing which will be held three months hence. The prizes and premiums total an even 1,000,000 Marks. The cost of the tickets is 3,000,000 Marks. Since the lottery vendors are all volunteer workers who give their services and get no commission, the net "take" of the Winter-Help from several lottery-series sold during the season totals a handsome sum.

Still other money-making devices exist, the best-known of them being the One-Dish Plan. Each month during the autumn and winter a certain Sunday is set apart as the sacrificial day. On that Sunday, every patriotic German is supposed to contribute to the Winter-Help the cash difference between the cost of a normal Sunday dinner and that of a single-course meal. In all public eating places nothing else is served during the noon hours, so foreigners also must comply. The cost is trifling for the meal itself, but I should hate to have it as a steady diet, consisting as it does of a plateful of stewed onions, cabbage, and potatoes, graced by a lone miniature meat-ball compounded of the cheapest grade of hamburger. In private homes families are not legally compelled to restrict themselves to one-course meals. They can actually eat as they choose. But they are practically compelled to contribute their cash offering in any case. A Brown-Shirt always appears at the door, and the offering is assessed on tariff-rates proportionate to the family's social status and known living-standards.

The foreigner doesn't learn that last item unless he happens to have German friends who tell him things. All he usually knows about is the box-collections, the lottery vendors, and the sad experience of a one-dish lunch in a restaurant or hotel. He may learn that annual contributions to the Winter-Help average well over 400,000,000 Reichsmarks—nearly $200,000,000 at the official rate of exchange. The foreigner may marvel that so prodigious a sum could be raised by the methods he has observed. As a matter of fact, it isn't. Most of the money comes in through a carefully worked-out schedule of contributions assessed on corporations, business firms, and individuals from the wealthiest down to all but the poorest peasants and laborers.

Your Nazi acquaintances probably won't mention this to you. If they do, they will almost certainly tell you these are merely patriotic suggestions for voluntary contributions, properly graded. Technically, they are telling the truth, since Winter-Help offerings are legally "voluntary." In the first days of the Nazi regime, quite a few persons took this literally and refused to contribute. That, however, was likely to be followed by unpleasant consequences; so prescribed sharing has become well-nigh universal.

Here, again, we encounter what I have already stated to be a cardinal aspect of Nazi Germany—the fact that what the foreigner sees and casually learns may be only a slight indication of what goes on behind the scenes.

So much for the way Winter-Help funds are raised. How are they spent? That is a controversial point.

Nazis assure you that these huge sums are efficiently managed and all go for the purposes intended by the donors. They point out that most of the work is done by unpaid volunteers, so the administrative overhead should be small. This may be true, but there is no way of checking such assertions because no detailed, audited balance-sheets are published. Some foreign observers tell you that Winter-Help funds have been diverted to other purposes, much as the still vaster Labor Front funds are presumed to have been, according to some assertions by foreign critics of the Nazi regime.

I do not know where the truth lies in this matter, so I merely raise the point in order to make a balanced picture. From what I actually saw and learned, it seems to me that much of the Winter-Help funds is actually spent on the poor and needy, and that the institution does a lot of good in many ways. So let us take a look at the Winter-Help to see what it is, how it works, and what it accomplishes.

The Winter-Help began in the autumn of 1933— the first year of the Nazi regime. It was a terrible time, with over 7,000,000 registered unemployed and 17,000,-000 in dire need. This latter figure included both unemployed and unemployables, especially the aged and the very young. The previous winter, the last under the Weimar Republic, had been grim. The Government dole had, to be sure, enabled the poor to keep body and soul together, but that was about all; and the outlook for the coming winter was equally gloomy.

Then the Fuehrer spoke. His word was: "No one shall suffer from hunger and cold!" So Hitler announced a new organization, run by the Party, to be known as the Winter-Help. It was not a substitute for

Government aid; it was an *addition to* that aid, designed to bridge the gap between the low minimum of State charity and a somewhat more tolerable standard of life. The aim was to provide coal and garments sufficient to keep a household fairly warm and decently clothed; to supply a bit more food; to distribute Christmas dinners, trees, and children's toys at the beloved Yuletide. It even promised to step in and relieve unexpected accidents and misfortunes for which the victims were in no wise to blame.

That very first season, the Winter-Help "delivered the goods." The Party got behind it to the last man, woman, and child. Over a million volunteer workers donated their services. Vast amounts of food, fuel, and clothing were mobilized and distributed. The hearts of the poor were cheered—and warmed towards the new regime. That was the intention; for the Winter-Help was officially described as: "The instrument which enables us to make the most comprehensive appeal to the spirit of national solidarity." In short, an extremely effective form of domestic propaganda.

The more I studied the Winter-Help, the more it appeared to me as an amazing cross between the Salvation Army and Tammany Hall. It would be unfair to put down the whole business as just cold-blooded politics. All the good-will mobilized, the unselfish effort donated, the goods distributed to deserving persons— those things are real, no matter what the attendant political motive. Think what it means to numberless "forgotten men"—and women, to be thereby lifted a bit above the squalor line; to have their drab lives unexpectedly brightened, especially at Christmas time. Perhaps all the poor do not share equally in those benefits;

perhaps good Party members get the best of what's going, while ex-Communists are often overlooked. Nevertheless, so many poor people get something that the
effect on popular feeling is great and cumulative. And
the tendency must be toward winning the good-will of
the populace for the Nazi regime. It is the little things
that count in getting and holding popular favor. Tammany in New York learned that long ago; and the Nazis
are as clever and far more efficient than Tammany ever
dreamed of being.

What we may term the Tammany-Salvation-Army
technique comes out in everything the Winter-Help
does. Picture to yourselves a typical case. A Winter-
Help volunteer enters a sordid tenement dwelling in
the poorest section of Berlin's East End. He or she
brings the family a basket of food, a packet of clothing,
a tiny Christmas tree, or fuel tickets good at the nearest coal-dealer's. "Good morning!" is the cheery opening. "I bring you this with the Fuehrer's Greetings!"
Then comes a bit of friendly chat. On leaving, the visitor extends an arm in salute with the inevitable: *Heil
Hitler!* Is it not well-nigh inevitable that the answering
"Heil" comes spontaneously from grateful hearts?

Such is the Winter-Help and what it signifies. Now
let us go on to consider the even larger social-service
organization of which the Winter-Help is itself organically a part. This vast institution bears the appalling
title of *Nationalsozialistischevolkswohlfahrt!* Broken
down into plain English, that Teutonic jawbreaker
means National Socialist People's Welfare. It's even
too much for the Germans, so they always speak of it
as NSV.

NSV, though essentially a Party enterprise, is techni-

cally a voluntary organization supported by nearly
11,000,000 members who pay dues with a minimum of
one Reichsmark per month. It has over 1,000,000 active
workers, of whom only about 20,000 are paid, these being trained social-service specialists in various lines.
The vast majority of NSV workers contribute their
spare time, and they do it generously—many of them
as much as three hours per day. Like everything else in
Nazi Germany, NSV is elaborately organized from a
supreme head-center in Berlin down through regional,
provincial, and local sub-centers until it reaches the
ultimate unit—the so-called "block" of forty or fifty
families. There can be no doubt that NSV is generally
popular; otherwise it would be difficult to conceive of
11,000,000 persons paying regular dues and over 1,000,-
000 contributing so generously of their time the year
round. Mere compulsion could not bring that about.
What, then, is the reason? The answer to that query
involves an understanding of a social set-up and attitude toward life which is radically different from ours.

First of all we should realize that NSV, like its
Winter-Help affiliate, is *not* a substitute for Governmental assistance to the poor and needy. In Germany,
total destitution has long been rare, thanks to the system of social welfare begun under the old Empire more
than half a century ago, and extended under both the
Weimar Republic and the present Nazi regime. Most
Germans are thus legally protected against dire poverty
and downright starvation. NSV *supplements* State aid
in various ways. And it does so, not in our sense of
"charity," but as a *duty* which the socialized nation,
the almost mystical *Gemeinschaft,* owes to each of its
members.

Another important point to be understood is that, despite all the assistance which it gives to the poor and weak, NSV is even more interested in helping the fit and strong to be fitter and stronger. It seeks to energize the individual by making him constantly feel that he is organically part of the whole nation, and that he literally has the whole nation behind him—so long as he in turn does his duty and seeks to serve the nation of which he is an integral part.

In the Nazi social-service system, the Winter-Help has specialized functions. It is concerned chiefly with the relief of temporary difficulties and transient weaknesses or breakdowns of morale. NSV takes care of the long pull and deals with social problems which are solvable only in the remote future.

One of the axioms of National Socialism is that the family, rather than the individual, is the true unit of society. For this reason, NSV tries in various ways to integrate individuals into healthy, prosperous, fruitful families. Hence its special efforts for the welfare of mothers and children. Its largest and most important section is that known as *Mutter und Kind*. The size of this special organization can be visualized when we learn that it has some 26,000 offices covering every part of the Reich, with medical staffs and assisted by about 230,000 matrons of homes, kindergarten governesses, communal sisters, and nurses. Their activities are manifold, though their aim is not clinical; rather is it investigative and educational. Mother-and-Child stations are neither hospitals nor sanatoria. When bad conditions are detected, they are turned over to hospitals or State charities. But mothers by the million have visited these stations, or station agents have visited mothers in their homes. For instance, all infants up to the age of two years are medically examined and the parents are given advice as to proper care and feeding. Through affiliated organizations, the stations complete their preventive and educational work by enabling mothers and children most in need to have special care, take vacations, go to kindergartens, and so forth.

A striking instance of the meticulous way in which NSV seeks to foster the public health is its special subsection called *Bettenaktion*. Medical research has established the fact that nothing is more important to health and personal efficiency than good, restful sleep. Subsection "Bed-Action" sees to it that each individual has his own bed—and a comfortable, sanitary one, at that. In the past few years, it is officially stated that fully 1,000,000 beds have been distributed free of charge to persons unable to pay for them.

Another important field of service is the raising to normal status of distressed or depressed areas. Certain remote regions, such as the mountainous districts of Lower Bavaria and the Eiffel hill-country in the Rhineland, were chronically impoverished and unable to improve their condition out of their own meager resources. NSV pours aid of all kinds into these abnormal districts until today, according to official accounts, some of them have been quite transformed.

Like the other quasi-public institutions of the Third Reich, NSV gets out a tremendous volume of educative literature about its own activities. Booklets, pamphlets, illustrated sheets, and small charts are printed and distributed wholesale to the general public, either free or at very slight expense. Its Berlin headquarters maintains a permanent exhibition including large illuminated wall-maps, colored charts, miniature models, and a stereopticon lecture lasting nearly an hour. Its foreign relations representative, Erich Haasemann showed me through, explained in detail, and invited me to visit some of its Berlin activities. The most interesting of these was its distribution center, which I visited next morning.

This center is housed in a rambling old building several stories high in the market district near Alexanderplatz. It is thus handy to the working-class quarters. Here needy persons come with their distribution-certificates—a sort of chit enabling them to get required articles, both clothing and furniture. They get these chits on recommendation from their *Blokwart,* the official who looks after each block of forty families. Incidentally, there are nearly 450,000 such units in Greater Berlin.

The Blokwart makes it his business to know intimately the circumstances of each family in his unit. He visits them frequently in their homes, and to him they make known their troubles and requests for aid. Here is how it works: an outdoor laborer needs a new sheepskin-lined jacket. He shows his old one to the Blokwart, who sees it is no longer serviceable. "That's right," says the Blokwart, "you've got to have a new jacket if you're going to be efficient on that job of yours these cold winter days. For you to get sick and perhaps land in the hospital would be bad business for the nation. So here you are. Go and pick one out at the center tomorrow after working hours." Down goes our workingman, presents his chit, and is shown to the proper department, where hundreds of jackets, of all sizes, hang on long racks. Like all lines, they are in somewhat different styles and in diverse colors. This is to avoid uniformity in appearance. That aids *morale* by satisfying personal tastes and heightening the wearer's self-respect. If all NSV recipients were dressed alike, they would have a depressingly "institutional" look. It is really extraordinary how such psychological factors have been carefully thought out!

I roamed around that warehouse for an hour, looking at huge stocks of everything from clothes and shoes to beds and baby-carriages. Everything seemed to be of good quality, well-made, and of surprisingly tasteful appearance. I was asked to note that there were *full* lines of everything, including even the most unusual "out sizes" which might not even be made commercially, much less carried in ordinary store stocks. For instance, I was shown a pair of boots so huge that it did not seem possible a human being could have such big feet. Nevertheless, I was told that a few did exist. Those persons were known. So NSV was prepared for them.

NSV does not manufacture its own supplies. They are bought in the open market, but they must be made by local manufacturers. Prices are thus not strictly competitive—at least, on a national scale. The idea is to spread work and keep local money at home.

These are only the high-lights of a subject with many ramifications. However, they may suffice to give a general idea of the importance of NSV in the Nazi scheme of things and in its hold upon the people. Such social services tend to win popular support for the Nazi regime and reconcile the masses to conditions which otherwise might breed discontent and even revolutionary unrest.

XV. SOCIALIZED HEALTH

"THE TREATMENT GIVEN A TUBERCULOUS PATIENT IS partly determined by his social worth. If he is a valuable citizen and his case is curable, no expense is spared. If he is adjudged incurable, he is kept comfortable, of course, but no special effort is made to prolong slightly an existence which will benefit neither the community nor himself. Germany can nourish only a certain amount of human life at a given time. We National Socialists are in duty bound to foster individuals of social and biological value."

It was the official in charge of the Tuberculosis Section of the Public Health Service headquarters who spoke. He was an earnest young man with reflective eyes and a precise manner of speech. His was only one of many departments devoted to the combating of every notable Germanic ill, from cancer to flat feet. Here the myriad strands of a nationwide organization head up in a big building near Nollendorfplatz.

I had become accustomed to elaborate publicity methods in all the national headquarters of Governmental or Party institutions, but I think this one deserves the prize. The whole building was one series of exhibits, while the detailed educational literature was all-inclusive. As usual, I was given a liberal sampling, sent next day to my hotel. They went to swell a collection of data which filled a hand-trunk by the time I left Germany.

I have that public health literature spread out before me as I write. There are some twenty pamphlets, dealing with general or special topics, including a detailed bibliography of the best books available in the entire field. Some of the pamphlets are illustrated with cuts and diagrams. I note especially the one dealing with foot troubles, which contains a whole series of exercises. Then there are several single-sheet "dodgers." Here is one entitled: *Advice to Pregnant Women.* This consists of a series of wood-cuts. First, the things she should do: Sponge-bath on arising; take a quiet walk; wear proper clothes—as indicated; brush her teeth before retiring; take a good sleep in a comfortable bed. Now the *don'ts:* heavy lifting; high reaching; bending long over the washtub; bending low to get into that bottom drawer; standing too long a time; drinking and smoking; wearing high-heeled shoes; getting shaken up—as on a motorcycle; finally, losing one's temper. At the bottom of the sheet, proper articles of diet are visualized. Others in this pictorial series cover matters like Preparation for Motherhood, and Care of the Baby.

The pamphlets deal with all sorts of things. Here are several on specific diseases—tuberculosis, cancer, foot troubles, infantile paralysis, venereal diseases, and so forth. There are several more on sex—the best ages for begetting children; advice to parents on handling children during adolescence; advice to youths and maidens—these last preaching strict morality, though from a patriotic rather than a religious basis. Lastly, there are a few miscellaneous topics, including diet, exercise, and avoidance of liquor and tobacco. All these are inexpensively gotten up for mass distribution.

Before I started on my tour of investigation, the general director, Dr. Eckhard, had given me a general background discussion, as Germans always do. He stated that the general theory and structure of the German public health system goes back to Bismarck's day. The outstanding development under the Third Reich is thoroughgoing co-ordination of various departments and organizations. Structurally, therefore, no great changes have taken place except the establishment since 1933 of a complete system of cancer centers throughout Germany. It is in the spirit and tempo of the Public Health Service that we discover the vital difference between the present and former times. The Nazi attitude, subordinating the individual to the collective good, is well expressed in the remarks of Dr. Eckhard's subordinate with which this chapter began.

Dr. Schramm, the eminent surgeon whom I met at my first dinner-party in Berlin, undertook to continue my education in Public Health. One of the points he stressed was the good general level of health, due largely to the health-insurance law by which even the poorest are assured full medical treatment. People are urged to seek medical advice periodically or for any worrisome symptom, and since it costs them nothing personally, they do it gladly. All medical men are legally bound to give a certain portion of their time to insured patients; patients have the right to choose the doctor or surgeon they wish to consult, and they even have the right to be sent to the private hospitals of such medical men, if he customarily sends his patients to those institutions. Dr. Schramm took me to the hospital of which he was chief surgeon. It was a fairly large private institution, with about 150 beds. Some wards were for insured patients. I spoke with several of them. They were all workingmen. Their health insurance allowed them up to one year's hospitalization, with pocket money. After that, if not cured, I was told they were taken care of out of the public health funds indefinitely. Incidentally, Dr. Schramm informed me that cotton is so short in wartime Germany that absorbent cotton has become scarce. It is now saved for vital uses. Ordinary dressings are made of paper, and appear to serve quite well.

Another interesting point I learned was the progress made in the fight against venereal diseases. Anyone infected must at once consult a doctor, under heavy legal penalties. Since he or she can get free treatment and choose the doctor, they are glad to comply. Privacy for the case is assured by having the doctor send in a report to the health authorities bearing a number, the name and address of the patient remaining in his files. But if the patient does not come regularly or fails to comply with directions, the doctor discloses the patient's identity and coercive measures are taken. Anyone spreading infection is punished by a sentence of at least six months in jail. This sentence is mandatory. Wealth and social position are of no avail. The result of all this is a sharp drop in social disease rates. Fresh syphilitic infections have become rare. There is still considerable gonorrhea, but much is hoped from the new treatment with sulfanilamide. The war has thus far not notably affected the situation. Soldiers are so well trained in prophylaxis and are subject to such heavy punishment for carelessness that there has been scant spread of venereal disease by them.

I spent an instructive morning visiting an accident and out-patient clinic, to see how that aspect of public health was handled. This clinic was maintained for workingmen; all of them, of course, insured. The approach was not prepossessing. It was on the fourth floor of a dingy warehouse-like building, and was reached by a freight elevator. Once inside, however, I was astonished at the completeness and modernity of the equipment. X-Ray and Roentgen-Ray machines, sun- and violet-ray lamps, mechanical and hand massage, up-to-date operating-room—everything seemed to be there. An American woman, the wife of a bone specialist, who accompanied me, was frankly astounded at what we saw. She knew about such matters, and she told me that she had never seen anything professionally finer at home. Perhaps the most significant point was the cheapness with which the clinic was conducted. I was shown the cost-sheets, and found that the average charge made for patients to their associations was less than one dollar per day.

Another important aspect of public health is housing. The officials concerned with this phase showed me several new developments, from inexpensive workingmen's apartments, through single and double-house settlements, to upper-middle-class "model villages," all on the outskirts of Berlin. However, I wasn't satisfied with what was officially shown me, surmising that everything would be the best of its kind. So I got a foreign journalist who knew about such matters to steer me around the poorest quarters. I was on the hunt for slums.

My colleague told me I wouldn't find anything very bad, because Berlin had no real slums, as most countries reckon them. But he promised to show me the worst there were, and we spent the greater part of a day poking about. Our starting point was Alexanderplatz, formerly a very tough district and a Communist stronghold. Today, it is a humdrum traffic and shopping center. The worst section nearby has been almost entirely rebuilt with municipal apartment houses for workingmen. They are plainly and simply built, and the rents are very cheap. The heart of this extensive development is Horst Wessel Platz, named after the famous Nazi hero and martyr who was murdered by Communists in an old tenement (now torn down) which faced the present square.

After that we radiated in easterly segments; some of the oldest tenement sections drab and dreary, especially in the gray light of a cloudy autumn day. But none of them were run-down, and no dirt or rubbish was to be seen. My colleague informed me that the Nazi Government has forced landowners to clean up and repair even the oldest tenements. This was originally started as part of a compulsory "make-work" program during the early years of the Nazi regime. In some tenement courtyards I saw small, shedlike buildings (somewhat like the "alley dwellings" of Washington, D. C.) which once had evidently been lived in. However, such structures have all been condemned as living quarters. So are all cellar tenements. The general impression I got from these workingmen's quarters was that of a rather low average standard of living, yet above the squalor line.

The nearest to slumlike conditions I discovered was in and about the Grenadierstrasse. There the very poorest class lives, including many foreigners and a considerable number of Jews. The tenements look sordid, with few clean curtains or flowers in the windows, as was the case nearly everywhere else. Many of the passers-by looked as sordid as their abodes. The Jews, understandably, had a fear-ridden, sullen air. I tried to find out whether ghetto conditions existed, in the sense that Jews were concentrated in certain tenements. Apparently this is not the case. In one tenement, where I saw nothing but Jews about, I asked a postwoman just going in to deliver mail if this were a purely Jewish place. With the frank callousness one so often encounters, she answered disdainfully, *"Ach, nein.* Jews, Gypsies, all sorts of trash live here!"

Germany's coldly efficient system of public health is strikingly shown by the scientifically notable sanitary job it has done in Poland. Although none of us foreign journalists were allowed to visit the Polish zone, I was fortunate in having a long conversation with almost the only foreigner who was permitted to go there. This man was Dr. Junod, a Swiss and a high official of the International Red Cross. Dr. Junod is an expert judge of sanitary conditions, with many years of service in the Red Cross and long experience in the Ethiopian and Spanish Civil wars. He visited Warsaw, Poland's shattered capital city, about mid-November.

He told me that what the German health authorities had done to Warsaw since its capture in late September was a miracle of scientific efficiency. Though the houses were still largely in ruins, the streets were immaculate—he did not see even bits of waste paper blowing about. The water and lighting systems had been restored and the population generally inoculated against typhoid. The prostitutes had been listed and were carefully examined at frequent intervals. Most striking of all, the urban masses, habitually filthy and verminous, had been deloused wholesale. The delousing stations parted a man from his clothes, both going through different cleansing processes. These were so nicely synchronized that the naked individual usually met his garments at the other end—both clean and freed from local inhabitants. The clothes were dry, since they had been subjected to a blast of hot air which desiccated them almost immediately.

About the more important aspects of the lives of the people through whose city those unlittered streets ran, I was able to gather little.

Nevertheless, the result of this intensive health campaign was an utter transformation of public hygiene in the short space of two months. Thereby a great peril had been averted. Sanitary conditions immediately following the German conquest were so bad that, unless heroic measures had been speedily taken, mass epidemics would have been inevitable. This would have endangered not only German-occupied Poland but Germany itself. If such epidemics had spread into the Reich, the consequences might have been catastrophic, for the habitually cleanly Germans have no such partial immunity to filth diseases such as typhus as the Poles have acquired through having been chronically exposed to them. It was clearly not for the Poles, therefore, but for the benefit of the invaders that this miracle of sanitary science had been invoked.

XVI. IN A EUGENICS COURT

NOTHING IS SO DISTINCTIVE IN NAZI GERMANY AS ITS IDEAS about race. Its concept of racial matters underlies the whole National Socialist philosophy of life and profoundly influences both its policies and practices. We cannot intelligently evaluate the Third Reich unless we understand this basic attitude of mind. Unfortunately such understanding is not easy, because the whole subject has been so obscured by passion and propaganda.

I have long been interested in the practical applications of biology and eugenics—the science of race-betterment—and have studied much along those lines. During my recent stay in Germany I supplemented this academic background by first-hand investigation, including discussions with outstanding authorities on the subject. These included both official spokesmen such as Reichsministers Frick and Darré, and leading scientists —Eugen Fischer, Fritz Lenz, Hans Guenther, Paul Schultze-Naumburg, and others. Through their recommendations I was able to sit beside the judges during a session of the Eugenic High Court of Appeals.

As is well known, the Nazi viewpoint on race and the resultant policies are set forth by Adolf Hitler himself in the pages of *Mein Kampf,* the Bible of National Socialism. The future Fuehrer therein wrote: "It will be the duty of the People's State to consider the race as the basis of the community's existence. It must make sure that the purity of the racial strain will be preserved. It must proclaim the truth that the child is the most valuable possession a nation can have. It must make sure that only those who are healthy shall beget children and that there is only one infamy: namely, for parents who are ill or show other defects to bring children into the world. But on the other hand it must be branded as reprehensible to refrain from giving healthy children to the nation. Herein the State must come forward as the trustee of a millennial future, in face of which the egotistic desires of individuals count for nothing. Such individuals will have to bow to the State in such matters.

"In order to achieve this end the State will have to avail itself of modern advances in medical science. It must proclaim that all those people are unfit for procreation who are afflicted with some visible hereditary disease, or are the carriers of it; and the State must adopt practical means of having such people rendered sterile. On the other hand the State must make sure that the healthy woman will not have her fertility restricted through a financial and economic system of government which looks on the blessing of children as a curse to their parents. The State will have to abolish the cowardly and even criminal indifference with which the problem of social provision for large families is treated, and it will have to be the supreme protector of this greatest blessing that a people can boast of. Its attention and care must be directed towards the child rather than towards the adult."

When we analyze Hitler's pronunciamento we observe that he is here dealing with two very dissimilar things. The first of these concerns differences between human stocks. Hitler assumes that such differences are vitally important and that "the purity of the racial strain" must be preserved. Therefore, logically, crossings between them are an evil. This is the Nazi doctrine best described as *racialism.*

The interesting thing is that Hitler does not here stop to labor the point. He takes it for granted as self-evident and passes on to other matters which he treats in detail. These concern improvements *within* the racial stock, that are recognized everywhere as constituting the modern science of *eugenics,* or race-betterment.

The relative emphasis which Hitler gave racialism and eugenics many years ago foreshadows the respective interest toward the two subjects in Germany today. Outside Germany, the reverse is true, due chiefly to Nazi treatment of its Jewish minority. Inside Germany, the Jewish problem is regarded as a passing phenomenon, already settled in principle and soon to be settled in fact by the physical elimination of the Jews themselves from the Third Reich. It is the regeneration of the Germanic stock with which public opinion is most concerned and which it seeks to further in various ways.

There are one or two German ideas about race which, it seems to me, are widely misunderstood abroad. The first concerns the German attitude toward Nordic blood. Although this tall, blond strain and the qualities assumed to go with it constitute an ideal type in Nazi eyes, their scientists do not claim that Germany is today an overwhelmingly Nordic land. They admit that the present German people is a mixture of several European stocks. Their attitude is voiced by Professor Guenther when he writes: "The Nordic ideal becomes for us an ideal of unity. That which is common to all the divisions of the German people is the Nordic strain. The question is not so much whether we men now living are more or less Nordic; the question put to us is whether we have the courage to make ready for future generations a world cleansing itself racially and eugenically."

Another misconception is that the Nazis regard the Jews as a distinct race. To be sure, that term is often used in popular writings and many ignorant Nazis may believe it, but their scientific men do not thus defy obvious anthropology. They therefore refer to the Jews as a *Mischrasse*. By this they mean a group which, though self-consciously distinct, is made up of several widely diverse racial strains. It is because most of those strains are deemed too alien to the Germanic blend that the Nazis passed the so-called Nuremberg Laws prohibiting intermarriage between Jews and Germans.

Without attempting to appraise this highly controversial racial doctrine, it is fair to say that Nazi Germany's eugenic program is the most ambitious and far-reaching experiment in eugenics ever attempted by any nation.

When the Nazis came to power, Germany was biologically in a bad way. Much of her best stock had perished on the battlefields of the Great War. But those war losses were surpassed by others during the post-war period, due to the falling birth-rate. Economic depression, mass-unemployment, hopelessness for the future, had combined to produce a state of mind in which Germans were refusing to have children. The birth-rate dropped so fast that the nation was no longer reproducing itself. Furthermore, the lowest birth-rates were among those elements of highest social value. The learned and professional classes were having so few children that, at this rate, they would rapidly die out. At the other end of the scale, the opposite was true. Morons, criminals, and other anti-social elements were reproducing themselves at a rate nine times as great as that of the general population. And those lowest elements were favored in their breeding by the welfare measures of the Weimar regime. Statistics indicate that it cost far more to support Germany's defectives than it did to run the whole administrative side of Government—national, provincial, and local.

As the Nazis saw it, they had a two-fold task: to increase both the size and the quality of the population. Indiscriminate incentives to big families would result largely in more criminals and morons. So they coupled their encouragements to sound citizens with a drastic curb on the defective elements. That curb was the Sterilization Law.

The object of the statute is set forth in its official title: An Act for the Prevention of Hereditarily Diseased Offspring. The grounds for sterilization are specifically enumerated. They are: (1) Congenital Mental Deficiency; (2) Schizophrenia, or split personality; (3) Manic-Depressive Insanity; (4) Inherited Epilepsy; (5) Inherited (Huntington's) Chorea; (6) Inherited Blindness; (7) Inherited Deafness; (8) Any grave physical defect that has been inherited; (9) Chronic alcoholism, when this has been scientifically determined to be symptomatic of psychological abnormality.

It should be understood that all these defects and diseases have been proven to be hereditary by scientists throughout the world. It was estimated that at least

400,000 persons in Germany were known to be subjects for sterilization. But the law specifically forbids sterilization for any non-hereditary cause. Even mentally diseased persons, habitual criminals, and ordinary alcoholics cannot be sterilized. Each case up for sterilization must be proved beyond a reasonable doubt before special district courts, and appeals from their verdict can be taken, first to a regional court of appeals, and ultimately to the High Appellate Court sitting in Berlin.

Such are the provisions of the Sterilization Law. So many charges have been made outside Germany that it is being used to sterilize politically undesirable persons that I particularly welcomed the opportunity to study at first-hand the High Court's proceedings. Parenthetically it should be noted that the term "sterilization" does not mean castration. The law specifically prescribes methods which involve only a minor operation and result in no diminution of sexual activity other than incapacity to produce offspring.

Germany's Eugenic Supreme Court sits in an impressive building at Charlottenburg, one of Berlin's western suburbs. I arrived just as court was opening. On the bench sat a regular judge in cap and gown. At his right was the celebrated psychopathologist, Professor Zutt, a typical savant with mild blue eyes and a Vandyke beard. At the judge's left was a keen-eyed younger man who was a specialist in criminal psychology and beside whom I sat during the proceedings. All three courteously explained points to me at frequent intervals.

Since this was the court of last resort, all matters came up to it on appeal from lower courts, and thus tended to be "hairline" cases. The thing that struck me most was the meticulous care with which these cases had already been considered by the lower tribunals. The dossier of each case was voluminous, containing a complete life-history of the subject, reports of specialists and clinics, and also exhaustive researches into the subject's family history. In reaching its decision, the High Court not only consulted the records of the case but also personally examined the living subjects themselves.

The first case I saw looked like an excellent candidate for sterilization. A man in his mid-thirties, he was rather ape-like in appearance—receding forehead, flat nose with flaring nostrils, thick lips, and heavy prognathous jaw. Not vicious-looking, but gross and rather dull. His life-history was mildly anti-social—several convictions for minor thefts and one for a homosexual affair with another boy when a lad. In early manhood he had married a Jewess by whom he had three children, none of whom had showed up too well. That marriage had been dissolved under the Nuremberg Laws. He was now seeking to marry a woman who had already been sterilized as a moron. The law forbids a non-sterilized individual to marry a sterilized person; so he was more than willing to be also sterilized. The lower court recommended sterilization.

All three members of the High Court interrogated the man at length. Questions disclosed the fact that he conducted a newspaper delivery route in the suburbs, that he was able to run this simple business satisfactorily, and that he answered the Court's queries with a fair degree of intelligence. The Court concluded that sterilization had not been proven mandatory and sent back the case for further investigation.

Case Two was obviously unbalanced mentally, though not an asylum case. Swinging a cane like a fine gentleman, he entered Court with an "air," which went incongruously with his shabby-genteel clothes and the battered felt hat tucked under his left arm. There was no doubt that he should be sterilized. The lower courts had decided he was either a schizophrenic or a manic-depressive, and both defects came under the law. But which of the two it was had to be clearly determined before the operation could be legally performed. This man wanted to marry an unsterilized woman, so he was strongly opposed to sterilization. His case-history showed two prolonged mental breakdowns, irrational violent quarrels, and queer actions. Ten years previously he had evolved a plan for a Utopian State and had been arrested when he tried to lay it personally before President Hindenburg. He answered questions intelligently, revealing education, but he got excited easily; and his eyes, which were never normal, became wild on such occasions. The Court inclined to think him a manic-depressive, but they also detected schizophrenic symptoms. Since they were not absolutely sure, the case was remanded for further clinical investigation.

Case Three was an eighteen-year-old girl. A deaf-mute, she talked through an interpreter. She was obviously not feeble-minded, but had a poor family record. The parents, who also appeared, were most unprepossessing. Her case had first come before the lower court two years ago. It then decided against sterilization because no hereditary deafness was shown in the family record. Recently it had recommended sterilization because several unfortunate hereditary factors in the family had been disclosed by further investigation. The High Court ordered the girl sent to a clinic for observation. It also ordered more research into the family record.

Case Four was a seventeen-year-old girl. The issue was feeble-mindedness. She certainly looked feeble-minded as she sat below the bench, hunched in a chair, with dull features and lackluster eyes. Left an orphan at an early age, she had had a haphazard upbringing. The record showed her to have been always shy, backward, and unable to keep up with normal schooling. At present she was employed as helper in a cheap restaurant. When her case first came before the lower court, its verdict was: Wait and see. Perhaps this is a case of retarded intelligence due to environmental factors, which will ripen later. But it did not ripen; so there were further hearings, at which two specialists had disagreed.

The members of the High Court examined this poor waif carefully and with kindly patience. She had no knowledge of or interest in even the most elementary current events. For instance, she barely knew there was a war going on. But the psychologist discovered that she was able to make change for small customers' bills in her restaurant and that she could perform other duties of her humble job. So the Court finally concluded that, despite her most unprepossessing appearance and her simple, childlike mind, she was not a moron within the meaning of the law and therefore should not be sterilized.

There were other cases that day, all conducted in the same painstaking, methodical fashion. I came away convinced that the law was being administered with strict regard for its provisions and that, if anything, judgments were almost too conservative. On the evidence of that one visit, at least, the Sterilization Law is weeding out the worst strains in the Germanic stock in a scientific and truly humanitarian way.

To turn from negative to positive eugenics, the first active measure for increasing both the quantity and quality of the population was the Law for the Promotion of Marriages. I have already mentioned the young Friesian milker and his wife who were enabled to furnish a home through a 1,000-Mark Government loan, 25 per cent of which was canceled on the birth of each child born to them. These loans are made to young couples, not in cash, but in the form of certificates for household goods; before being eligible for the loan, the couple must have passed medical and mental tests proving that they are sound, healthy stock. Since the law went into effect, more than 900,000 such loans have been made.

Another population stimulus was official grants-in-aid to large families in poor circumstances. This was later expanded to a regular system of child-allowances. The taxation laws were likewise revised to lighten the burdens which large families tend to bear. An example of this is the tax on salaries, which is 16 per cent for the unmarried and 10 per cent for a married man without offspring, but which decreases with each child until it vanishes after four children have been born. In all measures requiring official loans or allowances, only sound, healthy persons can benefit. It should be understood that these specific measures dovetail with all those social-welfare and public health activities discussed in previous chapters. Thus the entire system is permeated with the eugenic point of view.

These stimuli to population growth have produced remarkable results. In 1933, the year when the Nazis came to power, only 957,000 children were born—far below the reproductive rate for the nation. The very next year births had shot up to 1,197,000, and they increased steadily until, when the war broke out, they were running about 1,300,000 annually. This is entirely contrary to the general trend in other countries of Western and Northern Europe, where average birth rates are low, with slight changes during the past decade. Even Mussolini was unable to get as good results from his efforts at increasing Italy's population until he recently copied several measures from the Reich. And we should remember that Fascism seeks quantity production, without the eugenic requirements for quality that are in force in Germany.

Before closing this survey, we should note the psychological aspect of Nazi population policy. The rulers of the Third Reich do not stop with laws and economic regulations. They realize that, for the full attainment of their goal, ideology must be mobilized. So the German people is systematically propagandized for the upbuilding of what may be described as a racial and eugenic consciousness. Here, for instance, are the *Ten Commandments for the Choice of a Mate*. Couched in the exhortatory form of the German *Du*, this new racial decalogue is brought so constantly to the attention of every German youth and maiden that they must know it by heart.

Here is the text:

1. *Remember that thou art a German!* All that thou

art, thou owest, not to thine self, but to thy people. Whether thou willest it or no, thou belongest thereto; from thy people hast thou come forth. In all thou doest, bethink thee whether it be to thy people's best advancement.

2. *Thou shalt maintain purity of Mind and Spirit!* Cherish and foster thy mental and spiritual capacities. Keep far from thy mind and soul whatsoever is instinctively foreign to them, what is contrary to thy true self, what thine inner conscience rejects. Seeking after money and worldly goods, after quick preferment, after material pleasures, may often lead thee to forget higher things. Be true to thine own self, and before aught else be worthy of thy future life-mate.

3. *Keep thy body clean!* Maintain the good health received from thy parents, in order to serve thy people. Guard against expending it uselessly and foolishly. A moment's sensual gratification may lastingly wreck thine health and heritable treasure whereon thy children and children's children have a compelling claim. What thou demandest from thy future life-partner, that must thou demand of thyself. Remember that thou art destined to be a German Parent.

4. *Being of sound stock, thou shalt not remain single!* All thy qualities of body and spirit perish if thou diest without heirs. They are a heritage, a donation from thine ancestors. They exist as a chain, of which thou art but a link. Durst thou break that chain, save under stern necessity? Thy life is straitly bound by time; family and folk endure. Thy hereditary estate of body and spirit prospers in thy waxing offspring.

5. *Marry only for love!* Money is perishable stuff and ensures no lasting happiness. Where the divine spark

of love is absent, there can no worthy marriage endure. Wealth of heart and soul is the foundation of a lasting, happy union.

6. *As a German, choose a mate only of thine own or kindred blood!* Where like meets like, there rules true unison. Where unlike races mix, there is discord. Mixing racial stocks which do not harmonize leads to the degeneracy and downfall of both strains and peoples. The more unlike the mixtures, the faster this takes place. Guard thyself from such ruin! True happiness springs only from harmonious blood.

7. *In choosing thy mate, consider the ancestry!* Thou weddest not alone thy mate but also thy life-partner's forebears. Worthy descendants are to be expected only where worthy ancestors went before. Gifts of mind and spirit are just as much inherited as the color of hair and eyes. Bad traits are bequeathed precisely like lands or goods. Naught in the whole world is so precious as the seeds of a gifted stock; noxious seeds cannot be transformed into good ones. Wherefore, marry not the one worthy member of a bad family.

8. *Health is the prerequisite for even outward beauty!* Health is the best guarantee for lasting happiness, for it is the basis for both external charm and inward harmony. Demand of thy mate medical assurance of fitness for marriage, as thou thyself must also do.

9. *In marriage seek, not a plaything but a helpmeet!* Marriage is not a transient game but a lasting union. The supreme aim of marriage is the raising of healthy offspring. Only by the union of beings who are like in spirit, body and blood can this high goal be attained, to the blessing of themselves and their people. For each

race has its own ethos; so like souls can alone endure together.

10. *Thou shalt desire many children!* Only by engendering at least four children can the continuance of thy people be assured. Only by having an even larger number can the greatest possible proportion of the traits inherited from thine ancestors be surely handed down. No child wholly resembles another. Each child inherits different traits. Many gifted children greatly enhances the worth of a people and are the surest guarantees for its future. *Thou* wilt soon pass away; what thou givest to thy descendants endures. Thy people liveth forever!

What an amazing mixture of idealisms and propaganda! This Marital Decalogue is a striking instance of the Nazi attitude and methods.

XVII. I SEE HITLER

To meet and talk with adolf hitler, "der fuehrer" of the Third Reich, was naturally an outstanding item in my professional program when I went to Germany. I have already recounted how, my very first evening in Berlin, I met Herr Hewel, one of Hitler's confidential men. I did not fail to discuss the matter with him, but his reaction was not encouraging. For a long time past, he said, the Fuehrer had been seeing very few foreigners except diplomats in his official capacity as Chancellor of the Reich. Since the outbreak of war, no non-official foreigner had been received; nor was such an audience then in contemplation. However, Herr Hewel expressed interest in my plans and promised to see what could be done.

The officials of the Foreign Office and the Propaganda Ministry with whom I had introductory talks during the next few days were equally dubious. They flatly told me that, while an audience was remotely possible, an interview was out of the question. Let me explain that, in journalistic parlance, the two terms have a widely different meaning. An *interview* is granted with the express understanding that much of what is said will be permitted publication in the press, though certain remarks made during the conversation may be withheld as being "off the record." In an *audience*, on the contrary, everything said is "off the record" unless specific permission to publish certain remarks is granted. But there was no chance that such an exception would be made to me, because, when the current war broke out, a rule was adopted that any audience with the Fuehrer which might be given was with the clear proviso that no word spoken by him should be quoted. That logically excluded newspapermen, since for them an unquotable audience would have no professional meaning.

It looked as though I was up against a stone wall, but when I analyzed those conversations, I thought I saw a possible way through. Just one American writer had seen Hitler in the preceding two years. He was Albert Whiting Fox, well known for his magazine and press feature articles. After three months of diligent effort, Fox had seen Hitler shortly before the war. And, from what was told me, I gathered that Fox succeeded mainly because his purpose was to present a picture of Hitler the Man and his surroundings, rather than to get a statement of the Fuehrer's views on politics or other controversial matters.

The Nazi officials liked that idea, because they favored anything which would present the human side of their Leader to the outer world. More than one of his close associates expressed regret to me that the foreign public knew and thought of him only in his official capacity—occasionally declaiming over the radio, but otherwise an aloof, mysterious figure whom his enemies depicted as sinister, even inhuman. Indeed, these informants went on to say that they would have long since accorded reputable foreign writers and journalists permission to make first-hand studies

of Hitler and his environment but for the opposition of
the Fuehrer himself. It seems that Hitler dislikes having
his intimate personality and private life thus publicized.
He feels it would be undignified, and prefers being
known to the outer world for what he officially says
and does.

Realizing how these officials felt, I concentrated
along that line. I pointed out that, though I had come
to Germany as a journalist, I was there also with the
intention of gathering material for a book and for lectures to the American public. In those latter capacities,
the ban on quoting Hitler's remarks were to me relatively immaterial. An audience would serve almost as
well, if I were permitted to describe the circumstances
and portray the man himself as I saw him. It is to these
arguments that I ascribe chiefly the audience which,
after two months, was granted me. Indeed, this audience, the only one granted a non-official foreigner since
the beginning of the war, was given me explicitly in
my capacity, not as a journalist, but as a writer of books
and public speaker.

The memorable day was Tuesday, December 19,
1939. Shortly before one o'clock in the afternoon, a
shining limousine drew up in front of the Hotel Adlon
and a handsome young officer in dove-gray Foreign
Office uniform ushered me to the waiting car. Driving
down the Wilhelmstrasse, the car slowed before the
Chancery and blew a peculiar note on its horn. Like
most public buildings erected under the Third Reich,
the new Chancery is severely plain on the outside, with
a high doorway flush with the wall and normally always
closed. In response to the summons, however, the halves

of the entrance opened immediately, and the car drove slowly inside.

What a contrast to the plain exterior! I found myself in a large paved courtyard. Opposite the gate was a broad flight of stone steps flanked by two impressive gray stone figures. The flight led up to an entrance. On the steps stood several lackeys in blue-and-silver liveries, while near the entrance doorway was a knot of high officers in regulation gray-green uniforms. Through the entrance I glimpsed a foyer ablaze with electric light from crystal chandeliers.

Emerging from my car, I walked up the steps, to bows and salutes, and entered the foyer, where more lackeys took charge of my hat and overcoat. I was here greeted by a high official with whom I walked through the foyer into a magnificent hall, without windows but electrically lighted from above. This lofty hall, done in light-red marble inlaid with elaborate patterns, reminded me somehow of an ancient Egyptian temple. At its further end, more steps led up to an enormously long gallery of mirrors lighted by numerous sconces on the left-hand wall. Since this gallery was set at a slight angle, the effect upon me was of intense brilliance; much more so than a straight perspective would have afforded.

About half-way down the long gallery I observed a door on the right-hand side, before which stood a pair of lackeys. Through this door I passed, to find myself in a large room which, I was told, was the ante-chamber to the Fuehrer's study. In it were about a dozen high officers to whom I was introduced and with some of whom I chatted for some moments.

The whole build-up thus far had been so magnificent and the attendant psychic atmosphere so impressive that by this time I really did not know what to expect. I had the feeling that I was being ushered into the presence of a Roman Emperor or even an Oriental Potentate. The absurd thought crossed my mind that I might find *Der Fuehrer* seated on a throne surrounded by flaming swastikas.

At that moment I was bidden to the Presence. Turning left, I passed through double doors and entered another large room. To my right hand, near the doorway, was an upholstered sofa and several chairs. At the far end of the room was a flat-topped desk from behind which a figure rose as I entered and came towards me. I saw a man of medium height, clad in a plain officer's tunic with no decorations save the Iron Cross, black trousers, and regulation military boots. Walking up to where I had halted near the doorway, he gave me a firm handshake and a pleasant smile. It was the Fuehrer.

For an instant I was taken aback by the astounding contrast between this simple, natural greeting and the heavy magnificence through which I had just passed. Pulling myself together, I expressed in my best German my appreciation of the honor that was being shown me, calling him *Excellency,* as foreigners are supposed to do. Hitler smiled again at my little speech, motioned to the sofa, and said: "Won't you sit down?", himself taking the nearest chair about a yard away from me. My German evidently made a good impression, for he complimented me upon my accent, from which he inferred that I had been to Germany before. I assured him that he was correct, but went on to say that this was my first view of the Third Reich. To which he replied, with a slight shake of the head: "A pity you couldn't have seen it in peacetime."

The conversation of about twenty minutes which followed these preliminaries naturally cannot be repeated, because I had given my word to that effect. Hitler, however, told me no deep, dark secrets—heads of States don't do that sort of thing with foreign visitors. I think it is no breach of my agreement to say that much of his talk dealt neither with the war nor politics but with great rebuilding plans which the war had constrained him temporarily to lay aside. His regretful interest in those matters seemed to show that he still had them very much in mind.

Even more interesting than what Hitler said was his whole manner and appearance. Here I was, in private audience with the Master of Greater Germany, and able to study him at close range. Needless to say, I watched intently his every move and listened with equal intentness to his voice. Let me try to depict as clearly as possible what I observed.

There are certain details of Hitler's appearance which one cannot surmise from photographs. His complexion is medium, with blond-brown hair of neutral shade which shows no signs of gray. His eyes are very dark-blue. Incidentally, he no longer wears a cartoonist's mustache. It is now the usual "tooth-brush" type, in both size and length. As already remarked, his uniform is severely plain and seemingly of stock materials.

In ordinary conversation, Hitler's voice is clear and well-modulated. Throughout the audience he spoke somewhat rapidly, yet never hurriedly, and in an even tone. Only occasionally did I detect a trace of his native

Austro-Bavarian accent. The audience was not a mono-
logue. Although naturally he did most of the talking,
Hitler gave me plenty of chances to ask questions and
put in my say. He did not at any time sharply raise his
voice. Only when discussing the war did it become
vibrant with emotion; and then he dropped his voice
almost to an intense whisper. He made practically no
gestures, sitting for the most part quietly, with one hand
resting on the arm of his chair and the other lying relaxed in his lap.

Hitler's whole appearance was that of a man in good
health. He certainly did not look a day older than his
fifty years. His color was good, his skin clear and un-
wrinkled, his body fit and not over-weight. He showed
no visible signs of nervous strain, such as pouched eyes,
haggard lines, or twitching physical reactions. On the
contrary, appearance, voice, and manner combined to
give an impression of calmness and poise. I am well
aware that this description tallies neither with current
ideas nor with reports of other persons who have seen
and talked with him. Very likely those reports are just
as true as mine, since Hitler is said to be a man of many
moods. Perhaps I saw him on one of his good days; perhaps he intended to make a particular impression upon
me. All I can do is to describe accurately what I myself
saw and heard.

Three other persons were present during this audience. First of all, there was Herr Schmidt, the official
interpreter, present at all meetings of the Fuehrer with
foreigners and reputed to be master of many languages.
This time his services were not needed, so Herr
Schmidt sat quietly beside me on the sofa without
uttering a word the entire time. Equally silent were

the other two, who sat in chairs some little distance away. They were Foreign Minister von Ribbentrop and Herr Hewel, who had done much to bring the audience about. Hitler terminated the conversation by rising, shaking hands again, and wishing me success in the balance of my stay in Germany. He then turned back to his desk, whither von Ribbentrop had already gone and where two other men were standing. At some point during the interview a photograph had been taken of Hitler and myself in conversation. So unobtrusively was this done that I was not aware of it at the moment. The first thing I knew about it was when a copy was presented to me with the Fuehrer's compliments as a souvenir of the occasion. Since it was given me with the express understanding that it was not for publication, I cannot reproduce it here, as I should like to have done. I regret this, for it shows an interesting pose and would have helped greatly to visualize what I have attempted to describe.

From this audience emerge two outstanding contrasts. First, as already indicated, that between the magnificently staged approach and the simple, undramatic, almost matter-of-fact meeting with the man himself. Very likely this contrast was also deliberate staging. Anyhow, it made a striking effect.

The second notable contrast which occurred to me was that of this audience with Hitler and one I had years ago with his fellow-dictator, Mussolini. The two audiences were complete opposites. There isn't much stage-setting in reaching Mussolini at the Palazzo Venezia. The dramatic build-up really begins when you go through a little ante-chamber door and find yourself in an immense room, darkened by half-closed blinds, and with no furniture except a desk and a couple of chairs at the far end of the room. From behind that desk rises Mussolini, just like Hitler, but there the resemblance abruptly ends; for, instead of coming to meet you, you have to walk all the way across the room to him.

However, from the very start, you feel that Mussolini is intensely *human*. You get the fact that he is interested in you as a *person*. Also you sense that he is trying to sell you, not only his ideas but also *himself*. He wants to win your interest and admiration, and to attain that he employs the arts of a finished actor—uses his big, compelling eyes; thrusts out his chin; aims to semi-hypnotize you. It's all very intriguing. Perhaps, to an Anglo-Saxon, it's a bit too obvious. But it flatters your ego, just the same.

Nothing like that with Hitler. Though always pleasant and courteous, he makes no obvious attempt to impress or win you. When he talks, his eyes get a far-away look, and he sometimes bows his head, speaking abstractedly, almost as though to himself. Whatever he may be to his friends and intimates, I came away feeling that, however interested Hitler may be in people collectively, he is not interested in the average individual, as such. Of course, that is a personal impression. After all, I was just a foreign journalist who meant nothing to him or his scheme of things, and whom he had seen only on the advice of subordinates. But the same was true of Mussolini, who *had* shown a personal interest.

Another factor: personal charm. Mussolini has it. At least, he turns it on even in casual audiences. I felt his magnetic aura when I was two yards away from him.

I didn't get any such psychic reaction from Hitler; neither did I get any emotional "lift" from his conversation. This was perhaps the most surprising thing in my whole audience with him, because all that had been told me pointed to the exact opposite. My very first evening in Berlin, Herr Hewel had descanted to me on the *inspirational* value of personal contact with the Fuehrer, and all who were closely connected with him spoke in the same way. Dr. Ley, for instance, described at great length the need of continuous personal contact with Hitler, not only for specific advice but even more to drink in and be inspired by the constant creative emanations from the Fuehrer's constructive genius. For instance, Ley said that Hitler had once said to him: "If you wait until I summon you about something, then it is already too late." As a matter of fact, the Nazi inner circle foregathers with Hitler almost every day, especially at lunch time. The mid-day pause in Berlin's official life is admittedly timed to this *intime* luncheon-period.

Now I do not attempt to explain this seeming contradiction between my personal impression and that of all privileged Nazis. At first, I thought their statements on this matter was a sort of "Party Line." Yet the idea was expressed in so many diverse ways and with such differences in detail that I am inclined to think they really meant what they said. It's just one of those mysteries that you run into so often in present-day Germany. Like the Third Reich which he has created, what you first see in Hitler by no means indicates all that lies behind.

One last aspect connected with this audience—its rigid confidentiality. Long before I saw Hitler, I had had to give my word of honor that everything he might say when I saw him would be kept scrupulously "off the record." As the time for the audience approached, everybody concerned said to me in substance: "You know, by recommending you, we have in a sense vouched for you. If there should be any misunderstanding on your part, it would be—most embarrassing for us." I was given to understand that the Fuehrer felt strongly on the matter.

The climax to all this came when I returned to the Adlon after my audience and found a message from Herr von Ribbentrop, stating that he would like to see me later that same afternoon. At the hour appointed he received me and wasted no time getting to the point.

"You understand, of course, Dr. Stoddard," said he, "that today's interview with the Fuehrer must not be quoted in any way."

I was slightly nettled. "Mr. Minister," I answered, "long before this audience, I informed your subordinates and the officials at the Propaganda Ministry of my journalistic experience and my reliability for keeping a confidence and keeping my given word. I assume your subordinates have informed you favorably."

"Of course, of course," replied von Ribbentrop hurriedly, "but—"

Even this is not the whole story. Three days after my audience with Hitler I left for a Christmas holiday at Budapest, Hungary. Magyar newspaper colleagues of mine in Berlin had telephoned their editors I was coming, and naturally the audience had made me "news." So two editors of leading Budapest papers promptly gave me a fine luncheon, after which they proceeded to interview me with the introductory remark: "Now let's hear all about your interview with Hitler."

"Gentlemen," I had to tell them, "before I say another word, please understand that it was not an interview but an audience, and that everything said was very much 'off the record.' You must give me your word that, in whatever I say, you will publish this statement textually. If you agree, I will tell you what the Fuehrer looked like and under what circumstances I saw him."

They agreed, and, like good Magyar gentlemen, they did just what they promised. Their press accounts were, of course, promptly transmitted to Berlin. I knew nothing about it till I got back ten days later. Then I did, because officials met me with unusual cordiality. "What nice statements you made in Budapest," was the general refrain.

Thenceforth, all doors seemed to be open to me. In my last month in Berlin I got my most important interviews. Which would seem to indicate that, in Germany as elsewhere, keeping faith is a good thing at least for a journalist to do.

XVIII. MID-WINTER BERLIN

As the initial weeks of my stay in Germany grew
into months, the damp chill of autumn deepened into
the damp cold of winter—the first winter of the Second
Great War. The shortest days of the year drew nigh,
and in North Germany they are short indeed. Even at
high noon the sun stood low in the heavens—a sun that
gave scant light or warmth. Often the sun was hidden
by clouds. When the cloud-veil was thick, it was almost
like twilight, fading presently into the long winter night
with its inevitable blackout.

Slowly yet inexorably, war's impoverishing grip drew
ever tighter, producing cumulative shortage and scarcity. Its constricting presence could be literally felt.
Thanks to the efficient rationing system already described, you didn't notice it much in the bare necessities
of life, but it did hit all comforts and luxuries. Here,
uncertainties and disappointments were the order of
the day, symbolized by that dread word *Ausverkauft*—
"sold out."

Ausverkauft; how often you saw that sign! It was a
mental hazard that dogged your footsteps at every turn.
You found a brand of cigarettes that fairly suited your
American taste. Forbidden to buy more than one pack-
age at a time, you couldn't lay in a stock. All at once,
that brand was no longer on sale anywhere, and you

213

were told that it was off the market—permanently *ausverkauft*. You hit upon a cigar that suited your fancy. Impossible to buy a box, while your daily ration of five cigars in October dropped to three in December and to two per day when I left Berlin. Also, the chances were that long before then, that brand could be had no more. Suppose a few friends were scheduled to drop into your room for a chat. You went around the corner to buy a bottle of brandy for the occasion. Temporarily *ausverkauft*. Same with schnapps. All you could buy that day in the liquor line was an imitation vodka, made in Germany. And I may add that in mid-January, when the cold was at its worst, hard liquors vanished completely from the market.

One of the most annoying aspects of the situation was the deceptive appearance of the stores. They all kept up a good front. The windows were filled with attractive displays. But go in and try to buy any of it! Like as not, you would be told that those were only *Muster*—display-samples which were not for sale. The shops had been ordered to keep their windows full of goods even when stocks were almost bare, so as to create a prosperous atmosphere that would bolster morale. It was highly instructive to watch how the big department stores found goods to cover their counters. They did, but when you looked closely, you found that much of the stuff on sale consisted of things seldom wanted or of obviously poor quality. Quick "sellers" were chronically short, especially during the Christmas shopping season. I remember going into AWAG, formerly Wertheim's, Berlin's biggest department store, to buy a few toys for the children of a family I knew well in Berlin. It was at least a fortnight before Christmas, yet I found that everything I had in mind had long since been sold out.

Now these occurrences were not real hardships. They were merely annoyances. But multiply them many times a day, in conjunction with such matters as scratched-out dishes on restaurant or hotel menus, shortages of taxicabs, and the constant dread that you might lose or wear out some article of clothing which could not be replaced, and you found yourself in a chronic state of irritation which wore on the nerves. Most of the foreigners I met, with the exception of a few old hands who were thoroughly "salted," told me that their dispositions were being slowly but surely ruined. This was especially true of Americans, who were apt to be cross and jumpy after a few months' stay in Germany.

All this applies particularly to foreigners. We have already pointed out that the Germans, long toughened and hardened by misfortune, are not affected to anything like the same extent. But they, too, felt the grim undertow which was sucking down their living-standards. No class was exempt. Indeed, war's leveling process hit the poor less obviously than it did the rich and well-to-do. I would go into homes displaying every evidence of wealth and comfort. At first sight, nothing had changed. But those families could no longer entertain much because they could buy only a few luxuries beyond their food-rations; they could not bring out their fine linen and napery because they had no extra soap to wash them with when soiled; they had to use the subway or walk because their fine motor-cars had been either commandeered by the government or laid up for lack of gasoline. And didn't they hate this sort of thing!

It was in such homes that I heard the bitterest complaints.

The Christmas season was especially revealing. It showed how slim is the margin the German people now has for good cheer. Yuletide is especially dear to German hearts. Even the very poor strain themselves to make a real celebration, particularly for the children. I have already described how the Government did its bit by allowing men to purchase a Christmas necktie and women a pair of stockings without recourse to their clothing cards. Other official relaxations were a slight raising of the food rations for the month of December, and a special food bonus for Christmas week. This munificent release worked out, per person, at about one-eighth of a pound of butter, the same amount of *Ersatz* honey, one extra egg, and a little chocolate cake and candy! Lastly, there was a temporary increase in the sugar ration and permission to buy certain flavoring extracts and spices. Since the regular bread-flour ration was already ample, German housewives were able to bake their traditional Christmas cakes and marzipan—in moderation. Boughten sweets, however, were scarce. There was a cake and candy shop near my hotel, and I noted the daily queue of persons waiting eagerly to enter for the short period in which that shop was open for business. When the daily stock had been sold out, the shop closed for the day.

I did not witness the actual Christmas celebration in Germany, because I spent the holiday season in Hungary. But I was in Berlin until December 22nd, so I saw all the preparations. They were rather pathetic. In the department stores, crowds of shoppers would mill about the counters, looking for Christmas gifts. Most of the stuff on sale was clearly unsuitable for that purpose. Nevertheless, the most unlikely articles were bought, for want of something better. Everybody seemed to have money enough. The trouble was that their Reichsmarks simply couldn't connect with what they were after. That typifies what goes on in Germany all the time. It's a sort of reverse inflation. Money doesn't increase notably in quantity, but what you can buy with it dwindles away.

That is the reason why Germans tend to spend so much on amusements of all kinds. Despite the blackout and curtailed transportation, moving-picture houses, theaters, and the opera are filled to capacity. The same is true of cafés, bars, and night-clubs, where Germans throng to drown their sorrows according to their pocketbooks in beer, schnapps, or champagne. The Germans today drink much more than they normally do, so the night-life is stridently hilarious. I saw a good deal of drunkenness; and I may add that when the German sets out to do some serious drinking, he makes a good job of it. Seldom does he acquire a fighting jag. Usually he just gets maudlin until he sinks either to the floor or into the gutter, as chance directs.

One of the drawbacks to a big time in Berlin is that you must quit early unless you are near home. Otherwise you will find no return transportation. The subways and most trams stop at 1.00 A.M., and buses retire even earlier, while there are virtually no taxis. I recall one poignant occasion when I forgot the schedule. I emerged from a night-club in a driving rain, three miles from my hotel and with not the faintest idea how to get there on foot. Of course there were no taxis, since a chauffeur whom the police discovers parking or cruising near any resort of pleasure loses his license. The friend who had brought me thither stuck by me as we roamed the wet streets in search of a conveyance. At last a taxicab hove in sight, and my companion brought it to a halt by yelling: "Here's a foreigner! An American! He has a legal right to ride!"

After a hard day's work, I did not always feel like spending the evening writing in my room. The same was true of other foreign journalists living in downtown hotels or who had night work in downtown offices. Some months before my arrival in Berlin, the Propaganda Ministry had tried to help the foreign press corps by having special privileges extended to a certain restaurant called the *Taverne* with the idea of making it the evening rendezvous for newspapermen. One could get certain foods like egg dishes, unobtainable elsewhere, while taxis were allowed to stand outside. Also, the place was furnished with a number of regular "Ladies" whom the journalists nicknamed "Himmler's Gals," because they were supposed to be *Gestapo* (political secret police) agents waiting to vamp the unwary and extract information from them. However, the *Taverne* prostitutes, the high prices and the noise soon got on the nerves of the North European and American correspondents.

The Propaganda Ministry, heeding our complaints, soon found a new place for us which was eminently satisfactory. This was a private dining-room in the *Auslands Club,* a really distinguished organization on Leipziger Platz. Here the food was excellent, the service quick, and prices surprisingly moderate, considering what you got for your money. Accordingly, we Americans, together with the best of the North European correspondents, made our quarters a real club of our own, dining there frequently and spending the evenings in conversation. On dark, cold winter nights, I cannot describe how grateful I was for that snug haven.

In many ways the life of the foreign press corps in Berlin is a hard one, professionally as well as personally. I cannot praise too highly my American colleagues, who do fine work on the most difficult and also the most thankless assignment in Europe today. I have already described the technical side of our professional existence and the generally good relations existing between foreign journalists and the officials with whom they have regularly to do. The only time those relations threatened to become strained was when the Russo-Finnish War broke out. Red Russia's invasion of Finland raised stormy echoes in the foreign press corps, and the German Government's attitude in the matter did not tend to calm us. Since this is a good instance of Nazi propaganda methods, towards both foreigners and its own people, it seems worth describing in some detail.

The Government's basic standpoint was that it sat on the sidelines watching objectively a matter which was not its concern. At first, it did its best to play down the affair. During the diplomatic crisis which preceded the war, and even after fighting had actually started, the Government spokesmen in our daily press conferences refused to take things seriously and foretold a peaceful settlement. German newspapers either tucked brief items in inconspicuous corners or printed nothing at all. Only when the war was well under way did they make even a partial attempt to present the news.

In its attempt to mold German public opinion, it was revealing to see how the official thesis evolved from day to day. First we were told that Soviet Russia sought merely to safeguard its outlet to the Baltic Sea, and that the Finnish Government was very foolish in refusing to grant Moscow's moderate demands. We were also told that those demands were fully justified by geography, history, strategy, and what-have-you. Next came an assertion that Russia was trying to throw off the shackles imposed upon her after the Great War by unjust treaties that constituted an "Eastern Versailles." If Finland rashly attempted to perpetuate this intolerable *Diktat,* she must suffer the logical consequences of her folly. The final link in this chain of reasoning brought England into the picture. The newspapers at first hinted and then openly stated that British diplomacy was chiefly, if not entirely, responsible for Finland's stubborn resistance to Russian pressure.

Well, if you heard only that side, and if you either forgot or didn't know what had happened in the past, perhaps the German official thesis might have seemed reasonable. Otherwise it sounded pretty thin. When you mentioned the matter to well-informed Germans who weren't officials, they would shrug deprecatingly and then make a more understandable explanation.

"What do you expect us to do?" they would ask. "What *can* we do, under the circumstances? Here we are in a life-and-death struggle with Britain and France. Do you want us to offend Russia and perhaps find ourselves as we were in the last war—nipped between two fronts?"

So, most Germans seemed inclined to think that their Government was making the best of a bad business. But, in private conversation, intelligent Germans admitted that it *was* a bad business. And they displayed no love for Soviet Russia, either. Make no mistake about that.

The foreign residents in Berlin were practically solid in their sympathy for Finland and their condemnation of the Soviets. The Americans, especially, were furious. One of the ways in which we gave vent to our feelings was by raising our glasses to the toast: *Skoal Finland!* whenever we took a drink. We newspapermen were especially fond of doing this in the Kaiserhof bar. You will remember that the Hotel Kaiserhof is the Nazi social stronghold, and at the cocktail hour its bar, a large room with many tables, is apt to be filled with big guns of the Party. We journalists would often slip in there for a drink and a chat after our afternoon press conference at the Propaganda Ministry just across the Wilhelmsplatz from the hotel. We were thus sure of a distinguished audience when we raised our glasses and gave our defiant toast. We had our answer all ready, in case any Nazi remonstrated, by pointing out that the German Government had officially emphasized entire objectivity to the Russo-Finnish conflict, and that therefore it was no breach of etiquette on our part to show where our sympathies lay. The Nazis must have realized this; because, aside from a few heavy stares, no objection was ever made. Indeed, I imagine that such demonstrations by the press representatives of many neutral nations may have given some of our Nazi hearers a sense of moral isolation which could not have been agreeable.

The most interesting vantage-point from which to watch both official and foreign attitudes was at the daily press conferences at the Foreign Office, which I have already described. Whenever the Finnish question arose, as it often did, the usually cordial atmosphere would grow a bit tense. Of course, impeccable politeness prevailed on both sides. But the press queries were sharply searching, while official answers frequently had an acid flavor.

I certainly didn't envy the Government spokesman, those days. Usually, he was Dr. Braun von Stumm, an able man, though with a temper of his own. He needed all his ability, for he had to keep a somewhat tortuous official record straight, and dodge or parry questions shot at him by clever, quick-witted men and women on a highly delicate topic. And he visibly showed the strain he was under. As the questions piled in, he would redden, and I could see him squirm, mentally as well as physically. On more than one occasion, those days, he reminded me of the bull in a Spanish *corrida,* pricked by the barbed darts flung at him by agile *banderilleros.* When he thought the matter had gone far enough, he was apt to announce brusquely that the Russo-Finnish topic had been fully covered for the day, and that we should shift our queries to other matters.

One other outstanding aspect of Berlin life should be included in the picture. This was the great cold. On top of an unusually inclement autumn, it started in about mid-December. From then on, one cold wave after another rolled over us, fresh from the Russian steppes. Morning after morning, it would be below zero, Fahrenheit. With a rise of only a few degrees during the short winter day, the cold hung steady and tightened its grip. Since it was a damp cold, its penetrating quality was far greater than our winter weather.

Those cold waves covered all Europe. I found even lower temperatures in Hungary, though with a drier air, and I watched the mighty Danube river fill with ice floes during the Christmas season until it was frozen solid by New Year's Day.

The severest blow which the hard winter dealt Europe was an almost complete stoppage of inland water transportation. We in America make comparatively little use of our rivers. Europe, on the contrary, is covered with an interlocking system of navigable rivers and canals on which much of the slow freight is moved by barges. By the turn of the year, that entire system was frozen up, so water-borne freight movements were paralyzed. That threw a prodigious burden on railway lines already overworked or on motor trucks strictly rationed for gasoline.

Nowhere were winter's blows harder to parry than in Berlin, one of the world's great metropolitan centers with a population exceeding four million souls. Even in normal times this implies an elaborate supply system, much of it by water. For instance, I was informed that 40 per cent of Berlin's coal ordinarily comes by barge. The sudden crisis precipitated when the great cold began in mid-December was rendered all the more serious by the fact that three months' strict food and fuel rationing had made it impossible for the thrifty and forehanded to lay up any stocks.

Great credit is due the Government for the way it handled the situation. Truly heroic efforts were made, and disaster was averted. Yet widespread suffering was inevitable. Living as I did in one of Berlin's leading hotels, I personally experienced little of all this. The Adlon continued to be well heated, and I saw no perceptible difference in the quality of my food. But, when I returned to Berlin immediately after New Year's, I heard sad tales on every hand of ill-heated houses or apartments and skimpy domestic menus. Even potatoes and cabbages grew scarce, because they froze on the way to market and were spoiled. Train schedules were cut to the bone. When I left Germany at the end of January by that famous flyer, the Berlin-Rome Express, my journey was full of unpleasant incidents. I felt I was getting out just in time, and what I learned afterwards amply justified my foreboding.

An amusing aspect of the wintry scene was the enormous overshoes issued to policemen on post before public buildings. I presume they were stuffed with felt, straw, or some other cold-resistant material. Anyhow, the *Schupos* waddled along their short beats like mammoth ducks, and seemed somewhat self-conscious when passers-by glanced at their foot-gear.

Berliners did not wholly lose their proverbial wit and caustic sense of humor. Curses at the weather were often interlarded with jests. The best joke I heard was uttered by the coatroom man at the *Auslands Club*. When I came there to dine one bitter December night, I gave him my opinion of the weather in the shape of a loud "Brrrh!" Quick as a flash, he replied, with a sly wink: "Yeah. The first export out of Russia!"

To tell the truth, I was a bit fed-up with this war-time Berlin life. Much of my hardest work was still ahead of me, and I had a long time to go before I could get through. I needed a break, and I could think of no better place than Budapest, Hungary; a city of which I have always been fond, and where I have old friends. So, three days before Christmas, I left Berlin for the holidays in a land where I could escape from black-outs, food-rations, etcetera, at least for a short time.

XIX. BERLIN TO BUDAPEST

THE BEST NIGHT TRAIN IN GERMANY ROLLED INTO THE Friedrichstrasse Station. At least, it ought to be the best, because it's the only all-sleeping-car train in the Fatherland, and it runs between Berlin and Vienna, the two metropolitan cities of the Third Reich.

It was three days before Christmas. I had been warned that the holiday traffic would be heavy, so I had engaged my berth nearly a fortnight in advance. I had also been positively assured when I bought my ticket that there would be a dining-car on that de luxe train, so I had eaten nothing since lunch. As meals in Germany don't stand by you very well these days, I was good and hungry.

The best night train in Germany was half an hour late, though it was made up in the Berlin yards and had stopped at only two stations before reaching mine. Meanwhile I had stood on the darkened platform and watched the crowds storming the outgoing trains. Never before had I realized so fully the shortage of Germany's rolling-stock. The railway authorities were quite incapable of handling the holiday traffic. When the day-coach section to Vienna ahead of mine arrived, it was like an aggravated subway rush. The coaches, already well-filled from previous stations, were jammed to overflowing. I pitied that close-packed mass of humanity, condemned to stand up all night, and thanked my lucky stars that my train took only those whose passages were booked.

At length I climbed aboard my sleeper, found my compartment, deposited my hand luggage, and sought the porter to ask my way to the diner. He shook his head sadly.

"There isn't any on tonight, sir," he answered.

"What?" I stormed. "But they assured me—"

"I'm sorry, sir, but we don't have a diner aboard."

"Well, then," I said, clinging to a last hope, "haven't you anything in your buffet?"

"Nothing to eat, sir; only beer and liquors."

"Well, what can I do?" I asked in desperation.

"There's one more stop in Berlin, sir. You may be able to get something on the platform if you're quick."

The train was just drawing into that station, so I dashed down the steps and made for the dimly lighted little buffet. Only packaged goods to be seen! I bought two small boxes of crackers and made a flying leap for the train which was about to get under way. Those crackers, washed down with two bottles of beer, constituted my dinner.

A traveler must needs be somewhat of a philosopher, so I proceeded to look on the bright side. My car was relatively new, my compartment comfortable and clean, while hunger is a good sauce even for crackers. Midway in my reflections I was disturbed by raucous voices in the corridor. I opened the door and found several angry men and women gesticulating with the conductor. I presently gathered that one of the sleeping cars had broken down when the train was made up and had not been replaced; so some thirty passengers with perfectly good tickets had no place to sleep. This reconciled me to my lost dinner like nothing else.

I turned in early; the bed was excellent and the car well sprung; I slept long and well. There is an old saying that he who sleeps dines, but I disproved it when I awoke from my slumbers next morning hungry as a wolf. The best night train in Germany was over two hours late, so I knew I would miss my connection for Budapest. That, however, was a minor detail beside the question of food. Rather hopelessly, I asked the porter.

"Oh, yes, sir," he answered brightly. "We switched one on early this morning. Last car in the rear."

Electrified, I lightly trod a long series of cars until I reached the diner. Of course, I knew in advance that I would get nothing more than rolls, butter, and imitation coffee. Still, after two months in Germany, that didn't faze me. Blithely I took out my food-cards; and, since I was a bit ahead of the game, I recklessly tore off a double allowance of butter. About this time the waiter came up. He looked at my pile of coupons and shook his head.

"Sorry, sir," he announced, "but we have no butter— and no rolls either; just sliced bread."

"All right," I sighed, "bring me some honey or a bit of jam."

"Sorry, sir," came the reply, "you're a bit late, so the honey and jam are also out."

My famous breakfast thus whittled down to three slices of dry bread dipped in the *Ersatz* mixture which German wits have dubbed *West-Wall Coffee* because it is "untakeable"!

The best night train in Germany pulled into Vienna nearly three hours late. I had a seven-hour lay-over before the next train for Budapest, Hungary, left at six o'clock that evening. The day was cold and foggy, and I was cold and hungry. I knew Vienna well of old, and had been there a short time before, so I took a long walk to get a bit of exercise and finally dropped into a little place I remembered to get an early lunch.

An hour before train-time I ambled over to the station. That was certainly a good hunch, as events were to prove! First of all, I had to deposit my Reichsmarks before leaving Germany; and that took some time because I had to wait in line. The real trouble, however, developed when I turned in my ticket at the gate. In the waiting-room beyond, I glimpsed a tight-packed crowd of people.

"What's the matter?" I asked the ticket-taker.

"Passport control," he answered shortly.

"But I thought that was done at the frontier," I said in dismay.

"It's done this way here," he barked. "Move on! Don't block the gate."

With a bag in one hand and my typewriter in the other, I charged the rear of that crowd and wormed my way into the press. Craning my neck, I glimpsed two officials examining passports behind a long table. Just two of them to handle that mob! And how leisurely they were about it! Slowly they scanned each passport thrust into their faces by frenzied hands, making copious notes and asking questions from time to time. Dismayed at this deliberation, I glanced at the station clock and saw it was a quarter before six. Gradually I forged to the front, and one of the officials took my passport, scanned it, and gave it his O.K. With four minutes to spare, I hastened to the train and found a compartment. Leaning out of the window, I hailed the conductor.

"How long will the train be delayed for all those folks back there in the control room?" I queried.

He looked at me severely. "We leave at six sharp," was his crisp reply.

Sure enough, on the hour, he blew his whistle and the train started, with unfortunates running vainly down the platform in its wake. I hate to think of the number left behind, forced to spend a night in a strange town, perhaps with insufficient funds, and very likely with families anxiously wondering what had happened to them, since no private telegrams can be sent across the border.

This train was fast and kept to schedule. It is only about fifty miles from Vienna to the Hungarian frontier, and the interval was occupied by inspections from various officials examining your luggage, checking up on your money, and giving your passport the once-over a second time.

Until we reached the border, of course, the windows were kept tightly curtained. Then the train stopped, started, stopped once more. Cautiously I peeked past a corner of the curtain. We were in a brilliantly lighted station bearing the big neon sign *Hegyeshalom*. On the platform stood policemen and railway officials in strange uniforms. Through the uncurtained windows of the station I could see a restaurant with counters laden with foodstuffs. I was in Hungary—a land of peace and plenty! Standing up in my compartment, I gave three loud *Ellyens!* Which is Magyar for *Hooray!*

To enter Hungary from wartime Germany is literally to pass from darkness into light. The sense of this grew upon me with every kilometer the train made toward Budapest, the Hungarian capital.

First and foremost, a meal in the dining car which, accustomed as I had become to German fare, seemed a dinner fit for the gods: a big basket heaped with crisp, all-wheat bread, butter *ad lib.,* a meat entrée with sour-cream gravy, and so on down to a cup of good strong coffee. Such viands may not sound startling to American readers—but just you live a couple of months in wartime Germany, and you'll understand.

Another wonder was the approach to Budapest—a great city twinkling and sparkling with lights. To one fresh from blacked-out Germany, it seemed like fairyland. Then the taxi drive through brilliantly-illuminated streets thronged with Christmas shoppers lingering before windows filled with tempting displays—it seemed just too good to be true. A sound night's rest in an excellent hotel, followed by a breakfast memorable for such unheard-of delicacies as orange-juice, eggs, and coffee with whipped cream completed my sense of liberation.

At first sight, therefore, neutral Hungary seemed as peaceful and normal as America. But of course I realized that Hungary does not enjoy our blessed isolation, set as it is squarely in the midst of war-torn Europe. How far had its everyday life been affected by the storm raging just beyond its borders, and what were its prospects for the near future? Those were the two questions I set out to investigate as I sallied forth from my hotel next morning and walked down a majestic promenade beside the broad river Danube to keep my first appointment.

I was glad to be in Hungary, not merely to get a vacation but also for professional reasons. Hungary is the key nation in the whole Central European small-state constellation, while Budapest is an ideal vantage-point from which to survey the entire mid-European situation, including both Germany and Italy. Since Hungary is neutral, you can meet all sorts of foreigners, including both sets of belligerents, and get their respective points of view.

During my ten days' stay I met and talked with a considerable number of important personalities, Hungarian and foreign, including the Prime Minister, Count Teleky; the Minister for Foreign Affairs, Count Csaky; ex-Premier Bethlen; Tibor Eckhard, an important Parliamentary leader; and other men prominent in Hungarian national life. Count Csaky was the only one among those mentioned whom I had not known in former days, and since the Magyars are warm-hearted folk who have the knack of easily resuming interrupted friendships, it was pleasant as well as rewarding.

One of the most charming qualities of the Magyars is their informality. This applies to all classes, and is due mainly to the fact that the whole spirit of the country is profoundly aristocratic. The Magyars consider themselves to be a master-race, innately superior to their Balkan neighbors. This may not be so agreeable for the neighbors, but it does promote good social relations and national solidarity among themselves, and is pleasant for foreign visitors. I never saw a Magyar with an inferiority complex. Nobleman or taxi driver, they respect themselves and one another, with neither condescension nor servility. That is one advantage of an aristocratic society, where each one knows just where he stands in the social scale. Hungary is thus almost exempt from those plagues of other lands—the vulgar ostentation of plutocrats and the ostentatious vulgarity of proletarians.

The apex of the Hungarian social pyramid is the aristocracy. It is a real aristocracy, and it effectively runs the country. This ruling class is not confined to the titled nobility; it includes likewise the very numerous gentry. Those two groups have a strong sense of mutual cohesion, best exemplified by the way they habitually address one another in the familiar second-person singular —the Magyar equivalent of the German *Du*.

Though Hungary was outwardly normal, I found it inwardly nervous, as was natural when one considers its ticklish international situation. All the personalities with whom I conferred chatted freely but asked me not to quote them directly.

One thing they all agreed on—the Magyars are thoroughly at peace among themselves. Imminent dangers from abroad have united an instinctively patriotic people. Domestic politics stand adjourned, and the existing Government appears to have not only popular support but also popular confidence in its ability to guide the nation safely and to further its best interests. Although the Hungarian army was on a war-footing while I was there, there had been no general mobilization. In the capital itself I saw relatively few soldiers. The bulk of the troops were massed to the north and east, along the most immediately-threatened frontiers. This absence of soldiers from the capital was, in itself, strong evidence of the domestic calm which prevails. Everyone assured me that the local Nazi movement, formerly so strong as to be dangerous, had greatly lessened since the beginning of the war, and that its leaders were discredited.

Hungary is an agricultural country, producing in abundance all the staple foodstuffs with large surpluses for export. Imported foodstuffs, however, were becoming scarce. This was chiefly due to foreign exchange difficulties. The Hungarian currency was still steady, but wartime expenses were a heavy burden on the treasury, and a prudent Government was taking no chances. So imports of all kinds were being curtailed. This hit the average citizen in such matters as coffee and clothing. The Hungarians are great coffee-drinkers, and any sudden deprivation of this cherished beverage would be keenly felt. The Government was therefore rationing coffee in indirect ways, chiefly by putting on a stiff war-tax and limiting sales. When I was there, you could get a cup of coffee, but at twice the former price. The Government had likewise forbidden the importation or manufacture of pure wool cloth. This, however, hit only the richer people who could afford all-wool clothing.

The re-exportation of imported articles was forbidden, and this ban was strictly enforced. People told me gleefully about one recent instance. It seems that a group of visiting German business men loaded themselves down with all sorts of things forbidden in the Fatherland, from Brazilian coffee to American shaving creams and toothpastes. At the border, the Hungarian customs officials spotted the loot and promptly confiscated it!

This little incident brings up one of the burning questions which agitate the Hungarian people—their relations with Germany. In normal times, the economic ties between Hungary and the Reich are not only close but mutually beneficial. Germany, especially since the annexation of adjacent Austria, offers the best natural market for Hungarian foodstuffs and other raw materials, while Germany is able to supply Hungary with manufactured articles on unusually favorable terms.

But today, conditions are not normal. German industry has been so disrupted by the war that it can no longer supply Hungary with the quantity and quality of manufactured goods desired along many lines. On the other hand, German needs for Hungarian produce grows by leaps and bounds. This wide gap between deman and supply has caused growing economic tension between the two nations, with important political implications. The Hungarians have no intention of allowing themselves to fall wholly into Germany's economic sphere. They know that, should this happen, they would soon be sucked dry by wartime Germany's pressing economic needs, with no commensurate benefit to themselves. That is what has happened to the German protectorate of Bohemia-Moravia, and what may happen with Slovakia. The canny Magyars do not want to follow suit.

However, Hungary is in no position to take too stiff an attitude towards its giant neighbor. So long as Germany can obtain considerable quantities of food and industrial raw materials from Hungary under existing arrangements, it is to the interest of the Germans to have Hungary remain neutral and peaceful. The more normal Hungarian life is, the better its economic system will function and the more it will produce. But Germany demands a large share of the resultant surplus, even though the Reich cannot momentarily pay for it by a full exchange of goods. The Hungarians know that they must meet the Germans halfway or risk most unpleasant consequences. So they continue to sell largely to the Reich, despite the fact that it means a further increase of German debit balances. They feel that a disguised tribute is worth the price, so long as it is kept within bounds. As one Hungarian statesman remarked to me candidly, "We know it means piling up more blocked Marks; but—better get Marks than soldiers!"

None of the Hungarians I talked to seemed to me pro-German. But neither did any of them sound pro-Ally. England was strongly criticized for the way she was even then holding up goods destined for Hungary on ships stopped by the British naval blockade. They all wanted to keep out of the war if it were humanly possible, and expressed no strong ideological preferences. Mainly, they thought the outcome of the war highly uncertain, with complete victory unlikely for either Germany or the Allies.

One eminent personage—remember I am under obligation to give no obvious clues as to identity—expressed this viewpoint as follows: "The chances are that the military stalemate in the West indicates that *this* war will end in a draw. But such a peace may be only a truce, followed by another war in the not-distant future. It may be twenty or thirty years before our poor old continent can find a genuine settlement. There are so many problems to be solved—for instance, the problem of Russia, which has recently become even more complicated. Britain does not seem to realize that eighty million Germans in the heart of Europe must be given some hope of an adequate future. Until they get it, they will make continual trouble, even though the Allies win the war and Germany is carved up. The greatest ultimate danger in this war, should it be unduly prolonged, is the degradation of the German standard of living to the full Russian level. In that case, we might see those two peoples really get together permanently—which would be a frightful danger for Western civilization. But few Englishmen visualize this, and even fewer Frenchmen. The French, in particular, seem to want to 'finish up Germany'—which is, of course, impossible."

The only prominent person I talked with who thought an Allied victory almost certain was equally pessimistic about the ultimate consequences. The reason for his pessimism was that he thought the Germans would hold out so long that victors and vanquished alike would be ruined and sink into common anarchy.

Another political leader gave me some interesting sidelights on Hitler and his foreign policy. This man had first become acquainted with the future Fuehrer at the very start of his political career. Hitler at that time appeared to my informant to be a fanatically intense, simple-minded man, limited in education and outlook. His chief criticism of Hitler was that, though the Fuehrer has since learned the technique of politics to a marvelous degree, he has not acquired a commensurate understanding of the larger aspects of what he does. According to my informant, Hitler made his great mistake when he got his agreement with Stalin, *and then* invaded Poland. If he had used the Russian agreement as an instrument of diplomatic pressure, the Poles would soon have had to do everything Hitler wanted, and there need have been no war.

What interests Hungarians most intensely in the field of foreign affairs is their relations with their Central European neighbors. In the peace treaties which followed the Great War, Hungary lost large slices of territory to Czechoslovakia, Jugoslavia, and Rumania; and of the inhabitants of those lost lands at least 3,000,000 were Magyars. To get back the lost blood-brothers has been the absorbing passion of this supremely patriotic folk. They did so in large part, as far as their claims against Czechoslovakia were concerned, when that country was conquered by the Germans and Hungary was awarded a share. Hungary has, for the time being, soft-pedaled claims against Jugoslavia, because both countries now want peace in Central Europe for various reasons. Hungary's chief goal is to recover the Magyars of mountainous Transylvania, which she lost to Rumania. That remains a burning issue in all Magyar hearts. One of the most powerful organizations in Hungary today is the Revisionist League, staffed entirely by Transylvanian exiles who work continually to bring about the reunion of at least 1,500,000 Magyars with their homeland. I conferred at length on this question with Dr. André Fall, the head of the League, and his colleagues.

There can be no doubt that Hungary would go to any lengths in order to recover Transylvania, if the opportunity ever presents itself, and its statesmen watch with lynx eyes each move on the diplomatic chessboard with this in mind. However, for the moment, they feel that this issue must be subordinated to the general situation, especially the danger from Russia which, they believe, menaces not only Hungary but the rest of the small nations of Central Europe, including Rumania itself.

It is the specter of Russia which haunts Hungarian minds. I could seldom talk politics in Budapest without having that grim topic bob up. Most Hungarians believe that Stalin has his eyes on Central Europe and plans to strike for its domination. Some think the attack will come soon. And it is generally agreed that such a Russian onslaught would set all Central Europe in flames.

Fear of Russia is nothing new for the Magyars. Before the Great War, Czarist Russia set itself up as the Big Brother to the Slav peoples of Central Europe and the Balkans, and the ultimate goal of that policy was a great "Pan-Slav" federation with Russia as its natural head. But that would have spelled the destruction of Hungary. The Magyar race, brave, energetic, but not very numerous, stands midway down the Danube valley, thereby separating the Slavs of the north and east from those to the west and south. Should the Pan-Slav ideal ever be realized, the Magyars would be practically obliterated.

When Russia went Bolshevik during the Great War, Pan-Slavism gave place to the Communist policy of World Revolution. That, however, didn't end the feud between Russians and Magyars. Indeed, war-torn Hungary was presently overrun by Bolshevik agents who put over a local Communist revolution headed by the notorious Bela Kun. This Communist regime was soon overthrown by Admiral Horthy who formed a conservative government that has ruled Hungary ever since.

That was a body-blow to Soviet Russia which has never been forgotten. Moscow regards conservative Hungary and its aristocratic rulers as a bulwark of reaction, and would like nothing better than to encompass its overthrow.

So long as Russia was shut away from Central Europe by a strong Polish buffer state, Hungary had little to fear from Moscow. But the partition of Poland between Soviet Russia and Nazi Germany at the beginning of the present war gave the Soviets a common frontier with Hungary. This was an ominous change for the Magyars. To be sure, the new frontier ran along the crest of the rugged Carpathian Mountains, and was thus easy to defend. But further eastward the Carpathians become Rumanian. There we touch the thorny question which not only embroils Rumania and Hungary, but prevents them from combining effectively against the Russian peril which menaces them both.

Hungarian leaders with whom I talked admitted that this inability of Hungary and Rumania to pursue a common policy against possible Russian aggression might ultimately be fatal to both of them. But such an understanding was impossible without a prior settlement of the Transylvanian question in a sense favorable to Hungarian aspirations. As one eminent personage frankly put it to me: "No Hungarian Government could openly aid Rumania unless Transylvania were first ceded. The people would tear any statesman to pieces who did that. A benevolent neutrality would be the utmost we could risk."

Russia has had a bone to pick with Rumania ever since the latter seized the province of Bessarabia while Russia was in the throes of revolution. Russia has never

reconciled herself to Bessarabia's loss and would undoubtedly like to get it back again. Some of my Magyar
informants did not think that Russia would make war
on Rumania merely to recover this province. An invasion of Bessarabia would therefore imply the first step
toward the larger goal of Balkan domination.

Few Hungarians thought that Rumania could long
defend itself against Russia single-handed. They had a
poor opinion of the Rumanian army and considered the
internal situation most unstable. As one personage put
it: "Just now, everything in Rumania depends on one
man—King Carol. Should he disappear, anything might
happen." Furthermore, there seemed good reason for
believing that, the instant Russia struck from the east,
Bulgaria would strike from the south to recover her
lost province of Dobrudja, likewise taken by Rumania
as a war prize. Should Rumania collapse suddenly, like
Poland, Russian armies might rapidly occupy Transylvania, a natural fortress from which they would domi-
nate the Danube valley.

That is the supreme peril which threatens Hungary.
And the Magyars assured me that, to avert that danger,
they are ready to fight even against the longest odds.
If Russia should stop short with Bessarabia, Hungary
might not move. But the instant Russian troops went
further, the Hungarian army would strike to occupy
Transylvania. At the start, at least, this would spell war
against Rumania rather than against Russia. But the
Magyars would regard this as a preventive occupation
to forestall a Russian invasion. If Hungary should sit
still, it would soon be at Russia's mercy, because its
present eastern frontier is an arbitrary line drawn across

open country which could not be defended against a powerful opponent.

Should Hungary occupy Transylvania under those circumstances, imagine the diplomatic tangle which would ensue! Britain and France have given Rumania a guarantee treaty similar to the one they gave Poland. They sidestepped Stalin's occupation of eastern Poland because they didn't then want to fight Russia. But could they ignore a direct Russian attack upon Rumania? And if they did declare war on Russia, what would they do when Hungary committed an act of war against Rumania—in order the better to fight Russia—against whom Britain and France had at least technically begun hostilities?

At first sight it might look as though Hungary would be courting almost certain destruction to fling itself single-handed at the Russian colossus. The Magyars, however, feel they would not stand alone. They believe Mussolini could not tolerate Russian domination of the Balkans and Central Europe. Therefore Hungary counts upon Italian aid. Indeed, I was informed from what seemed to be a reliable source that, even then, a large number of Italian planes and pilots were discreetly tucked away "somewhere in Hungary," ready for eventualities.

If Mussolini did what the Magyars expect him to do, we glimpse another amazing diplomatic tangle. Here we would have Hungary, Italy, Britain, and France, all fighting Russia. What would be the relations of this singular quartette amongst themselves? Remember that Hungary would be also fighting Rumania in defiance of an Anglo-French guarantee, while Italy would be at least nominally on good terms with Germany, her Axis partner but the Anglo-French arch-enemy.

Such were the diplomatic and military crossword puzzles with which my Magyar informants were busying themselves, those crisp winter days of my sojourn in Budapest. They were keen analysts, yet, somehow or other, I personally didn't believe that Stalin was going to put on the big show they were expecting—at least, not for some time. The main reason for my skepticism was that I had come straight from Germany. And two months of intensive study and observation there had made me certain of one thing—Germany didn't want to see the war spread to Central Europe and the Balkans. Why not? *Because that's where Germany eats.*

Most of the food and a large part of the raw materials which Germany can import overland come from precisely those regions. So long as the nations there are at peace, their economic life is fairly normal, and they thus have large surpluses for the German market. But the instant war breaks out there, exports to Germany stop. And it wouldn't help the Germans much if their armies overran the whole region, because it would be so devastated in the process that even German efficiency would need a year or two to get things running again as well as they run today.

That being the situation, can we imagine Germany standing by and letting Russia start something which, to the Reich, would be an unmitigated disaster? We know that Berlin and Moscow have a pretty definite understanding. It is almost inconceivable that the German Government cannot exert enough pressure upon Stalin to prevent him from carrying out a policy which, for Germany, might prove fatal.

Those, at any rate, were the arguments I put up to

Hungarian friends and acquaintances in the closing days of December, 1939. And, as I write these lines the following spring, they seem to be still valid. That, however, does not mean that Hungary can be sure of maintaining her neutrality, set as she is on the mid-European crossroads, with all its latent dangers. Small wonder that my Budapest friends tended to be nervous. The longer I tarried in that charming capital, the more I got the feeling that its peaceful and extremely congenial existence might be shattered almost any day.

Yet, for the moment, everyday life ran smoothly, and people made the most of it in the pleasure-loving Magyar way. On New Year's Eve, when all Budapest turns out for a grand jollification, I foregathered with newspaper colleagues at their favorite eating-place to celebrate.

It was an unpretentious place on the outside, but it had an inner room, the walls decorated with Magyar rural scenes done by local artists; enlivened by a gypsy orchestra. And how those Tziganes could play! The Old Year's final hours passed all too swiftly with good food, fine wine, witty talk, and much jollity. When the midnight hour struck, a chimney sweep appeared with his traditional broom made of small twigs, and each of us broke off a piece for good luck. After him came another man bearing in his arms a sucking pig. To assure good fortune in the coming year, everybody tried to touch the little animal, and if possible to pull its curly tail.

My friends and I then left for a promenade along avenues crowded with revelers, equipped with tin horns and rattles, wearing paper caps over their ordinary headgear, bedecked with badges, and waving streamers mostly in the national colors—red, white, and green.

There was plenty of inebriation, but it was all good-natured. Everyone was having a royal good time, and the weather helped—crisp, but not too cold, and with a light powdering of snow which gave just the right seasonal touch.

We ended up in an *Espresso Bar*. These characteristically Budapest institutions are small coffee shops where the delectable drink is made by driving live steam through pulverized coffee, which is then served in small cups. The process extracts every bit of aroma and makes a beverage strong enough to take your head off. However, it goes well after a big evening. One of our party, a young man from the Revisionist League, apparently needed it; for when we entered the place he announced in stentorian tones that he was a Transylvanian. Whereupon all hands, including the waitresses, applauded loudly and laughingly shouted: *Ellyen!*

New Year's Eve marked the close as well as the climax to my Budapest interlude. Shortly after noon of New Year's Day found me in a train-compartment, Vienna-bound. I own to a regretful pang as I recrossed the frontier; left behind me gay, friendly, neutral Hungary; and entered war's shadow once more.

Incidentally, I re-entered Germany equipped with sundry eatables—sausages, smoked and spiced; a precious kilo of butter; and a bottle of the best *baratsk*, apricot brandy, which is a Hungarian specialty. Those luxuries were to help out a bit in Berlin. But, for my immediate needs, I took along several large ham sandwiches. I wasn't going to go foodless a second time on "the best night train in Germany," with which I was to connect that same evening at Vienna. However, the laugh was on me. This time, the famous express *had* a dining-car!

XX. THE PARTY

"THE PARTY." THAT IS THE COMMONEST PHRASE IN Germany today. It denotes that all-powerful organization, NSDAP (National-Socialist-German-Workers-Party) which dominates, energizes, and directs the Third Reich.

Just what is the Party, and what are its relations with the Nation, the State Administration, and those numberless organizations characteristic of German life? That was one of the first questions I put when I got to Germany. Knowing as I did the range of official literature, I supposed I would be promptly handed a neat manual setting forth the whole subject in the meticulous Teutonic way. What was my amazement when the Propaganda Ministry informed me that no such manual existed, the reason alleged being that the system was more or less fluid and that changes were continually taking place.

Accordingly, I had to piece the current picture together, bit by bit. You never can be sure, at first glance, what is "Party" and what isn't. For instance, I at first took it for granted that all the Brown-Shirt S.A. and Black-uniformed S.S. men I saw were Party members. Presently I learned that this was not true; that many of them were candidates, qualifying themselves for membership by meritorious service. As for the organizations,

245

some are "Party," others "State," still others are intermediate, while one or two, like the National Labor Service (*Arbeitsdienst*), were started by the Party but are now under State control. It was all very confusing. Indeed, I frankly admit that even now I haven't got a wholly clear idea of the scheme in all its complex details.

The reason for this seeming confusion appears to be that National Socialism, though a revolutionary movement, evolved as a regular political party with a complete organization of its own, until, by the time it came to power, it had become virtually a State within a State. Instead of merging itself with the State, or vice versa, this separate organization has been maintained. Of course, all branches of the State are headed by prominent Party men, and their higher subordinates are usually Party members. Indeed, a man may simultaneously hold a State and a Party office. But, in such cases, both the offices and their functions are kept consciously distinct from each other.

When Nazis try to explain to you the interactions of State and Party, they usually say that the Party is like an electric motor running a lot of machinery. This motor is the great energizer. It revolves very rapidly and tries to make the machine go at top speed. The machine, however, tends to run at a regulated tempo, toning down in practice the motor's dynamic urge. The Party urges ever: "Faster! Faster!" The officials of the State Administration, however, charged as they are with actual responsibilities and faced with practical problems, act as a machine "governor," keeping progress within realistic bounds.

Dr. Robert Ley, head of the Labor Front, occupies

the post of Organization-Leader for the entire Party, and on this exalted phase of his activities his views were enlightening.

"Dr. Ley," I asked him in an interview, "for a long time I've been studying the various organizations you direct. I think I've learned considerable about them, yet I know I haven't got the whole picture. Will you explain to me briefly the basic principles underlying all of them? And will you also explain their relations to both the Party and the State?"

It was late afternoon. We were sitting in a cozy reception-room adjacent to the Doctor's study, in the restful atmosphere of tea, cakes, and sandwiches. For some moments, Dr. Ley sipped his tea reflectively.

"Let's see how I'd best put it," he said finally. "As to our basic ideas, they are very simple. First of all, the principle of natural leadership. By this we mean the proved leader who by sheer merit has fought his way up from below to supreme command. This is best exemplified by Adolf Hitler, our Fuehrer, whom we believe to be an inspired genius."

By this time Dr. Ley had fairly warmed to his subject. His gray eyes shone with enthusiasm.

"Our second principle," he went on, "is absolute loyalty and obedience. So long as a plan is under discussion, it is carefully weighed from every angle. Once debate is closed and a decision is made, everyone gets behind it one hundred per cent. But behind both those principles is a third which is even more fundamental. This is what we call the *Gemeinschaft*—the organic unity of a people, founded on identity of blood. Germany is fortunate in being racially united. That is the ultimate secret of our harmonious strength."

"Thanks for the explanation," said I. "Now would you mind going on and telling me how, on those foundations, you have built up the various organizations you direct, and how they stand to the Party and to the State?"

"Before I do that," Dr. Ley answered, "let me make clear what the Party and the State mean to each other. The National Socialist Party, as others have doubtless told you, may be likened to a motor which supplies the energy by which an elaborate machine is run. To change the simile, we may also compare the Party to the advance-guard of a column of marching troops. Its duty is to pioneer, investigate, make everything safe. The State, on the other hand, is the main body which occupies the ground won and puts everything in final order. One of the outstanding features of the Third Reich is that the Party can, and does, make all sorts of experiments which would be impossible for State officials, tied down as they are by legal regulations and red tape."

"Would you mind making that a bit more specific?" I ventured.

"All right," he said. "Take me, for example. I'm not a State official. I'm purely a Party leader whose duty it is to prepare such experiments and set them going. Within my field, I have almost boundless freedom of action. For instance, when the Fuehrer ordered me to put through the People's Automobile (*Volkswagen*) Plan, I got the large sums needed. Of course I am held rigidly responsible for results. If I botched a job, I'd immediately be called to account. But so long as things go right, I don't have to waste my time explaining to all sorts of people just what I'm doing. With us, it's efficiency that counts."

"Do your experiments always succeed?" I asked.

"Not always," Dr. Ley admitted. "And when, after a full and fair trial, they are found to be impracticable, we frankly give them up. Sometimes, again, we find an idea to be theoretically sound but, for one reason or another, premature. In that case we lay the idea aside, to be tried again under more favorable circumstances. But when an experiment has proved sound and workable, the Party presently hands it over to the State; which then, as it were, anchors it firmly into the national life by giving it permanent legal status. That's what has actually happened with the institution we call *Arbeitsdienst*—the universal labor service required of young men and women. It started as a social experiment run by the Party. Now, having proved itself out, it is a regular State matter."

"Which means," I suggested, "that the Party is thereby free to take up still other social experiments?"

"Exactly," he nodded. "And we have so many measures, not merely for bettering life materially but for enriching it as well. We believe the more work we give men to do, the more enjoyment we must give them too. This applies to all grades of persons, with recreation furnished them according to their abilities and tastes. It is not a leveling process—rather is it a grading process, putting people in their right places."

"To each man according to his abilities?" I remarked.

"Absolutely," said Dr. Ley. "We are always on the lookout for ability; especially capacity for leadership (*Leitungsfaehigkeit*). That precious quality confers upon an individual the right to an agreeable life, a fine mansion, and many other good things. But the instant he shows himself unworthy of his position, he loses them all and is cast aside. National Socialism plays no favorites. While princes and rich men have not been deprived of their titles and wealth, none of them have any prescriptive right to prominence in the Third Reich. If a prince in the Party (and we have them) shows capacity for leadership, he goes ahead. Otherwise, he stays in the background."

So much for this exposition of Party principles, from its organizational director—to be taken with the usual grain of salt between theory and practice. Now a few words as to the growth and character of Party membership, as gathered from various official spokesmen.

Down to January 30, 1933, the lists were open to all persons who cared to join. Up to that time the Party was fighting for its very life and every recruit was welcome. On that epochal date, the triumph of National Socialism became virtually assured. At the moment, its membership totaled approximately 1,600,000. These veterans, who joined while success was still doubtful and helped put it across, still enjoy a certain prestige faintly reminiscent of the "Old Bolsheviks" in Soviet Russia. The Nazi "Old Guard" hold most of the leading posts and are generally regarded as most trustworthy. This explains why one sees relatively few aristocratic types in the upper ranks of the Party today, because not many joined up before 1933.

Although a rush to get on the band-wagon began at once, the Party welcomed new members until the following May, when its ranks had swelled to 3,200,000— just 100 per cent. The lists were then closed to individual joiners, but were still held open to members of certain nationalistic organizations like the *Stahlhelm* until 1936, when the Party had 4,400,000 adherents. Thenceforth, accessions were rigidly scrutinized. In fact, applications were discouraged; the Party sought the man, rather than the man the Party. The rule now is that membership is earned only after two or three years' faithful service in some form or other. It takes an outstanding act of merit in Party eyes for a man or woman to be admitted in lesser time. Much of the unpaid work of the country, such as volunteer service in NSV (previously mentioned), Winter-Help drives, or food-card distribution, is done with this in mind. Exceptionally distinguished activity is required for such persons to rise high in the Party organization. Able technicians may soon land good jobs, but that is different from getting into the directing upper crust. I was told that less stringent rules had been in force for candidates from Sudetenland and Poland after the acquisition of those regions, and that the total membership now approximates 6,000,000. After all, that is not a very large figure in comparison with the 80,000,000 Germans who inhabit the Greater Reich. The Party is thus still fairly exclusive, though if we add the families of members, the Nazi bloc probably numbers close to 20,000,000.

Theoretically, any young man or woman of unmixed "Aryan" blood is eligible when they come of age, and it is from the ranks of youth that the Party strives to recruit its membership. However, even here candidates must have an unblemished record, from a Party standpoint, in the Hitler Youth, and must be vouched for by their local Party Group. Formal admission takes the form of a solemn oath taken in front of the swastika flag, with the right arm upraised in the Nazi salute. The oath consists of a pledge of unconditional obedience to Adolf Hitler and the Party, after which the neophyte subscribes to a long list of commandments, the first one being: *The Fuehrer is always right.*

From the rising generation, the Party thus selects for membership those young men and women best conditioned for its purposes. And from this already selected group is recruited the *Schutz Staffeln* (Defense Detachments), commonly known as the S.S. This is the Party's private army. Originally it was a relatively small elite section of the Brown-Shirt Storm Troopers. But after the Party assumed power the S.A. men were assigned mainly to routine patriotic duties such as collecting for the Winter-Help. The S.S., on the contrary, became the Party's mainstay in upholding its all-pervading influence and authority. I was unable to learn its precise numbers, but I understand its present strength to be at least 200,000, organized into regiments, brigades, and divisions, just like the regular army itself.

Furthermore, the S.S. serves as a training school for both the ordinary police force (*Schutz Polizei*) and the Political Secret Police—the dread *Gestapo*. All three allied organizations are headed by Heinrich Himmler, who built them up to their present efficiency and thus wields a power in the Reich presumably second only to that of the Fuehrer himself.

The typical S.S. man is tall and blond, young or in the prime of life, with fine physique enhanced by careful athletic training. As Nora Waln aptly puts it, he has "the daily-dozen-followed-by-a-cold-shower look." As he strides along in his well-tailored black uniform with its symbolic death's-head insignia, he is clearly cock-o'-the-walk—and he knows it. It is interesting to observe how civilians instinctively give him the right-of-way on the sidewalks or in subway trains.

These S.S. may in many ways be compared to the Janissary Corps of the Old Ottoman Empire. To begin with they are picked men—picked for fanatical loyalty to the Party, for health and strength, and for unmixed "Aryan" blood. Before attaining full membership in the corps they undergo rigorous training, Spartan in character, which is best characterized by Nietzsche's famous dictum: *Be hard!* Well-poised hardness both to self and to others is their outstanding attitude. When discussing with foreign residents some harsh or ruthless aspect of the Nazi regime, they would often say: "That's the S.S. mentality coming out."

As might be expected, the S.S. have a strong *esprit de corps*. Their pride in themselves and their organization is unmistakable. Every aspect of their private lives must conform to strict standards and is carefully supervised. For instance, when they marry (as they are supposed to do in conformity with the Nazi eugenic program), the bride must be equally "Aryan," must pass exacting physical tests, and is expected to attend special courses in domestic and ideological training. The pair are thus deemed well-fitted to play the rôle required of them and to produce plenty of children for that biological aristocracy which is destined to be the natural rulers of the Third Reich. In return, S.S. families are well taken care of. Two of the best housing developments I was shown in the Berlin suburbs were for S.S. households.

I understand that the *Gestapo,* or Secret Police, are equally well disciplined and looked after, but of course they are invisible to ordinary view. I recall an amusing instance on this point. Some time after my arrival in

Berlin I was chatting with a high Nazi acquaintance, who asked me casually: "By the way, how many *Gestapos* have you seen since you got here?"

"None—that I could recognize," was my reply.

He laughed heartily. "A good answer," he said. "And you never will—unless they want you to."

Well, there was one *Gestapo* that I did want to see— the Big Chief of them all—Heinrich Himmler himself. But I was told that seeing him was almost as difficult as getting an audience with the Fuehrer, because he systematically shuns publicity and is therefore journalistically one of Germany's most inaccessible personalities. Naturally, that made me all the more eager to interview him. I finally did, the very day before I left Berlin. It was one of those by-products from my enhanced popularity which I encountered when I returned from Budapest, and which was undoubtedly due to my having strictly kept my word regarding the Hitler audience. Journalistically, this was a clear "scoop," for I was told by the Propaganda Ministry that mine was the first interview Himmler had ever given a foreign correspondent.

Like so many of my experiences in Nazi Germany, the whole affair was quite different from what I had imagined. Off-hand, you would say that the redoubtable Himmler's headquarters would have a mysterious or even a sinister atmosphere. But it didn't. It is a stately old building, made over into offices. You need a special pass to enter, but I went with an official, so there was no delay. Ascending to the second story by a broad stone stairway, we were quickly shown the Chief's quarters, and passed through a suite of offices, light, airy, and tastefully businesslike. There, young men and women were busy with typewriters and filing-cabinets. If the men had not been in uniform, I might have imagined myself about to meet a big corporation executive. Certainly, there was no "police" atmosphere about the place, secret or otherwise; no obvious plainclothesmen, gimlet-eyed sleuths, or other "properties" of a similar nature.

When I finally entered the inner sanctum I was met by a brisk-stepping individual of medium height who greeted me pleasantly and offered me a seat on a well-upholstered sofa. Heinrich Himmler is a South German type, with close-cut dark hair, a Bavarian accent, and dark blue eyes which look searchingly at you from behind rimless glasses. He is only forty years of age—extraordinarily young for the man who heads the whole police force of the Reich, commands the entire S.S., and has charge of the vast resettlement program whereby hundreds of thousands of Germans from the Baltic States, Russia, and Northern Italy are coming back willy-nilly to their racial and cultural Fatherland.

Those are certainly three big jobs for one individual. How he does it all is hard to understand. But you get at least an inkling when you meet and talk with him. The longer you are in his presence, the more you become conscious of dynamic energy—restrained and unspectacular, yet persistent and efficient to the last degree. Also you begin to glimpse what lies behind his matter-of-fact exterior. At first he impresses you as a rather strenuous bureaucrat. But as he discusses his police duties, you notice that his mouth sets in a thin line while his eyes take on a steely glint. Then you realize how formidable he must be professionally.

It was this aspect of his activities that I first broached. "I certainly am glad to meet one of whom I have heard so much," was my opening remark. "Perhaps you know that, in America, we hear rather terrible things about the *Gestapo*. Indeed," I added with a smile, "it is sometimes compared to the Russian Cheka, with you yourself, Excellency, as a second Dzherzhinski!"

Himmler took this in good part. He laughed easily. "I'm sure our police organization isn't half as black as it's painted abroad," was his reply. "We certainly do our best to combat crime of every sort, and our criminal statistics imply that we are fairly successful. Frankly, we believe that habitual offenders should not be at large to plague society, so we keep them locked up. Why, for instance, should a sex-offender who has been sentenced three or four times be again set free, to bring lasting sorrow to another decent home? We send all such persons to a detention-camp and keep them there. But I assure you that their surroundings aren't bad. In fact, I know they are better fed, clothed, and lodged than the miners of South Wales. Ever seen one of our concentration-camps?"

"No," I answered, "I wasn't able to get permission."

"Too bad I didn't know about it," said Himmler. "There you'd see the sort of social scum we have shut away from society for its own good."

That was all very fine, but I felt that Himmler was hedging a bit. So I proceeded: "You refer there to criminals in the general sense of the term. But how about political offenders—say, old-fashioned liberals? Is any political opposition tolerated?"

"What a person *thinks* is none of our concern," shot back Himmler quickly. "But when he acts upon his thoughts, perhaps to the point of starting a conspiracy, then we take action. We believe in extinguishing a fire while it is still small. It saves trouble and averts much damage. Besides," he continued, "there isn't any need for political opposition with us. If a man sees something he thinks is wrong, let him come straight to us and talk the matter over. Let him even write me personally. Such letters always reach me. We welcome new ideas and are only too glad to correct mistakes. Let me give you an example. Suppose somebody sees traffic on a busy corner badly handled. In other countries he could write a scathing letter to the newspapers saying how stupidly and badly the police run things. A hundred thousand people who may never have even seen that corner might get all excited, and the prestige of both the police and the State itself might suffer in consequence. With us, all that man has to do is to write us, and I assure you the matter will be quickly righted."

Feeling this traffic simile was a bit ingenuous, I tried to lead him back to the point he knew I had in mind. I nodded sympathetically and said, "That sounds reasonable. But how about a political matter? For instance, take a man like Pastor Niemoeller?"

I felt that ought to bring some reaction, because the Pastor is poison-ivy to most Nazis. Only a few days before, one fairly prominent member of the Party had grown red in the face at the mention of Niemoeller's name and had hissed: "The dirty traitor! If I had my way, I'd order him put up against a wall and shot!"

Himmler took it more calmly. He merely raised a deprecating hand, replying: "Please understand, it was a political controversy which got him into trouble. We never interfere with matters of religious dogma." Then, after a moment's pause, he added: "If foreign attacks upon us in this affair would cease, perhaps he could be more leniently dealt with."

It was clear that Himmler didn't wish to discuss the subject further. His eyes narrowed slightly and a frown appeared above the bridge of his nose. Seeing there was nothing more to be gained on that line, I took another tack.

"Tell me something about the basis of your S.S. organization?" was my next question.

"The *Schutz-Staffel*," answered Himmler blandly, "represents the best and soundest young manhood of our race. It is founded on the ideals of self-sacrifice, loyalty, discipline, and all-round excellence. Besides being soldiers, the S.S. has many cultural sides. For instance, we have our own porcelain factory, make our own furniture, and do much scholarly research. When you leave me, I shall have you taken to the barracks of the *Leibstandart* here in Berlin, the elite regiment which guards the Fuehrer. There you will see the type of young manhood of which the S.S. is so justly proud."

"And now, Excellency," I went on, "a few words, if you will, about your resettlement policy?"

"That policy," replied Himmler, "can best be expressed in the words of our Fuehrer: 'To give lasting peace to our eastern borders.' For centuries, that region and others in Eastern Europe have been chronically disturbed by jarring minorities hopelessly mixed up with one another. What we are now trying to do is to separate these quarreling elements in just, constructive fashion. We have voluntarily withdrawn our German minorities from places like the Baltic States, and we shall do the same in Northern Italy. We are even marking out a

place for the Jews where they may live quietly unto
themselves. Between us and the Poles we seek to fashion
a proper racial boundary. Of course, we are going about
it slowly—you can't move multitudes of people with
their livestock and personal belongings like pawns on
a chessboard. But that is the objective we ultimately
hope to attain."

Himmler talked further about his resettlement policies, carefully avoiding the tragic aspects that they involve. He then returned briefly to the subject of his
S.S. At that point, a smart young aide entered and
saluted.

"The motor is ready, sir," he announced.

"To see the Life-Guards," explained Himmler. "I
certainly want you to get a glimpse of my men before
you leave."

So saying, the redoubtable head of the *Gestapo* gave
me a muscular handshake and wished me a pleasant
homeward journey.

It was a wretched day in late January, cold as Green-
land and with swirling spits of snow to thicken the
blanket already on the ground. As Himmler's car
reached the suburbs, it swerved and swayed ticklishly in
hard-packed snow-ruts. However, the S.S. man at the
wheel was a splendid driver and got us to our destination safely and with celerity.

Hitler's Life-Guards occupy the former Prussian Military Cadet School. The buildings are old, though well
kept up. The one exception is the swimming-hall, a
magnificent new building with a pool so large that I
judged nearly a thousand men could bathe together
without too much crowding. The Commandant—a hard-
bitten old soldier, small, wiry, and dark-complexioned,

in striking contrast to his young subordinates who were all blonds of gigantic size—proudly told me how it happened to be built.

It seems that the Fuehrer came out one day to see how his Life-Guards were housed. At that time, the swimming-hall was an old structure capable of accommodating only one company at a time. Hitler looked it over and frowned. "This is no fit place for my *Leibstandart* to bathe," he announced. "Bring me pencil and paper!" Then and there he sketched out his idea of what the new swimming-hall should be. And on those lines it was actually built.

Such is the "Party" and such are the men who control its destinies. What are we to think of this amazing organization and of its aggressively dynamic creed which so uncompromisingly challenges our world and its ideas?

One thing seems certain: The National Socialist upheaval that has created the Third Reich goes far deeper than the Fascist regime in Italy, and is perhaps a more defiant breach with the historic past than ever the Communism of Soviet Russia. This the Nazis themselves claim with no uncertain voice. Listen to what Otto Dietrich, one of their outstanding spokesmen, has to say on this point:

"The National Socialist revolution is a totalitarian revolution. . . . It embraces and revolutionizes not only our culture but our whole thought and the concepts underlying it—in other words, our very manner of thinking. Hence it becomes the starting point, the condition, and the impelling force of all our actions. . . . We are crossing the threshold of a new era. National Socialism is more than a renascence. It does not signify the return to an old and antiquated world. On the contrary, it constitutes the bridge to a new world!"

Outside of Germany, most persons seem inclined to think that the "new world" envisioned by the Nazis would not be a very desirable abode. However, that does not alter the fact that we are here confronted by a revolution of the most radical kind, and that its leaders are revolutionists from the ground up. Furthermore, though most of them are still relatively young in years, they are all veterans hardened by prolonged adversity and scarred from many battles. They are the logical outcome of the quarter-century of hectic national life which we have already discussed. In my opinion, therefore, both they and their movement may be deemed *normal by-products of an abnormal situation.*

To give one instance of the grim school wherein they were fashioned, let me cite an episode from my own experience. In mid-summer of the year 1923, I sat in my room at the Hotel Adlon, discussing with a German the deplorable position to which his country had then been reduced. I had just come to Berlin from a trip through the Rhineland and the Ruhr, where I had watched the passive-resistance campaign against the French invaders, seen the black troops, and studied other aspects of that tragic affair. Now, largely in consequence of that desperate maneuver, the Mark was slipping fast to perdition, national bankruptcy was at hand, and utter ruin loomed in the offing.

As my guest discussed the seemingly hopeless situation, he was visibly in agony. Sweat stood out on his forehead. Suddenly, his mood changed utterly. Flinging back his head, he burst into truly blood-curdling laughter, best described by the German phrase *galgenhumor* —gallows-humor. Still shaking with his macabre mirth, he leaned forward and tapped me on the knee.

"Millions of us have already died, on the battlefield and from the British hunger blockade," he chuckled. "Perhaps millions more of us will perish, and we shall surely be ruined. No one can tell what trials await us, and the world will do little to assuage our agony. But, no matter what happens, it will be mainly the weak and soft who will perish. Soon, the good-natured, easy-going, pot-bellied German will be no more. Dr. Stoddard, let me make you a prophecy. If this goes on, in about fifteen years you will see a New Germany, so lean, so hard, so ruthless, that she can take on all comers—and beat them!"

The desperate spirit of the cornered man I talked to on a long-gone summer day typifies merely one phase of the bitter schooling which made Germany's present rulers what they are. In post-war Britain, a phrase was coined to depict their English counterparts. That phrase was: *The Lost Generation.* But if that were true of the war-scarred youth of Britain, how infinitely truer was it of German youth! Well, those war-youngsters are now in the saddle. So what we see in Germany is—*the lost generation come to power.*

From the moment I first looked at those rulers of the Third Reich, I felt there was something about them which, from my American viewpoint, was—queer. As I analyzed them, I realized that it was a sort of twisted cynicism combined with a hard ruthlessness. And when I listened to their life-stories, I saw it could scarcely be otherwise. Most of them had entered the war as volunteers when they were mere boys. One, I recall, was only fifteen at the time; others were not much older. These burningly patriotic lads went through the hell of a losing war, culminating in crushing defeat. Then their abased spirits were given a savage tonic by joining the Free Corps formed to combat the attempt at a "Spartakist" revolution. Joyously, they killed Communists for a while. After that, some of them tried to go to college or into business; but few of them could adapt themselves to the life of the Weimar Republic which they hated and despised. Some of them went abroad, adventuring; the rest sulked and brooded until their ears heard a sudden trumpet-call. It was Nazidom's brazen clarion: *Deutschland, Erwache!* "Germany, Awake!" They listened to Adolf Hitler's oratory which stressed all the longings of their embittered hearts—and they fell under his hypnotic spell. Into the ranks of the Storm-Troops they went, with additional years of fighting as they killed more Communists and "mastered the streets." Then, at last, victory—and undisputed power.

Such, in a nutshell, are the Nazis, as I analyzed them. The rest, only war's awesome arbitrament can decide.

XXI. THE TOTALITARIAN STATE

WE HAVE JUST SURVEYED THE PARTY. IN THE LIGHT OF what we there saw, we can now more intelligently examine its relation to the State. Furthermore, we may observe the relations of both State and Party to certain aspects of German life not previously discussed, such as Law, Crime, Finance, Business, and Religion.

Before so doing, however, I will venture a few words of caution. Much of what I am about to say is so strange and so repellent to our mode of thought that the reader will very likely find himself in a sort of Alice-in-Wonderland realm of ideas, wherein almost everything seems upside-down from his point of view. He will therefore be tempted to dismiss the whole business as either hypocritical camouflage or arrant nonsense.

That, however, would be a shortsighted attitude. After months of intensive study and innumerable conversations with representative Nazis, high and low in the Party scale, I am convinced that the "Old Guard," at any rate, are for the most part, fanatical zealots. If the Nazi thesis were a dialectic screen hiding mere lust for power and pelf, it would never have converted so large a portion of the traditionally honest, idealistic German people. If the Nazi leaders were just a band of cynical adventurers, with tongue in cheek and wholly "on the make," it would be far easier to deal with them.

Yet, whatever may be their aims, they are quite unscrupulous in their methods. Hitler has proclaimed, times without number, that the end justifies the means, and his disciples consistently follow that frank gospel. The Nazis are thoroughgoing propagandists—the cleverest I have ever come up against. They have evolved a propaganda system which is all-pervasive, and at its head stands Dr. Goebbels, generally recognized as the greatest master of the subtle art that our epoch has produced. Nazi spokesmen will paint verbal pictures for you which may sound alluring. When I listened to them, I kept firmly in the back of my mind the thought that I must take nothing for granted. I knew in advance that the speakers would not hesitate to overstress or suppress, and that the upshot might be something which, though literally true, would be a partial and distorted one.

However, just because they do not hesitate to present matters in propagandist fashion, we should not jump to the conclusion that there is nothing solid behind the presentation. There is clever intelligence in the Party, and lots of painstaking thought has been devoted to elaborating its program and perfecting the ideas upon which the program is based. National Socialism is not a mere farrago of nonsense; somehow it hangs together— *provided you accept its premises.* That's the trouble with most argumentation. People ignore or slide over premises and then wrangle bitterly over conclusions.

With this little *caveat,* or admonition, let us proceed.

Nazi political theory stems from an intimate union of four distinct elements, each of which is conceived by them in a special (and, to us, highly unfamiliar) sense. They are: Folk, State, Party, and Leader. We have already mentioned two of these basic factors: the

Gemeinschaft, the organic unity of a people founded on community of blood; and the *Fuehrerprinzip,* the principle of Supreme Leadership, incarnated in Adolf Hitler.

In Nazi eyes, the *Gemeinschaft* concept is best expressed by the word *Volksgemeinschaft;* literally, Folk-Community. Note the difference between this and our idea of a nation. To us, a nation means the sum-total of all persons now living in the territory of a sovereign State who owe allegiance to it. The Nazi Folk or People differs from the traditional nation both in time and in space. Having a racial basis, its living members are links in a vital chain which includes both the dead and the unborn. Furthermore, all its blood-brothers are organically members, even though they live far from the political center of the Folk. Thus, persons of German blood throughout the world are presumed to have a sort of mystic tie with the Third Reich, no matter what their technical citizenship. On the other hand, resident Jews are not, and cannot become, full-fledged Reich citizens. They are merely Reich subjects.

As for the Party, it is officially defined as "the incorporation of the German conception of the State and is indissolubly bound up with the State." But note also this: "The Party does not owe its position to the State; it exists in its own right. Actually the present State existed ideally in the Party before it was established in fact." Lastly, the Party is itself incarnated and sublimated in the person of its supreme Fuehrer.

To Americans, these are, of course, strange concepts. To show the extent to which Nazi thinking differs from ours, take the title I have given this chapter. To my mind, *The Totalitarian State* is the best way to characterize for American readers a regime which controls, commands, and directs everybody and everything within its supreme authority. But Nazis don't like the term, and Dr. Erich Schinnerer, a specialist on Nazi jurisprudence, registers his objection as follows: "The relation between People and State shows how false it is to characterize the National Socialist State as a totalitarian State. A State which itself works for an end and is not an end in itself cannot in any sense be called a totalitarian State, in which the center of gravity has been shifted to the disadvantage of the individual. In such case the defenseless individual is confronted by an all-powerful State. But the National Socialist State exists to serve the People and therefore each member. Each German is a member of the whole and therewith called upon to co-operate in the life of the State. The term, totality, properly applies to the National Socialist *Weltanschauung,* which is embodied in the whole people and activates every branch of national existence."

How are we going to reconcile such assertions with self-evident facts? As I see the matter, it is just one more instance of what I have repeatedly pointed out in these pages: the wide discrepancy between theory and practice in the Third Reich. And the reason for that is clear. National Socialism is a *revolution* which is still in the emergency stage. Even though this emergency may have been largely self-made, it nevertheless exists. Unless conditions become easier, we may expect a continued regime of practical martial law, with most of the fine theories put away in moth-balls.

Anyhow, the Third Reich is a completely co-ordinated and utterly unified State, wherein every trace of the old Federalism which existed under the Empire and persisted in modified form under the Weimar Republic has been swept away. The Federal States have been abolished. In their place are *Gauen,* or provinces, which designedly cut across State lines with the avowed intention of making the inhabitants forget their historic local attachments. That was what the French revolutionists did when they abolished the provinces of royal France and cut the country up into Departments. This was done so arbitarily that the French Departments have never developed much vitality. The Nazis claim that they have avoided this mistake by laying out each Province as a logical region based on a combination of history, geography, economics, culture, and common sense.

Dr. Wilhelm Frick, Minister of the Interior, is responsible for the transformation of Germany's internal administrative set-up which has taken place under the Nazi regime. Dr. Frick is much older than his colleagues, though he does not look his 63 years with his lithe, spare body, and alert attitude. Furthermore, he has behind him a long career in the Government service dating back to the Empire. The administrative remolding of Germany is thus in experienced hands. His motto is that of all Nazis: *One Folk, One Reich, One Fuehrer!*

The logical application of the basic principles just discussed is perhaps most evident in the field of jurisprudence, especially on its criminal side. All legal differences between different parts of Germany were promptly abolished and a uniform procedure established. Far more important was the change in the spirit and character of the law itself. That profound change is well explained by its author, Dr. Franz Guertner, Minister of Justice, who says:

"National Socialism looks upon the community of the nation as an organization which has its own rights and duties, and whose interests come before those of the individual. When we speak of the nation, we do not confine ourselves to the generation to which we happen to belong, but extend that term so as to comprise the sum-total of the generations which have preceded us and those that will come after us. This view has found expression in the National Socialist doctrine: *Gemeinnutz vor Eigennutz*—The Common Weal before individual advantage. It dominates National Socialist policy, and its natural corollary is that the rights of the individual must be subordinated to those of the community. The protection enjoyed by individuals is not based on the assumption that their particular rights are sacrosanct and inviolable, but rather on the fact that all of them are regarded as valuable members of the national community, and therefore deserve protection. . . . National Socialist ideas on justice thus differ fundamentally from those which prevailed under the preceding regime."

Some Nazi ideas of justice do, indeed, seem to "differ fundamentally," not only from those in Germany under the Weimar Republic but from those today in force elsewhere. In the world at large, the accepted idea is that legal codes have two basic functions: to regulate human relations and to protect the individual citizen against arbitrary official action. The first is embodied in civil and criminal law, the second in bills of rights. Both of these Nazi jurisprudence throws into the discard.

Any act deemed deserving of punishment may be dealt with under the "unwritten law," described as "the healthy sense of justice of the German people." The penalty is meted out "by analogy" with those in the existing code. The aim is to replace the former concept: "No punishment except through law," with the novel dictum: "No crime without its punishment." Also, punishment may be retroactive. This has been especially common in political cases, where persons have been condemned by Nazi courts for acts done under the Weimar Republic which were not then illegal. Likewise, the definition of treason has been greatly expanded, and such cases are dealt with by the dread "People's Tribunal," whose proceedings are secret and whose judgments are usually the death penalty. In the Third Reich, political offenses are deemed the greatest crimes, and are dealt with most severely. No safeguards exist in such cases for the individual citizen. The Nazi concept that the collectivity must at all costs be safeguarded here attains its logical conclusion.

In the sphere of ordinary criminal law, Nazi justice, however severe, has undoubtedly got noteworthy results. Under the Weimar Republic, crime was widespread. Old American residents of Berlin have told me about the conditions which then prevailed. Burglaries, holdups, and petty thieving were common. The poorer quarters of Berlin were unsafe for well-dressed pedestrians at night.

Today, Berlin is one of the safest cities in the world for even the most prosperous-appearing person. The general blackout makes no difference. I remember how Dr. Froelich laughed when I asked him about this.

"You bet our streets are safe," he said. "And I'll tell you why. Any holdup or robbery during the blackout hours is punished with death. The case comes before a special court, and two hours after a verdict of guilty, the offender's head is off on the guillotine!"

Scanning the papers for local items during my residence in Berlin, I found that statement was no exaggeration. During my entire stay, I caught only a few instances of holdup cases, mostly bag-snatchings at subway entrances by young hoodlums who were caught in every instance save one. Holdup cases seem to be given a fair trial, judging by a case I read about which concerned a drunken man who accosted passers-by and ordered them to hand over their money. The first "victim" laughingly pushed the wavering inebriate aside, thinking it a bad joke. The second person accosted, a woman, screamed, and brought a policeman promptly to the scene. At the trial, a specialist on alcoholism reported that the culprit was too drunk to realize what he was doing. So he got off with a prison sentence instead of losing his head.

One reason why there is so little wartime crime is that, the very first day war broke out, the Government started a general round-up of all persons with noteworthy criminal records, who were thereupon removed from circulation in concentration-camps for the duration of the war. This was merely an extension of the indeterminate detention of habitual offenders which Himmler referred to when I interviewed him. The Nazis see no reason why society should be plagued by persons who have demonstrated their chronic inability to avoid committing offenses. And they stay in concentration-camps for life, unless the camp authorities are convinced that they are reformed.

The Nazis are robust pragmatists.

Nazi achievements in finance and industry are generally regarded as deep, dark mysteries abroad. To me, the answer is very simple: *An absolute dictatorship over an industrious, resourceful people.* That is the basis of everything that has happened. Let's see how it has worked out in detail.

First, how did they get the money for a colossal rearmament program, coupled with other expenditures on an equally lavish scale? Easy enough. "Money," in the sense of a national currency as distinguished from actual gold and silver, is anything a Government says it is— so long as the people will accept it as such. The Nazi Government said the Reichsmark was the sole legal tender, and the policeman on the corner stood ready to enforce that decree in every case. There was no alternative, because no German could legally export his marks and turn them into foreign currencies; neither could he hoard dollars or pounds sterling, because whatever foreign currency he held must be promptly turned into the treasury in exchange for marks at the official rate. Anyone trying to dodge those rules flirted with the death penalty.

The only way the rules could have been nullified would have been a general popular refusal to accept the official tokens in ordinary transactions. That would have spelled rebellion; and this in turn could have occurred only through a general breakdown of confidence, not merely in the value of the currency but also in the whole Nazi regime.

An important factor which has predisposed Germans to retain confidence in the Reichsmark is their general monetary attitude. The terrible inflation of 1923 which reduced the value of the old mark to zero, destroyed in German minds faith in money. Henceforth they regarded the currency as a *token* of value—what economists term "the right of action" whereby desirable property of all kinds can be obtained.

Of all this the Nazi rulers were well aware. They knew that the one thing which would immediately shake public confidence would be to start the printing-presses and turn out a flood of money, thereby precipitating a *currency* inflation similar to that of 1923, which remained a horror in German minds.

The Nazis foresaw another danger as soon as their huge spending program got fairly under way. This was a *credit* inflation. If the economic law of supply and demand were allowed free play, prices would go sky-high, and the Reichsmark's purchasing-power would drastically decline. So they clamped on a complete price-system. In previous chapters we saw how wages, salaries, goods, and materials are kept in line, and how everybody knows in advance just about how much they will take in and pay out. So money and prices were both kept stable in relation to each other.

How did the Nazis actually finance their ambitious projects with neither currency nor price inflation? They did it in a number of ways. Fluid capital was regimented and either invested according to orders or diverted into Government loans. Profits were skimmed off by drastic taxation. Above all, consumption was kept down and living standards were lowered by what I have called a process of *reverse inflation*. I have described the way Germans can find fewer and fewer desirable things to buy with their money except life's bare necessities.

The upshot has been that the German people have themselves financed astounding expenditures by literally taking it out of their own hides. But a heavy price has naturally had to be paid, and this price has become rapidly heavier, especially in the last two years. By 1938, evidence accumulated that the furious pace of Nazi *Wehrwirtschaft* (really War-Economy) was running into the economic law of diminishing returns and was likewise entailing serious physical and psychological overstrain in every class of society. We saw this in our surveys of the peasantry, the industrial workers, women, and youth. We can observe the same symptoms when we view another important figure, the business man.

How the Nazis regard business and have fitted it into their co-ordinated scheme is authoritatively set forth by Dr. Wilhelm Bauer, one of the head officials in this field. He says:

"The basis for all Government intervention in business in Germany is to be found in the National-Socialist conception of the relation between business and the State. According to our theory, business is subordinated to the State. Formerly, it was believed that the fate of the State and of the nation lay in business, for it was said that business was of such great importance and so powerful that it controlled the State and determined State policies. In the National-Socialist State the relation between business and State is just the contrary. Today the State or State policy controls or rules business. . . . This means that the State is not concerned with economic conditions as long as they do not conflict with the welfare of the nation. The principle of private initiative has been maintained. However, where it seems necessary to bring business into line with the welfare of the nation, the State will not hesitate to intervene and direct business into the desired channels. In Germany, contrary to the usual belief, we have no 'planned economy,' but rather a 'directed' economy if I may use such an expression."

A "directed economy" seems to me a good phrase which well describes the way things have gone with business in the Third Reich. Unlike Communists, Nazis are not obsessed by dogma; neither are they enamored of logic. Their aim is maximum efficiency for their cause, and they will not hesitate to do seemingly inconsistent things if they think this best calculated to get what they are after. They have no theoretical objection to private business, and they realize it will not function without profits. But only such business as benefits the State by being privately run is allowed to remain in private hands. As for dividends, they are limited to about 6 per cent. Taxation plus price-controls make it hard for any business to pay more than that. However, when a business does manage to jump those hurdles, excess profits are either siphoned off into Government loans or reinvested as officialdom directs. Meanwhile the average business man is so regimented and so increasingly enmeshed in minute regulations and general red-tape that he feels himself virtually a cog in a machine. This trend has been greatly accentuated since the beginning of the war. Like everyone else, the business man is "in the army now."

Business men obviously do not like either their present status or the economic trend, which moves towards an ever-increasing degree of socialization. But they feel helpless and are cagey in expressing themselves. None of those I talked to would say very much. Here is a sort of composite report on those conversations: "German business, though closely controlled, still gives room for private initiative and profit-making. Controlled capitalism best expresses what now exists in the Third Reich. That, however, probably represents an advanced stage of a trend which is world-wide, since orthodox capitalism seems everywhere in rapid decline. One good feature in Germany is that class-antagonism has been greatly reduced; employers and workers both have their rights, and are kept up to their respective duties and responsibilities. The war is especially deplorable from the business aspect. If long continued, it must involve a rapid sinking of living-standards which will entail the gravest economic consequences. However, a total collapse of the economic structure is unlikely, because in Germany today everything is closely co-ordinated. The outlook for private business is thus not bright."

It is a noteworthy fact that I sensed much more latent discontent in business circles than I did among workers and peasants. Fritz Thyssen's flight from the Reich and his open breach with the Nazi regime may be symptomatic of what other big business leaders inwardly feel. However, I think it unlikely that they will follow Thyssen's example. Most business men presumably share the belief, so general in Germany today, that defeat in this war would spell the subjugation and ruin of their country. Furthermore, they believe that defeat would be followed by either Communism or chaos; and from both eventualities they have everything to lose.

The impasse between the Government and the church is inherently the most serious in German life today. It cuts very deep, involving as it does a clash between two sharply contrasted ideals. It far transcends ordinary policies. Among extremists in both camps it arouses intense emotion and provokes attitudes which seemingly cannot be reconciled.

Unfortunately I have little to say on this important subject, because I had neither the time nor the opportunity to investigate it properly. To be sure, I have read background literature, but to attempt a discussion of the problem on that alone would not fall within the purpose of this book.

There are, however, a few highlights on the struggle between the Government and the church which I should like to mention. To begin with, like other aspects of the Third Reich, little of the struggle appears on the surface. The churches are open and are well-filled, with no overt hindrance on attendance or services. The official attitude is that succinctly expressed by Herr Himmler in the interview he accorded me: "We never interfere with matters of religious dogma." Indeed, when you try to discuss the religious question with Nazis, they are apt to wave it aside as an annoying issue precipitated by a few incomprehensible fanatics. The average Nazi seems to be neither anti-religious nor anti-clerical; he thinks that the Church has its place in his scheme of things. But, like everything else, it should fit into the co-ordinated pattern of the Third Reich. Whoever dissents from or opposes that must be broken!

That explains the intense anger of most Nazis toward Pastor Niemoeller. He took direct issue with the whole Nazi regime, including the Fuehrer himself; and when at first he was lightly dealt with, he became still more vehement instead of falling silent. The cup of his offending ran over when he received widespread support from bitter opponents of the Third Reich in many foreign lands.

That's as far as you get with Nazis on the Church question. And non-Nazis don't usually like to discuss the subject. If they are not religious persons, it annoys them almost as much as it does members of the Party. If they have strong religious convictions, it is for them a topic both personally painful and possibly risky to discuss with a stranger.

XXII. CLOSED DOORS

THE FOREIGN CORRESPONDENT IN WARTIME GERMANY often feels as though he were living in a vast wizard's castle not especially well furnished and with many inconveniences. But he is hospitably received and well treated. Furthermore, the house-rules are clearly explained to him by the guest-warden who has him in charge. Over most of the premises he is free to roam at will.

But, as he ranges its interminable corridors, he discovers certain closed doors. Some of them are locked and bear notices strictly forbidding entrance. The correspondent knows that any attempt to break in will, at the very least, mean prompt expulsion from the castle. He will have committed a flagrant breach of those house-rules to which he has agreed. Other doors, though shut, are not locked. If he peeks inside, his action will be regarded with disfavor and he may become suspect. Still other doors may be opened to him on special request, but the rooms within will be so shuttered and his inspection will be so carefully supervised that he will probably get a very imperfect glimpse of what is there. Finally, the guest-wardens will tell him about certain rooms which he is not allowed to enter, though the correspondent will have his doubts concerning the accuracy of such accounts.

Under these circumstances the correspondent will naturally not get a complete picture of this wizard's castle and its contents, though if he is observant and industrious he may see and hear quite a few things not intended for his eyes and ears. He will also piece out his fragmentary knowledge by chats with fellow-guests and by snatches of gossip picked up or overheard from the servants. If he stays long enough, he will acquire a fairly clear idea of what it is all about, though there are a few mysteries that he presumably will never be able to unravel.

The undertone of wartime Germany was grim. This was most evident in Berlin and reached its climax at its official heart, in and about the Wilhelmstrasse. At night, especially, the effect was eery. I know it well, for I lived just around the corner and often traversed the famous thoroughfare in the late hours. After nightfall the west side of the interminably-long block between Vossstrasse and Unter den Linden is closed to foot traffic. Red lights gave warning, backed by police and military guards in front of the Chancery, the Fuehrer's residence, and other official buildings, including the Foreign Office. The east side, where walking was permitted, was also guarded. As I walked warily in the blackout, I would often glimpse the looming figure of a gigantic *Schupo* standing motionless as a statue in some recessed doorway. Across the street, sentries paced their beats with heavy, rhythmic tread. For the rest, silence, save when a pair met. Then I might catch an interchange of deep guttural salutations. Two or three small blue lights, spaced at intervals, indicated the entrance to Ministries. Closed motor-cars might be seen entering or leaving the Residence by its semi-circular drive. Despite the stringent blackout, an occasional ray of light from curtained windows revealed intense activity going on far into the night.

The whole atmosphere of the place was uncannily mysterious. I sensed that, like every passer-by, I was intently watched by many pairs of hidden eyes. This I proved the first time I stopped for a moment to bend down and tie a shoe-lace. Instantly, a beam of light from a powerful electric torch shot out from across the way, to see what I was up to. I purposely tried the same trick on subsequent occasions, with the same result. This sense of intent surveillance was hardly pleasant. I was glad to turn the corner onto the "Linden" and slip into my hotel.

The doors most tightly barred to us correspondents were the military and naval zones. This was natural, and nobody could legitimately complain about what every nation does in wartime. During my entire stay in Germany no correspondent was allowed to get anywhere near the West-Wall, which is not a "wall" but what military men call a "position in depth"—a fortified zone extending back many miles from the frontier.

The other implacably closed door was that into the German-occupied area known as the Gouvernement-General of Poland. Toward the close of the September *Blitzkrieg* campaign, a large party of journalists were taken to Poland on a tour of observation which had its climax with Hitler's triumphant entry into Warsaw. Then the portals were slammed shut and triple-barred.

One American special correspondent, Kenneth Collings, did defy the rules and brought out an exciting story; but he had a very rough time of it and nearly got shot as a spy. Also he had to get out of Germany immediately thereafter.

Berlin buzzed with rumors about conditions in Poland, but I never talked with anyone who had actually been in Poland except Dr. Junod, the Red Cross official already mentioned, and a German whom I met casually on the train from Berlin to Vienna in the Christmas season. My chat with him was too brief to get much information, but he did show me a whole sheaf of special permits he needed there as manager of a factory which had been taken over by the Germans. They revealed an incredibly regimented life. He needed a permit (*Ausweis*) to be on the streets after 8.00 p.m.; to drive a car at all, and another to drive at night; also at least a dozen others, some of these being to get raw materials and shipping privileges. Jokingly, I asked him whether he didn't need an *Ausweis* to kiss his wife. He laughed and said: "Not yet, but it may come to that!"

Some of the rumors around Berlin were very lurid. One of the most persistent which went the journalistic rounds was that the Nazis were systematically killing off all troublesome Poles; that *Gestapo* and S.S. men went from village to village, rounding up those denounced by resident secret agents and machine-gunning them into a common grave which the victims had been previously forced to dig. I mention this, not to assert its credibility, but to present a picture of the rumor and gossip which are passed around when authentic news is unobtainable. The general impression among foreign journalists in Berlin was that rough work was going on in Poland. If that was an unjust inference, it's the Nazis' own fault for keeping out reliable neutral observers who could have written objective, unbiased accounts.

So much for locked doors. Now for those, normally shut, but which you might enter under special circumstances. Outstanding in this category is the Protectorate of Bohemia-Moravia. You need a special card to go there. I obtained one but never used it because I couldn't take the time to make such a trip worth while. Any journalist who arrives in Prague chaperoned by the German authorities doesn't see or learn much. He is thereby suspect, and no patriotic Czech will dare come near him. Even when you have proper introductions you must proceed cautiously in making your contacts, chiefly so as not to betray those you want to meet. And that means quite a long stay.

I got a certain amount of first-hand information from foreigners who had been there and on whom I could rely. Naturally, I cannot disclose their identity. They told me that the German army and regular civil functionaries had behaved fairly well and wanted to reconcile the Czech population by tactful treatment. Most of the troubles which occurred were due to the Party, especially to young local Nazis, many of whom grossly abused their authority. I was told that the student riots of late October were repressed with excessive severity and much cruelty. The number formally executed was probably not greatly in excess of that officially announced, but many were so badly beaten up by the S.S. that they died in consequence, while the number of those deported to concentration camps in Germany was very great.

I was likewise informed that the suppressed hatred of the Czechs, especially toward the local Germans, was gruesome; that even the Czech women kept carving knives sharp to stick into the bellies of Teutonic neighbors if the right time ever came. My informants had heard that large quantities of small-arms and machine-guns were safely hidden in various parts of the Protectorate, making possible effective guerilla warfare, should the German armies be defeated at the front and the Reich show signs of cracking. However, the Czechs are a disciplined people, too canny to rise prematurely and thereby expose themselves to the terrible vengeance they know would be in store. Hence, though the Protectorate may be a potentially eruptive volcano, the fires are well banked and little should immediately take place.

Most interesting among the closed doors through which one may take a peek are those labeled *Unrest* and *Jews*. I have already remarked that, while militant discontent with the Nazi regime undoubtedly exists in Germany, it is probably not as widespread as is often alleged by exiles. *Organized* unrest has burrowed so deeply underground that foreigners know almost nothing tangible about it. A few long-resident journalists seem to have direct contacts, but of course they cannot write on the subject; neither do they give out much specific information. This is wise, both for their own sakes and to avoid all possibility of implicating "inside" informants.

The most reliable information I got at first-hand on the condition of the Jews was from two Jewish families to which I bore introductions. One was formerly wealthy, the other had been well-off. Both were living in reduced circumstances. Their properties were impounded and managed by quasi-public institutions, though they received enough from the incomes to manage decently. At one of these homes I was surprised to meet "Aryans" of standing who expressed no apprehension in consequence of having kept up friendly relations with my hosts.

I was told that, while the situation of the 20,000 Jews still in Berlin was a hard and distressful one, there had been no organized violence against them since the great synagogue-burning riots of November, 1938. Jews were occasionally beaten up or otherwise mistreated; several instances had occurred after the Munich attempt on Hitler's life. But my informants said they thought such acts were due to the initiative of Party subordinates rather than to official policy.

The most difficult aspect of their existence arose from the continual limitations and discriminations which they suffered. The majority of stores, shops, and restaurants have entrance signs which read: *Jews Not Wanted,* or *Jews Not Allowed to Enter.* These prohibitions are widely enforced; so it is difficult for Jews to shop or get a meal away from home. They are, however, allowed to register with local tradesmen and legally to enter within certain hours. Jews are given regular food-cards, but no clothing cards were issued to them while I was in Berlin.

All Jews must carry about with them a special identity-card which must be produced whenever required by anyone authorized to demand it. They are not supposed to go to the central portions of the city, and I never saw one on the Wilhelmstrasse, Unter den Linden, or adjacent sections. Jews may not legally be out of their houses after 8.00 P.M.; nor can they go to ordinary places of amusement at any time.

The Jews naturally find such a life intolerable and long to emigrate. But that is most difficult because they can take almost no money or property with them, and other countries will not receive them lest they become public charges. Their greatest fear seemed to be that they might be deported to the Jewish "reservation" in southern Poland which the German Government is contemplating.

The average German seems disinclined to talk much to the foreign visitor about this oppressed minority. However, I gathered that the general public does not approve of the violence and cruelty which Jews have suffered. But I also got the impression that, while the average German condemned such methods, he was not unwilling to see the Jews go and would not wish them back again. I personally remember how widespread anti-Semitism was under the Empire, and I encountered it in far more noticeable form when I was in Germany during the inflation period of 1923. The Nazis therefore seem to have had a popular predisposition to work on when they preached their extreme anti-Semitic doctrines.

The prevailing attitude toward the Jews in present-day Germany reminds me strongly of the attitude toward the Christian Greeks and Armenians in Turkey when I was there shortly after the World War. The Turks were then in a fanatically nationalistic mood;

and, rightly or wrongly, they had made up their minds that the resident Greeks and Armenians were unassimilable elements which must be expelled if they were to realize their goal of a 100 per cent Turkish Nation-State. To accomplish this, they were willing to suffer temporary economic difficulties of a serious kind. In traveling through Asia Minor I came to towns and villages where business was at a standstill, houses stood half-finished, and fruit lay rotting on the ground, because Greek or Armenian traders, jobbers, and artisans had been driven out and there were no Turks competent to replace them. When I got to Ankara, the new Turkish capital in the heart of the Anatolian plateau, I took the matter up with Mustapha Kemal and other Nationalist leaders. In all cases, their answer was substantially the same.

Here was their line of argument: "We know what we are now undergoing, and what bad repercussions our policy may have on world public opinion. But we feel it is a vital national task. We believe that the Greeks and Armenians are aggressively alien elements, who monopolize many aspects of our national life. The more they prosper, the more harmful they become. By suddenly driving them out, we may have to suffer economically for ten, twenty, or even thirty years, until we have produced from our own people competent artisans and business men. What is that in the life of a nation? Under the circumstances, it is a price we are ready to pay."

In Nationalist Turkey, the determination to eliminate the Greeks and Armenians was motivated mainly by political and economic considerations. In Nazi Germany, the resolve to eliminate the Jews is further exacerbated by theories of race. The upshot, in Nazi circles, is a most uncompromising attitude. If this is not oftener expressed, the reason is because they feel that the issue is already decided in principle and that elimination of the Jews will be completed within a relatively short space of time. So, ordinarily, the subject does not arise. But it crops up at unexpected moments. For instance, I have been stunned at a luncheon or dinner with Nazis, where the Jewish question had not been even mentioned, to have somebody raise his glass and casually give the toast: *Sterben Juden!*—"May the Jews Die!"

Can Germany hold out? That is the query endlessly debated whenever foreign observers chat together in wartime Germany. It's a fascinating topic because it probably holds the key to the vital riddle of who will win the war. Germany lost the last war chiefly through the strangling effects of the Allied blockade which starved both the German people and German industry to the point of general collapse. If the new blockade works equally well, Germany is doomed. But if history does not repeat itself, then Germany may at the very least keep its present supremacy over Central and Eastern Europe. And that, in turn, spells a qualified German victory.

This isn't news. It is a simple statement of fact known to every well-informed person. I certainly realized its importance when I went to Germany to study the situation. And throughout the months spent there I did my best to get the answer. Among other things, I hobnobbed with the best-informed neutral observers I could find—resident journalists from various countries, diplomats, long-established professional and business men. Many of these foreign residents were specialists with a wealth of technical information.

From what those men told me, plus my own studies and observations, I learned a lot. But I didn't get the conclusive answer I sought. The evidence was usually fragmentary and often contradictory, while the experts differed violently among themselves. Some said that Germany's situation was getting desperate and its outlook almost hopeless; others maintained that Germany could last indefinitely and had virtually won the game. Between the two extremes lay intermediate viewpoints. So I left Germany somewhat in the mood of Omar Khayyám who came out by the same door wherein he went.

However, though unable to offer an assured Yes or No to the riddle of German war-prospects, I think it is possible to state the elements of the problem and fairly summarize the evidence. By setting forth what is definitely known and what can logically be inferred from the known facts, we will be in better position to draw reasonable conclusions and interpret the meaning of current happenings as they take place.

Ever since Adolf Hitler came to power in 1933, Germany has been rearming at an ever-quickening tempo. The result has been the most tremendous piling up of war material that the world has ever seen. But even this huge rearmament program is only part of the story. Germany's whole national life has been systematically put on a war footing. The Nazis frankly call it *Wehrwirtschaft*—a military economy.

An outstanding feature of war economics is secrecy.

As far as possible, outsiders must be kept from finding out what goes on. So, from the start, any disclosure of information affecting the national interest has in Germany been deemed an act of treason, punishable by death. Thus every phase of German preparedness, military or otherwise, has been shrouded in mystery.

Under these circumstances we see how hard it is to get the facts. Such statistics as have been published are notoriously partial and unreliable. Take the available figures on German imports during recent years. It is an open secret that vast quantities of strategic raw materials and essential foodstuffs have been bought abroad for direct army account and have never been reported in official trade tables. It is likewise known that a large proportion of regular imports have gone into special reserves; but how much has never been disclosed.

Of course, since the start of the war no figures whatever have been published, so the mystery steadily deepens. That is the main reason why even the best-informed foreign residents in Germany come to such widely differing conclusions on German ability to carry on the war against the strangling effects of the British blockade.

Although we are thus faced with many unknown or partly known factors, it seems nevertheless possible to reach conclusions which will hit somewhere near the truth. Under these limitations, I shall try to analyze Germany's war situation. The analysis naturally falls under four main heads: (1) military; (2) industrial raw materials; (3) foodstuffs; (4) national psychology, usually termed *morale*.

It is on the military factor that foreign observers in Germany are in closest agreement. Nearly all of them are convinced that the German army is highly efficient and splendidly equipped. They likewise were agreed while I was there that so long as Germany continued to wage a defensive war on one front, the West Wall appeared to be impregnable to direct attack. That does not mean that the Allies could not drive in deep salients by sacrificing enough men and metal.

Incidentally, while I was in Germany, its full manpower had obviously not yet been mobilized. Everywhere I went, I noted great numbers of fit individuals who were not in uniform. Also, the munitions plants ran full blast throughout the quiet winter months—a fact I learned from unimpeachable information. This continuous piling up of munitions was a significant indication that reserves of essential raw materials remained ample. Bearing in mind the rapidity with which war material becomes obsolete, the munitions industry would have been unlikely to carry on at that rate if there had been any immediate danger of vital raw-material shortages. Unless, of course, those munitions were earmarked for quick use on a major scale.

This brings us to one sharp difference of opinion I encountered on the military situation. Some foreign residents thought that Germany was strong enough to risk a great Western offensive in the spring or summer of 1940, either directly at the French Maginot Line or down through Holland and Belgium. That is certainly what high Nazis implied when they boasted confidently of their ability to wage a short war culminating in complete victory. However, most foreign observers told me they thought the odds were distinctly against the success of such a venture, especially in the war's first year. Such an offensive, the most tremendous military operation ever undertaken, would entail not only prodigious loss of life but an equally prodigious consumption of war material. These objectors did not think Germany as yet possessed the economic reserves, especially of oil and steel, to carry through a complete Western offensive to a successful conclusion. At best, it would mean a supreme gamble, with speedy collapse as the penalty for failure. They therefore concluded that, unless Germany was economically in such bad shape that she could not hold out long even on the defensive, the High Command would be unlikely to risk everything on a single thunderstroke.

The obvious conclusion to be drawn from these conflicting viewpoints was that, if Germany launched a Western offensive in the current year, it would indicate either great strength or great weakness.

All this emphasizes the vital importance of the second factor—industrial raw materials. The tragedy of Finland dramatically shows that the finest army is helpless without abundant supplies of every kind. In the same way, the German army would soon be defeated if its sinews of war should be cut.

So far as industrial plant and equipment are concerned, Germany seems amply able to supply its armies, maintain its civilian population above the destitution-line, and do a considerable amount of foreign trade. An important part of Hitler's gigantic preparedness program has been the systematic development of heavy industry, which is far ahead of what it was in the last war. By including Austria and Czechoslovakia, to say nothing of occupied Poland, we find that Greater Germany's plant capacity is approximately 50 per cent greater than in 1913.

Factories, however, can no more run without raw materials than armies can fight without supplies. And modern industry needs a wide variety of materials drawn literally from the ends of the earth. Foremost on the list stand coal, iron, and oil.

Germany has plenty of coal within her borders, while the seizure of Poland's rich coalfields, gives her a good surplus for export. But iron is a grave problem, while oil is undoubtedly her greatest weakness.

Germany lost her only high-grade iron mines when she ceded Alsace-Lorraine to France at the close of the last war. Recently the Reich has been developing various low-grade iron deposits as part of its famous Four Year Plan for industrial self-sufficiency. Collectively known as the Hermann Goering Works, these enterprises are economically wasteful; but since they are frankly a war measure, costs are a minor matter. These new works are just getting into full production. Details are a State secret, though it is believed their output will be considerable. Still, they cannot supply more than a portion of Germany's needs, and their product needs mixing with high-grade ores to yield the best steel. A domestic source of high-grade ore exists in Austria, but the field is too small to be of major importance.

The German Government is combing the country for scrap. During my stay in Berlin I often saw workmen removing iron railings even from the fronts of private homes, while the public was told to turn over every bit of old metal to official junk collectors. This does not prove that Germany is today faced with a crucial iron shortage. It does mean, however, that the Government is looking ahead and is taking no chances.

There can be scant doubt that the Reich has built

up large reserves of iron, as of other vital raw materials. Trade statistics show that, during the three years before the war, imports of iron ore increased notably, while imports of scrap and pig iron jumped 300 per cent. Furthermore, as already remarked, there is the likelihood of large purchases made abroad for direct official account which would not appear on the commercial records. The chances are, therefore, that Germany began the war with enough iron on hand to meet its needs for a considerable time.

Still, Mars, the War God, has a voracious appetite for iron, while German industry, running at top speed, requires much iron and steel for replacements. This is especially true of the overworked German railways. Shortly before the war broke out, a large construction program was started to remedy acute shortages of locomotives and rolling-stock, and it is unlikely that this was entirely shelved.

Where is Germany to find the necessary iron supplies for all this? Under the most optimistic estimates, the Reich cannot cover more than half its needs from domestic sources. The balance must come from abroad. With the British blockade barring the ocean lanes, the only accessible large-scale foreign source is Sweden. Even before the war, Sweden's extensive high-grade iron mines furnished Germany with nearly half of its imported iron ore. Obviously, this vital source of supply must at all costs be maintained. When I was in Germany, officials clearly intimated that Germany would unquestionably go to any lengths if Sweden stopped or notably lessened the flow of iron ore upon which German industry and the German war-machine so largely depend. This is a major factor in Germany's invasion of Scandinavia which began as these pages are being written.

Perhaps, in the long run, Russia can help cover the Reich's iron deficit, if German technicians succeed in putting Russia on an efficiency basis, as is reported they are now doing. However, that is what Germans call "future music," presumably some two years away. Meanwhile, it is interesting to note that Germany still gets iron from Luxemburg. Even more interesting are reports that some iron from French Lorraine finds it way to the Reich, in exchange for German coke which the French iron mines need for effective operation. This contraband trade apparently runs through neutral Belgium and is winked at by both sides. Though the French Government has denied these reports, they are not improbable. Such exchanges occurred in the last war, and are an historical commonplace. Even across the hottest battle-lines, barter usually occurs when the mutual benefits are sufficiently apparent.

Germany's iron and steel problem, though serious, does not seem to be insoluble. Anyhow, an acute shortage is unlikely to develop in the immediate future.

We now come to the crucial problem of oil, the weakest spot in Germany's industrial armor. I understand that the Reich's normal peacetime consumption of motor fuel averages between five and six million tons. During the past few years Germany has made herculean efforts to reduce her dependence upon foreign supplies. From elaborate borings under Government subsidy, oil fields were discovered which stepped up production of domestic natural crude by at least 300 per cent. Germany likewise produces large amounts of benzol, a by-product of coke. Most important of all, new chemical processes have made possible large-scale extraction of oil from Germany's extensive deposits of lignite, or brown coal. It is estimated that, from these combined sources, Germany at the start of the war was producing motor fuels to an annual total of something like three million tons—about half her peacetime needs.

Germany is now at war, and if her war machine were operating at full capacity, oil consumption would be stepped up to at least twelve million tons per annum. But, until the invasion of Scandinavia at least, the oil-devouring *Blitzkrieg* occurred only at the start and ceased when the brief Polish campaign was over. Thenceforth, the war became a *Sitzkrieg,* which took very little oil. Meanwhile the most rigid economies have been practiced. Private automobiles no longer run; buses and trucks operate on a mixture containing some 30 per cent of potato alcohol, while a vast fleet of laid-up merchant ships burns no liquid fuel whatever. It is reliably estimated that, under such circumstances, Germany's oil consumption ran below the normal peace-time level.

But this strange sit-down war could not go on indefi-nitely, so Germany might at any moment be faced with oil consumption on a tremendous scale. Is Germany prepared to meet the strain? The Reich has undoubt-edly accumulated large oil reserves. For years her im-ports have notably exceeded current needs, bearing in mind her domestic output. In 1936, imports totaled 4,200,000 tons; in 1937, 4,300,000; in 1938 they rose to nearly 5,000,000, and for the first half of 1939 they ran over 2,700,000 tons, indicating that some 5,500,000 would have been imported if war had not broken out in September.

Those are the official trade figures, which do not exclude the possibility of further imports on direct official account. However, it is improbable that these could have been very large. Oil is harder to conceal and store than most other materials. While in Germany I heard rumors of vast hidden pools, but I am inclined to disbelieve them.

Whatever the size of the Reich's oil reserves, the blockade dealt a heavy blow by cutting off imports from North and South America, which averaged 80 per cent of the total. It is interesting to note that, in 1938, Rumania supplied Germany with only 700,000 tons of oil, while Russia contributed the insignificant item of 33,-000 tons. Yet it is precisely on those two countries that Germany must rely if she is to avoid an oil famine that would probably be fatal.

Rumania, of itself, can hardly solve the problem. The Rumanian oil fields are on the decline. In 1938, Rumanian oil exports to all countries were less than 5,000,-000 tons, and those exports were allocated by definite agreements not merely with Germany but with Britain, France, Italy, and Balkan countries as well. Despite much strong-arm diplomacy, Germany has as yet been unable to get Rumania to grant the Reich more than its agreed allotment of 1,200,000 tons. Incidentally, very little Rumanian oil reached Germany during the severe winter months when the Danube was frozen and barge navigation became impossible.

Should Germany invade and conquer Rumania, its oil fields would be at the Reich's disposal. Such an invasion, however, even though successful, might on balance do Germany more harm than good. Oil wells and refineries would presumably be destroyed long before the German armies could seize them, and it is estimated that it would take a year to get the wells into production again, while refineries might take longer still. Besides, the whole Balkan region might be plunged into war, which is the last thing Germany wants at the present time, since she would thereby lose a major source of foodstuffs and raw materials, at least for a considerable period.

The key to Germany's oil dilemma seems to lie in Russia. The Soviet's Caspian oil fields centering around Baku are among the richest in the world, with an average yield of thirty million tons. Most of this is consumed in Russia itself, but there is a large surplus, much of which might be shipped to Germany. The chief difficulty is transportation, either across the Black Sea and up the Danube, or by rail overland a vast distance and at great expense. There is also the possibility that Anglo-French fleets and armies, allied to the Turks, may cut the Black Sea route, and even destroy or capture the Caspian oil fields themselves. That would indeed be a body-blow to German hopes. In that case, their only feasible Russian source would be the Polish oil fields of the Russian-occupied zone, whose annual output is a scant 500,000 tons.

Germany faces other problems in raw materials, though none so serious as that of oil. Russia can furnish manganese ore in abundance—given time. Copper, lead, chrome, and bauxite (the basis of aluminum) are suppliable from Central Europe and the Balkans. Ample zinc has been acquired with conquered Poland. Nickel, tin, and some rare alloys have been irrevocably cut off by the Allied blockade, except the nickel mines of northern Finland; but it is well-nigh certain that Germany anticipated those contingencies by storing amounts sufficient for her probable needs. A rubber shortage is largely averted by German synthetic *buna*.

Thus, unless the German war-machine stalls for lack of oil, it looks as though the Reich could weather the blockade, so far as industrial war materials are concerned, until communications with Russia are perfected and its huge eastern neighbor gets into fuller production a year or two hence. Naturally, this implies that Russo-German relations continue on their present footing. Should Stalin abandon his pro-German policy, the entire situation would change and Germany's raw-material prospects would become dark indeed.

Now for the food factor. We have already covered that phase so fully in preceding pages that little more need here be said. Reliable information indicates that the almost unprecedented cold of the past winter has damaged or spoiled a considerable proportion of the Reich's stored supplies of potatoes, cabbage, and other vegetables. That is a serious blow. Besides upsetting the schedule of food-rationing for human beings, it will make far more difficult the maintenance of the Reich's vast pig population, which is fed largely on a potato and sugar-beet diet. If a large percentage of Germany's pigs has to be slaughtered, that will in turn worsen the fat situation, which is Germany's most acute dietary problem.

We now reach the fourth and final factor in our analysis of Germany's war situation and prospects. This is the element of *morale*. It is the most difficult of them all to assess, because national psychology lies in the realm of the "imponderables" which can be neither statistically weighed nor numerically tabulated. With so many unknown or uncertain quantities to deal with, the best we can do would seem to be the drawing up of a sort of balance-sheet, listing the respective assets and liabilities.

To outward seeming, the Third Reich is as formidably prepared psychologically as it is in arms. For seven long years, Adolf Hitler and Paul Joseph Goebbels, acknowledged masters of propaganda, have systematically forged a naturally disciplined people into an amazingly responsive psychic unison. The result has been that, behind the world's mightiest military machine, we discern an even more formidable psychic mechanism— an entire people, 80,000,000 strong, welded into a living juggernaut of Mars, wherein each individual has his designated place and functions as a regimented unit in a complex synthesis such as perhaps only Germans can devise and run. Human history has probably never seen its equal—and its efficiency has already been dramatically proven. No one can have studied wartime Germany at first-hand without being deeply impressed. Yet mature reflection suggests that so prodigious and intensive an effort cannot be without its price. That price is psychic strain. The German people have been toughened and hardened by a generation of adversity. In the last seven years they have been psychologically trained down fine, like a boxer preparing for a championship bout or a football squad for the big game of the season. The question is, Are they absolutely "in the pink," or are they a bit overtrained? As I watched the average German's dull reflexes, I could not help wondering whether I did not behold a people physically still vigorous but spiritually tired.

What the answer is, I do not know. Probably the future alone can tell. Personally, I think that German morale is strong—but brittle. To vary the simile a bit, I believe it is like a rubber band, which can be stretched a long way without showing a sign of weakness—and then snaps!

To show what I mean, let's see what happened in the last war. Down to its very end, German psychology was extraordinary. To avoid any appearance of partiality, let me quote a British writer who studied this very matter during those crucial years.

Says Harold Nicolson: "I remember how, in the last war, the magnificent morale of the German people as a whole rendered it difficult for us at any given moment accurately to assess the state of German public opinion. A special branch of our Foreign Office was created for the sole purpose of ascertaining the true conditions within Germany. This branch interviewed neutral visitors, scanned every organ of the German press, analyzed the letters from home that were found on dead or captured Germans. Not only did these letters contain no hints of any weakening in the national will, but the women who wrote to their men at the front very rarely complained of the fierce ordeal to which they were being subjected. It was only when the final crash occurred that we learned how terrible the conditions had really been. Throughout those four ghastly years the morale of the German people was superb. Their trust in their leaders remained, unto the very last moment, unshaken; their obedience to their government was uniform; no word escaped them of the sufferings which they were being made to endure." And Mr. Nicolson concludes: "It will be the same during this war. I am not among those who believe in some sudden uprising of the German people. It is not the width and depth of German morale which we can question. What we can question is its duration."

I substantially agree with this British commentator as to the existence of a definite and sudden breaking-point in German morale, though I think it as yet far away. Where I disagree with him is in his conclusion. Mr. Nicolson believes that history will surely repeat itself; that if the Germans are confronted with a hopeless situation, they will throw up the sponge and surrender unconditionally, as they did in 1918. This may, of course, occur. Yet, from my stay in Germany, I envisage a more terrifying possibility.

As I traveled through Germany, I frequently saw a slogan painted on factory dead-walls. It read: *Wir Kapitulieren Nie!* The English whereof is: "No Surrender!"

In *Mein Kampf*, Adolf Hitler asserts that Germany's collapse in the last war was due to a "stab in the back" struck by Communists, pacifists, and others "unworthy the name of German." This historic version has been hammered home until it is devoutly believed by all Nazis, including virtually the whole rising generation. They are systematically taught that Germany is unbeatable. Yet they are also taught that if, by some almost inconceivable mischance, Germany goes down, everything else should go down too, because life thereafter would simply not be worth while.

This catastrophic doctrine can be best explained to American readers as "The Policy of Samson." To Germans, it might be more intelligible as "The Spirit of Hagen the Grim." Let me explain what I mean, first by an episode from my own experience, and then from a sally into Teutonic folklore.

In that depressing German summer of 1923 I met a group of men who gave themselves the seemingly paradoxical title of "National Bolshevists." They looked most unlikely candidates for the part, because they were typical Prussian army officers, monocles and all. Yet they were dead in earnest. Here, in substance, is what they told me, referring to the "passive resistance" campaign then being waged against the French invasion of the Ruhr: "We know what France wants—to smash the Reich. And France may succeed. But even though the Reich vanishes, the German people remains. And the Germans would then collectively become a modern Samson; unable to free himself, yet strong enough to disrupt and destroy. Should this modern Samson bring down the temple of Europe, he will bury all European nations beneath its ruins."

I have not forgotten that conversation with desperate men. Neither do I forget the *Niebelungenlied,* probably the clearest revelation of the primitive Teutonic folk-soul. Richard Wagner has immortalized it in his *Ring* operas, which Adolf Hitler has proclaimed the supreme musical expression of Germanic genius. Now, in the *Niebelungenlied,* the "front-stage" hero is Siegfried the Glorious. But there is another outstanding figure, equally symbolic. This is Hagen the Grim. Hagen it is who, from fanatic loyalty, kills Siegfried and ultimately precipitates that general destruction termed *Goetterdaemmerung*—"The Twilight of the Gods."

Whether, in the last extremity, the German people will, or can, loose a general orgy of destruction, I do not know. But I think that it is possible. I certainly gleaned some dread undertones during my stay in the Third Reich. Two of the highest Nazis I interviewed hinted plainly that if Germany found herself with her back to the wall, they would not hesitate to precipitate general chaos.

However, despite this *furor Teutonicus,* there would seem to be some method in the madness. Most Germans are unwilling to admit even the possibility of defeat. Those who do, couple it with remarks which amount to some such phrase as: "If we don't win, there will be no victor." What that means is about as follows: "If this war is fought to the bitter end, all Europe will be plunged into chaotic ruin. Then, with everybody down in the ditch together, we Germans, with our innate sense of organization and discipline, willingness to work hard, and knack of pulling together, can lift ourselves out of the ditch quicker than anyone else." The moral whereof was, of course, that, no matter what might immediately happen, the Germans were bound to win in the long run.

Thus, 'twould seem, hope springs eternal in the *Hagen* breast!

XXIII. OUT OF THE SHADOW

RETURNING FROM WARTIME EUROPE TO AMERICA IS A journey from darkness into light. Not until the war-torn Old World has sunk well below the ocean's horizon do you breathe freely once more.

I came out of Europe the way I went in—*via* the Brenner Pass and Italy. It was essentially the reverse process to my entrance four months previous. The great difference was that, instead of mid-autumn, it was now the coldest winter in many years. I left Berlin on an evening of Arctic chill. The record cold wave was at its height. Frozen switches, iced signals, clogged steam-pipes, and a defective electric generator so disrupted the schedule of the usually smooth-running Berlin-Rome Express that the trip was marked by extreme discomfort and interminable delay.

Once over the Brenner, things went better. The great cold was left behind the mighty barrier of the Alps; so was the worst of that grim atmosphere of war whose depressing influence you do not fully realize until it no longer envelops you. When I finally stepped from my train at Genoa, my port of embarkation, I was greeted by a mild sea breeze. The salty tang of it was a foretaste of my ocean path towards home.

Genoa is the port of embarkation now for nearly all Americans returning homeward. Our neutrality law forbids American ships from touching at French or British ports, so Northern Italy is the nearest neutral exit from both Western and Central Europe. Accordingly, the United States Lines has instituted a regular service between Genoa and New York, and when I embarked on the *Washington* I found myself among compatriots who had been sojourning all the way from Britain to Russia and the Balkans.

This gave me a fine chance to compare notes with fellow-Americans from many European lands, especially from England and France, about which countries I was most curious. The resident in wartime Germany is hermetically sealed from contacts across the battle-lines. So rigid is the veil of censorship that, in Germany, one gets only a vague and obviously distorted idea of the "other side." Now, for the first time, I could discover how Englishmen and Frenchmen were talking and feeling. And I learned this, not from foreign propagandists, but from my own people.

Aboard the *Washington* every aspect of material living was balm to my strictly rationed self, from the superabundant food to cherished trifles like finding miniature cakes of soap in my bathroom and being handed paper clips of matches with each purchase of cigarettes. There are so many genial aspects of American life which we thoughtlessly take for granted until we are suddenly deprived of them and are plunged into alien surroundings where we have to fuss and plan and almost fight to get the bare necessities of existence. Even more deeply satisfying is the sense that you are among your own kind who are not worried and harassed and ulcerated by nationalistic hatreds. Yes, it was great to be in the American atmosphere once more.

INDEX

Adolf Hitler Schools, 156
Agriculture, Nazi aim and policy in, 109-129
Amusement, German dependence on, 217
Arbeitsdienst. See National Labor Service
Aristocracy, training for a new, 156-157
Army, fraternization in, 77
"Army of the Spade," the, 141
Asendorf, Werner, 40
Athletics, emphasis on, 155-157

Balkans, the, 237 ff., 242, 298
Barred zones, 46, 279-304
Bauer, the German, 111-112
"Beautification of Labor," the, 135
"Bed-Action," 176
Berlin, 26 ff.; Nazi architecture in, 29; Hitler residence, 29-30; impassivity among people, 30; clothes, 31-32; taxis, 32-33; moving ordnance through, 36; blackout, 33, 57-58, 280-281; subway, 58; midwinter in, 213-224; Christmas in, 216
Bessarabia, 239-241
Bethlen, Ex-Premier, 231
Bettenaktion, the. See "Bed-Action"
Blackouts, 22, 33, 57-58, 280-281
Bodily development, emphasis on, 155-157

Boehme, Dr., 40
Bohemia-Moravia, surveillance of correspondents in, 46; conditions in, 283-284
Bohle, Wilhelm, 78
Bolzano, 21
Bratislava, 79-84
Brown-Shirt Storm Troopers, 169, 252
Budapest, en route to, 225-230; New Year's Eve in, 243-244
Business, Nazi control of, 274-276

Camps, Youth, 139-147
Cattle for Germany, 127
Christmas season in Berlin, 214-217
Church, conflicts with, 152-153, 277-278
Clinic service, 183
Clothing rations, 31-32, 92-96; Winter-Help distribution, 177-178
Coal for Germany, 293
Collings, Kenneth, 282
Correspondents, foreign, rules for, 41-46; telephone permits, 42-43; mail routine, 43; travel conditions, 45-46; zones barred to, 46, 279-304
Crime, Nazi principles in relation to, 268 ff.
Csaky, Count, 231
Czechs. See Bohemia-Moravia